A Father's Daughter

Domenic Marks

This book is dedicated to all the victims, survivors, and families who have had the misfortune of experiencing the impact of an Amniotic Fluid Embolism and to all the families who have, or had, a loved one suffering from the disease of addiction.

This story is your story.

Introduction

How do you begin writing a book about a personal tragedy?

How do you tell the story that is still being written?

I have never written a book before, but I've already accepted how this may play out. This book will tell the story of my daughter's life and our relationship from my perspective. This will require me to open the door to my family, my life, and my soul. This will expose my innermost thoughts. This will allow you, the reader, to come on in, make yourself at home, and see what I'm made of. Some of it will be good, and some of it will not.

These are my recollections of events. I know they may not be consistent with the memories of others. I own everything on these pages and will take any criticism with that ownership. This is a story of strength, resilience, and perseverance. But mostly, it is a story of love. The love that only a father can have for his daughter. It is about how that love was tested on numerous occasions. It is a story of the challenges and victories that we experienced together.

I hope that by reading this book, you come away with some items that may change your life. That you find something that touches you and permits you to reconsider your position or change your perspective.

So, begin turning the pages and walk in my shoes. It is a walk with many twists and turns, many ups and downs, many lefts when I should have gone right, and many rights when I should have gone left. I will make one guarantee, however…

It is a walk unlike any other.

The Beginning of Terror...

Amanda's water had broken, and our granddaughter was coming to see us. We sat in the waiting room in anticipation and excitement...but then a couple of staff members entered Amanda's delivery suite. A minute after they closed the door, we heard a code calling on the overhead speaker. At this point, more staff began rushing into Amanda's room. Daryl, Joe, Debbie, and I were starting to get concerned. I tried to stay calm and reassure the others that Amanda and the baby were in the best hospital possible. I began to think something terrible was happening to Mila. I kept thinking that Amanda and Mario had been through so many trials and tests throughout the pregnancy that to come out of it without a child would crush them.

More and more people were going into Amanda's room. I couldn't figure out where they were all going. It was like a clown car but in reverse. The door would occasionally open, and I could see a crowd of people in there, but I could not see what was happening. I knew I couldn't hear Amanda's voice, and I would have thought she would be more vocal if anything terrible happened to Mila.

Why didn't I hear Amanda's voice?! Why didn't I hear a crying baby?! After all the difficulties Amanda had in her life already, why was she having more?! What was she going to have to deal with now?! I was starting to lose my composure. What in the hell was going on in there?!!!

This Father's Daughter

My Roots

You may be asking yourself why you would read a book created by a guy who never wrote a book. You may ask what makes me so unique.

My answer to those questions would be that I have no special skills to try and achieve this endeavor. What I do have, though, is a story unlike one I have ever read or heard of before. I could jump right into the teeth of this story, but without some background on myself and my family, it would leave gaping holes in the story that would leave you unsatisfied.

So please indulge me while I provide the building blocks to this remarkable story I'm about to tell you.

I grew up in a small town in the Mon Valley of Pittsburgh, Pennsylvania. The Mon Valley was the hub of steel mills in western Pennsylvania, where fathers worked in these mills and made a living that provided a decent life for their families. My town was located between two steel mills and overlooked the Monongahela River. My father did not work in a steel mill. He was a cement mason. My dad didn't get into cement work until he married my mom. He now had his own family to support, and the job didn't require an extensive skill level. I don't believe he ever loved his line of work, but it took care of his family, and that was all that mattered to him. My dad dropped out of school at a young age. He often told me he dropped out because he thought he knew more than the teachers. But he always followed that declaration with how wrong he was in thinking that. Much later in my life, I discovered he dropped out of school because he needed a job to help his mom pay the bills. My grandfather was an alcoholic, and in my father's childhood, that problem was met with closed eyes and lips. In other words, you didn't see or say anything to anyone.

My dad's father was from Italy and did not speak fluent English. My earliest memories, I was probably 6 or 7, were of visiting my grandparents and my grandfather taking my sister, who was 18 months older, and me out for walks in his neighborhood. Somehow our walks would always end up at the neighborhood bar, where he would give us nickels to play shuffle bowling while he sat at the bar drinking. After a while, my father would come for us, and walk us back to my grandparent's house where some very angry Italian words would be exchanged between my grandparents. That was my first exposure to addiction, and unfortunately, it would become a returning problem in my life.

My mom was a stay-at-home mother who took care of the house, my younger brother, my older sister, and me. Her father was struck and killed by a car while walking with my uncle. My uncle was a young boy at the time, and the story was that my grandfather pushed his son out of the way of the oncoming car and gave his life in the process. My mother was fatherless when she was 12 years old. My grandmother had to get a job to support her three children, and my mom became the caregiver for her younger siblings. They were penniless, and while I don't have actual events to portray how this affected my mother accurately, she often would tell me how difficult her life was after her dad passed. It wasn't until I was in my twenties that I realized she harbored deep anxiety over how much money was available and the importance of saving money. I had to think it was during her formative years that this anxiety took root. It was the first time I ever encountered a loved one with anxiety. Later in life, I would encounter another family member with anxiety. It would be a more extreme case that lives to this day.

We lived in a home that, as I recall, was built by a riverboat captain. It was an old wooden 3-story structure built at the turn of the 20th century. It was white with dark gray trim and had a turret on the right side of the structure. The structure was so large that it could be seen from the other side of the Mon River. In its heyday, it was equipped with a nonworking elevator that permitted the housekeepers to live on the upper floor and easily access the main living area. I'm sure at that time, the house was very regal and was the envy of the neighborhood. By the time my parents bought it in 1960, it needed extensive work. My dad spent a significant amount of time remodeling the house. So much so that the remodeling never seemed to end.

My family was probably on the lower end of the economic scale, but if we were poor, I never knew it. I grew up in a time when I would run out the back door in the morning and not come home until dinner, and no one ever thought that was a problem.

My parents were devout Catholics, and as a young boy, I was indoctrinated into that lifestyle. I write that not as a knock-on Catholicism, but I remember, at an early age, I couldn't comprehend the concept of faith and believing in something because I was told I had to.

I lived during the years of the John and Bobby Kennedy assassinations and the Martin Luther King assassination. I grew up during the Vietnam protests and Nixon years. It was a time of skepticism, making me examine things I didn't fully understand. In my teen years, my religious beliefs became a part of that skepticism. Maybe it could be explained as me being a rebellious teenager. I believed more in science than faith, even though I do believe in my interpretation of God.

As a child, I was insecure, somewhat shy, and not too confident in who I was. I didn't think I was good-looking or, for that matter, anything worth looking at. I felt like I just blended into the background. I was of average height but weighed next to nothing.

I was not bullied as a child. I had my group of friends, and while we playfully insulted each other, it was never threatening to me or made me feel unsafe. My friends and I would play baseball, football, street hockey, or basketball whenever we could. I loved athletics, but I never pursued formal sports outside my early childhood because of my low confidence level in my ability.

I attended a public school in my neighborhood for grades one through four. My grade school was on top of a hill about three blocks from my home. I liked going to that school because all my friends were in class with me. My parents transferred me to a catholic school for grades 5 through 9. I was transferred because the 5th-grade teacher was very hard on my older sister and my mother feared that this same teacher would be just as hard on me. I'm not sure what occurred between my mother and this teacher that would lead her to believe this, but it must have been significant for my mom to want to transfer me like that. It also could have been my mom's anxiety retaking hold of her and this was her way of tamping it down.

I attended an all-boys catholic high school during my freshman year. Most of the boys from my Catholic elementary school were in the same classes as me, and it seemed like my freshman year was going to be a good time. That was proven to be wrong very quickly. The school's teaching staff was primarily comprised of Brothers of the Catholic faith. In my eyes, the Brothers were sadistic. They would not hesitate to resort to corporal punishment if their class rules were violated. I rarely faced their wrath, but I wasn't fond of what they did to my classmates. I think teaching by fear is not the best method, so before my sophomore year in high school, I asked my parents to let me attend a public high school. I could not see myself returning in the fall. I never told my parents about the Brothers' method of teaching. It's not because I feared they wouldn't believe me; it was because I knew they would disagree with this reason for transferring.

My sister was already in an all-girls Catholic high school, and I knew the tuition for our enrollment was stretching the family finances, so I used that to plead my case with them. My parents thought about it for a few days and decided I could transfer to a public high school. Looking back, it was probably one of the most significant decisions of my life.

My mother, father, and I shortly before I moved out of my
childhood home.

My Only True Love

My mother was devoted to and loved her children and wanted the best for us. In that vein, she wanted me in the worst way to become a politician. She was very involved in the Republican party and thought I had what it took to become a good politician. To this day, I'm still not sure where she came up with that assessment. In the summer before I began public school, I received the high school curriculum book, which listed required and elective classes, my mom and I reviewed it together. My mom wanted me to take a speech course in high school. She thought it would be an attribute that would significantly enhance my skill set for being a politician. I don't know why she thought this was a good career choice for me because I told her that to be a politician, you had to have the ability to "sell your soul" to succeed and that I didn't want to live my life like that. It's funny the things that occur that shape your future because I took the speech class to appease my mom and ended up meeting my first and only true love.

On the first day of my speech class, I walked into the classroom and noticed the room was set up in a "U" formation with the teacher's desk at the opening. None of my neighborhood friends were in this class. It wasn't their style. I found an empty seat, not concerned with whom I sat next to. I kept my eyes forward as other students entered the room and took the remaining seats around me. The class was comprised primarily of girls interspersed with a few boys. I was beginning to regret letting my mom talk me into taking this course. I couldn't give speeches. I never wanted to stand in front of a class and recite anything. Right now, I wanted to be anywhere but this classroom when I looked up from my desk and noticed that the girl sitting to my right was the most beautiful thing I had ever seen. She had dark brown hair, dark eyes, and the prettiest face I had ever seen. I was stunned! She literally took my breath away! I had the hardest time taking my eyes off her, but I was too shy to say a word to her.

The teacher called for our attention, so I had to stop staring at the angel to my right. On this first day of class, the teacher had us stand, place our books on our heads, and march around the room. It was an attempt to show us how good posture affects the projection of your voice. It was lame, but I did it, of course. When class ended, I was looking forward to the next day in speech class so I could focus on the vision of beauty that sat next to me.

After school that day, I prayed to God that I could find the strength to speak to this exotically beautiful girl, but I knew I wouldn't. I didn't have confidence in myself and feared the rejection that might come my way if I somehow found the courage to speak to her. Well, at least I could spend the class time glancing her way and thinking about what could have been.

The next day in class, I remember sitting next to her before the class began and telling myself to say something… to say anything… don't let this moment pass! But I didn't say a word… because I didn't have to! She looked over at me and said, "I hope the teacher doesn't make us march around the room today." I don't remember the rest of the conversation; I was lost in her beauty, voice, and aura, but those words led to a friendship, a long courtship, and finally, a marriage. I'll never forget those words. They changed me as a person and helped mold me into the man I am today. I will also be forever grateful to God and my mom for leading me to my soulmate, my wife Daryl.

The only girl I've ever dreamed about; My wife, Daryl

Starting a Family

In 1979 my future wife, Daryl, and I moved to southeast Florida once she was out of college. She had a degree in Medical Records Administration. Since each hospital usually only had one administrator, it was a tough market for an individual fresh out of school to break into. She had a job offer from Mount Sinai Medical Center on the bayside of Miami Beach.

I had an electronics degree from a technical school and obtained a job at a mainframe computer manufacturing company in Fort Lauderdale. I wasn't upset about moving so far from my family home in Pittsburgh. I didn't see eye to eye with my parents and getting out on my own and moving 1200 miles from them put me in a position where I had to learn to rely on myself and handle my problems. As a bonus, the winter weather in south Florida sure beat the weather I was used to in Pittsburgh.

Six months after moving to Fort Lauderdale, Daryl told me about a position in the Bio-Med Department at Mount Sinai. I applied, interviewed, and got the job. I couldn't have been happier. I had an excellent job in a beautiful city and was able to spend more time with Daryl. We would meet for lunch, eat by the bay behind the hospital, or go to a restaurant on Miami Beach.

We were married in November of 1983 and lived in a 10th-floor condo that Daryl's father purchased as an investment property. Daryl's parents would stay with us every winter for about three months. We got along well, and there were never any conflicts, so it was a sweet deal for all of us. Daryl and I protected their investment by taking care of the condo, and we paid them rent, which was not unreasonable.

Daryl and I decided to start a family, but it was difficult for us. We tried unsuccessfully for about a year or so to get pregnant. We were beginning to consider artificial means, but Daryl became pregnant in the fall of 1985, and we welcomed our son Dan on July 10, 1986.

Dan was the most beautiful baby I had ever seen. I'm not kidding. I'm not saying this as a biased father. He was beautiful! The first time I held him, I was thankful that he was healthy and had all his fingers and toes.

Daryl was induced into labor and had an epidural, so the delivery was relatively easy. After Dan was born, we could no longer stay in the condo. The condo association had a no-children-resident rule. We bought our first house in North Miami Beach and began raising our new baby.

Having a child is the most life-changing experience that one could ever have. You are responsible for your child's health, welfare, and upbringing as a parent. As an upcoming father, I tried to prepare myself for this enormous responsibility, but I didn't begin to feel the weight of it until Dan was born. Daryl's mother and father came to Florida to help us out, but after a month of being there, they had to return to their home.

One of my most memorable times with Dan was when he was an infant and would become fussy. I would lay on the couch, lay him on my chest, and rub his back until he fell asleep. I never felt more content. It was also an excellent time to nap since I suffered from sleep deprivation from having an infant in the house!

When holding Dan, I couldn't help but think how I had to make sure I was always available to him when he needed me. I had to ensure that I guided him in the right direction and let him make reasonable decisions. I remember thinking this would not be easy, and I hoped I was up for the challenge.

Daryl and I must have done something right with how we raised Dan because I am so proud of the man he is today.

Now Daryl and I had a plan for when we wanted to have our next child. We decided to wait about four years after Dan was born to begin trying to have a second child. We reasoned that by the time Dan was finishing college, our second child would be starting college, so we would not be placing too much of a financial strain on ourselves.

Daryl and I decided not to use birth control after Dan's birth because we anticipated the same difficulty getting pregnant that we experienced with Dan's conception. We didn't expect that 18 months after Dan was born, we would find out Daryl was pregnant with our second child! So much for our best-laid plans!

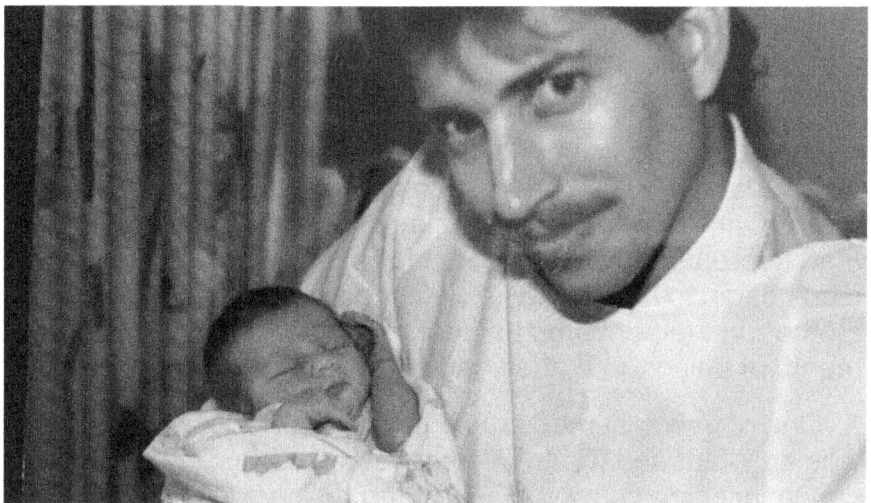

My son Dan on the day he was born

A Diva is Born

Daryl had a normal pregnancy with Amanda. Nothing was out of the ordinary at all. Daryl was getting close to her due date, and we hoped we could induce labor again.

Early in the morning of October 19, 1988, Daryl woke me and said she thought she might be in labor. She hadn't experienced labor pains with Dan, our first child, so she wasn't sure what she was experiencing. She called her doctor, who told us the best thing to do was to get to the hospital. As most expecting parents, we had a bag packed to go with us but what we didn't have was for someone to take care of our son. We had always hoped that Daryl would either go into labor or be induced during the day so we could utilize Dan being in daycare. That wasn't much of a plan, but it was all we had. So, all three of us piled into the car and headed to the Emergency Room at Mount Sinai. When we arrived, a doctor examined Daryl, and they immediately rushed her to the delivery room. She was so far along that they expected the baby to be delivered at any moment. It was about 4 am, and I had nowhere to take our son!

The daycare at Mount Sinai, where Dan went daily, was not open, and Daryl desperately wanted me in the delivery room. I did the only thing I could think of. I took Dan to the Medical Records Department where my wife worked and tried to explain to the two ladies who handled the midnight shift that their boss was having a baby and they were going to babysit my son Dan so I could be in the delivery room with Daryl. Neither of these ladies spoke good English. They were from Russia and worked the midnight shift so that they would have minimal contact with other hospital employees. They looked horrified as I thanked them and turned and left. I couldn't imagine doing that in today's world. I would probably be arrested for child abandonment.

I made it to the Delivery Room in time and witnessed the birth of our second child, whom we named Amanda Rose. We had a girl! I was so thrilled! Unfortunately, I had to leave the delivery room immediately to get Dan back from my wife's employees. I expressed my gratefulness for taking care of my son, but I'm not sure how much they understood what I was saying to them.

After I retrieved my son and Daryl was taken to a private room, we spent time as our new family of four. It was an extraordinary time for us. We felt so blessed to have two healthy children. Our life was complete.

I don't know how other fathers feel about their daughters the first time they hold them, but it was a moment of absolute love for me. I remember looking at her beautiful baby face and feeling the weight of being a father to a daughter. I knew my responsibility was to take care of this little girl for as long as I breathed. I knew at that moment that no matter what path she traveled or whom she brought into her life, I was always there to protect her and provide her with the support she needed in all she did.

I remember being alone with her for the first time, and I felt the need to verbally tell her that I would never abandon her or turn my back on her. I would be her knight in shining armor that would always protect her. When she was faced with the difficult moments that life throws at us, that I would be there to be her hero and support her. I promised her that she could always count on me no matter what.

Little did I know how severely those promises would be tested.

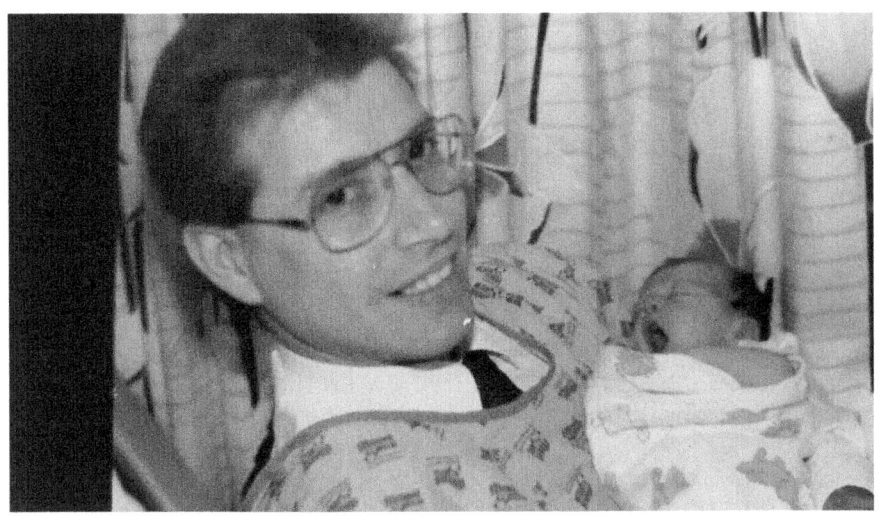

My daughter Amanda on the day she was born. Excuse the yawn… she had a rough day and was a little tired.

A Little Girl's First Year

My memory of Amanda's first year was that she was a happy child. She was cute as a button, and everyone who met her fell in love. By her first birthday, she had these big natural sausage curls in her hair that made her look like Shirley Temple. She was the apple of my eye.

She was extremely friendly and loved being with people. Her daycare caregivers loved being with her and never complained about her interactions with other children. She was a social being.

She and her brother got along most if she didn't try to play with his toys. But even when there was a disagreement, she was easily distracted by giving her something else to play with.

Her first 18 months were uneventful and typical for a little girl who was happy to be around others.

We were a happy family of four living in North Miami Beach, Florida, in a little pink house on a cul-de-sac with a canal where ducks would swim, just outside our backyard.

Movement

When my son Dan was born, Daryl began indicating that she wanted to move back to Pittsburgh. She was missing her family and wanted Dan to grow up knowing his family.

I will admit I had a tough time with this. I loved living in the Miami area. The winters were terrific. We enjoyed many festivals, street fairs, beaches, and weekend trips. I was struggling with leaving. We had been in the Miami area for almost ten years, and I felt like this was our home. I loved my job and the people I worked with. Going back to Pittsburgh was not on my radar.

When Amanda was born, Daryl's need to return to Pittsburgh amplified tenfold. Her parents and family pressured her to return so they could enjoy our babies. I was fighting this with all I had, but something changed my mind.

In August of 1988, I read a story in the local newspaper about what parents of elementary school children needed to be aware of. One item was the number and types of weapons confiscated at various elementary schools in the Miami area over the past school year. It was frightening to see the pictures of the tables filled with multiple kinds of weapons. There were even automatic handguns in the pictures!

Daryl and I lived in Miami during the Marielle Boat Lift and the Cocaine Cowboy Wars that took place immediately after that in the early 1980s. Everyone knew that Fidel Castro had emptied his prisons and sent the worst of his prisoners to Florida and what was occurring was somewhat because of that. We knew that if we stayed away from areas of concern or kept to ourselves, we would be fine.

We were never concerned with our safety throughout the turmoil that consumed parts of Miami during that time. It wasn't until I saw that newspaper article that I began to see this from a different perspective.

I was no longer just concerned with my and Daryl's safety, but now I had two children that I needed to consider. I had two little human beings counting on their mom and dad to ensure they were always safe and sound. In all the years I lived in Pittsburgh, I had never experienced or known these same concerns.

In the summer of 1989, I decided that my family's welfare was more important than my desire to stay warm in the winter.

We knew Daryl would have the most difficulty finding a job, so she began her search, and we put our home up for sale.

Johnstown PA

Daryl's job search was not bearing any fruit. The Pittsburgh healthcare market was a tough market to break into. There weren't many employment opportunities in the ranks of Medical Records Administrators. We hoped that her finding a job wouldn't be too difficult because we hated the thought of selling our home and moving into an apartment while her job search continued.

After a couple of months, a job opened at a hospital in Johnstown, Pennsylvania. Johnstown is about 70 miles east of Pittsburgh in the Laurel Highland Mountain range. Johnstown was a booming steel town beginning in the 1880s, but as the steel industry died, Johnstown had to adapt and transform itself. Johnstown's biggest claim to fame was the Great Johnstown Flood of 1889, which killed 2,200 people. While the flood was a tragedy, it displayed Johnstown's strong community spirit by rebuilding itself better than before. Today, Johnstown is home to about 22,000 people and has scenic natural beauty surrounding it.

Daryl flew to Pittsburgh, drove to Johnstown, and was interviewed. Within weeks she had the position. Our only concern now was if I could find employment. I went to college in Miami and obtained a degree in Computer Science. Johnstown is not at the epicenter of software technology, and we were concerned about me finding a job in my field.

Luckily, a company in Johnstown developed software for hospital laboratory systems. The company's founder was a physician at the hospital where my wife was going to be working. Word was passed to this physician about my skill set, and he arranged for me to be interviewed for a position as a software developer. I was able to secure that job, so this meant that Daryl and I were going to be employed and able to provide for our family without any income interruption.

We found a house to rent at the end of a dead-end street

which was surrounded and secluded by trees and shrubs. It had a log cabin feel and a working wood-burning fireplace in the main room. There was a jacuzzi tub in the second-floor master bath and a tennis/basketball court in the backyard. The rent was reasonable, and we had worked with the owner (who had moved to California) to be on a month-to-month lease.

We moved into our new temporary home in December 1989, just before the holidays.

Life in Johnstown

Within weeks of being in Johnstown, we had begun our jobs, placed our children in daycare, and started acclimating to our new environment.

Johnstown is a tiny town, and coming from Miami, it was quite a cultural change for Daryl and me. It wasn't easy at first. Johnstown was the opposite of Miami in size, temperature, and culture. There were no arts festivals every weekend or food festivals, or beaches. I missed those things, but I also knew a greater good was to be had, so I had to adjust my perspective to lessen the sting of not being in Florida any longer.

As time passed, we began to enjoy the close-knit family community of Johnstown and its slower pace of life.

Every Saturday, we would pack the kids in the car and make the 90-minute drive into Pittsburgh to visit the family we returned to connect with our babies. Daryl's sister Terry also had two children, a 7-year-old girl and a boy the same age as my son Dan.

Dan and his cousin Mike would play all day while Amanda would melt everyone's heart with her cuteness. She was a happy baby and loved being surrounded by her new, more prominent family. We would visit for most of the day, have dinner, and then head back to Johnstown, where we would spend Sunday either grocery shopping, visiting different areas of Johnstown, or relaxing with the kids.

Dan and Amanda loved their daycare, and Daryl and I were busy working and making new friends. It was easy to make friends in Johnstown, considering everyone knew everyone. I remember a morning that helped me fall in love with Johnstown.

Daryl usually left for work before I did. One morning she called me about 10 minutes after she left and told me she had a flat tire and was parked on the shoulder of the road. I told her I would be there so I could give her my car and she could get to work on time. By the time I got the kids in the car, it was probably 20 minutes before I got to where Daryl was. When I arrived, two vehicles were parked behind Daryl, and two guys were changing her tire! In Miami, Daryl had a better chance of winning the lottery than someone stopping to change a tire. I stayed with Daryl's car, let her take mine, and talked to the two men who stopped. It was refreshing to speak to two people with no agenda other than to help my wife out. They were even going to be late for their jobs but told me their bosses would understand.

This town and its people were extraordinary, and I was comfortable with our decision to move back to Pennsylvania. I was beginning to feel that Johnstown was a safe place to raise my kids. Only decades later, Johnstown would become no different from any other town or city in America. It would have the same major problem that every city, small or large, in America was struggling with… drug addiction.

Home Sweet Home?

Life in Johnstown was growing on my family. The kids loved their daycare, Daryl loved her job, and we all enjoyed our weekend travels into Pittsburgh to be with family. The cultural change between Miami and Johnstown became a distant memory.

We had been in Johnstown for over a year, and Daryl's quest to find a job in Pittsburgh had been fruitless. We knew it would be difficult to break into the Pittsburgh job market, and we were at a point where renting a home was losing its appeal.

We had moved from the first home in Johnstown to a small one-story brick home in Richland, a suburb of Johnstown. It was a nice place, but it was too small for us, and we were about four months from our lease expiring.

Daryl and I thought it was time to buy a home in Johnstown and raise our family there. At first, we began looking for homes for sale but then thought we could build a new house and have it to our specifications.

We found a local builder with whom we discussed our ideas concerning the home's construction. He knew our budget and went about scouting for available lots in the Richland area and designing the blueprints for our home.

After a few weeks, the builder contacted us and told us about a lot he found. He said it would be perfect for the home and asked us to meet him there to see for ourselves. We drove out to the lot and couldn't believe its beauty. The lot was halfway up the side of a large hill and looked down over an open field to a wooded valley below. There were a few other homes under construction on the hillside, but they were not close to the lot we were looking at. The lot was 2 acres in size and provided privacy along with the view. The other home lots were also roughly the same size, so you didn't get the cramped, congested feeling you sometimes have in a new plan.

The builder showed us how the back of the home would face the valley and how he planned to build us a wraparound covered porch that we could use to sit on and either relax or entertain others.

Daryl and I were so excited about the location. We needed the builder to complete the blueprints and see if he could stay within our budget. About one month later, the builder contacted us and told us he had blueprints ready for us to review.

We met with the builder and talked through the entire process of building. The blueprints for the home were all that we were hoping for. There was a wrap-around covered porch, a large eat-in kitchen, four bedrooms, three baths, an oversized two-car garage, and a finished basement.

The only problem was that the lot and construction would put us about $20,000 over budget. Daryl and I told the builder we needed time to consider the overage. Maybe we could find a less expensive lot, do without the wrap-around porch, or not have a finished basement. Daryl and I spent the next couple of weeks discussing it and decided we would build with the overage. It would stretch our budget, but we knew we would love our new home and not regret the additional costs over time. It was time to let our builder know our decision and begin the building process.

Pittsburgh Surprise

The spring of 1991 was quickly approaching in Johnstown and thus, so was the construction season. Daryl and I called our builder and asked him to meet to discuss the final plans and give him our decision to progress with the current blueprints.

A week before that meeting was to take place, Daryl received a call from the University of Pittsburgh Medical Center (UPMC). UPMC's main hospital was in the Oakland area of Pittsburgh. They had a job opening for a Health Information Manager and wanted to interview her. She quickly arranged the interview, and we delayed the meeting with the builder.

Two weeks later, Daryl found out she had the position, and now the ball was in our court to decide whether we wanted to move to Pittsburgh to be closer to our families or to remain and build the home of our dreams in Johnstown.

The decision was relatively easy. Family always came first. Having the ability to be within 20 miles of all our family and being able to spend more time with them was always at the top of our priority list.

Daryl accepted the position, so we met with our builder to give him the bad news, notified our jobs, and began looking for a home to rent in Pittsburgh. Life for our family was on the move again!

Pittsburgh North

Both my wife and I grew up in the southeastern part of Allegheny County, known as the Mon Valley, so we knew that we wanted to relocate to the northern suburbs of Pittsburgh due to the ease of the commute into the city. In the spring of 1991, we found a home to rent in Shaler Township. It was an older home with a lovely, enclosed brick back porch where Danny and Amanda could play.

The plan was for me to stay at home with the kids throughout the summer while I was looking for a job. Every day I would look through the want ads. The internet, while it existed, was not as it is today. No employers used the internet to search for candidates.

As my job search continued through spring and into the summer, I would spend my days taking care of the home, getting dinner ready, and keeping the kids entertained. There were other small children in the neighborhood, so Danny and Amanda had a few friends to play with, which made life a little easier for me.

Every Saturday, we would go to Daryl's parent's home, just as we did when we lived in Johnstown. The only difference was that now the commute was much shorter.

After being in Shaler for a couple of months, Daryl and I knew that the North Hills of Pittsburgh was where we wanted to buy a home. We talked about what we wanted in a home as a family.

The home I grew up in had a big backyard and a large cement patio. My dad, the cement mason, did all the work in putting that patio in place. He put up a basketball hoop, and my brother and I used that patio for basketball and street hockey. I remember how much I loved that backyard and patio growing up, so I hoped to have that for our children. Maybe not the patio, but the backyard was a must.

My wife wanted a master bath, a large walk-in closet, and a somewhat open floor plan. Danny and Amanda didn't have many demands. They only wanted a bedroom to call their own and a yard to play in. My wish list for our home was to have a level driveway along with the large backyard mentioned previously. I also wanted a game room.

The level driveway was so it wouldn't be difficult going in or out of the garage if it snowed, and it wouldn't be too hard to shovel that snow away. The large level backyard was for the kids to be able to play in and to make it easier to mow the lawn. The game room was also for the kids, so they had some place to entertain their friends. That never actually happened. The basement, where the game room was located, was rarely used by anyone, so several years later, I had the cellar refinished and turned it into a man cave. It was decked out in Pittsburgh sports memorabilia. I had painted the walls in the Pittsburgh Steelers colors, including the black, white, and gold player jersey stripe around the room and up the steps to the main floor. I put in a large-screen TV and surround sound. I loved that room and still miss it to this day. I must give a special "Thanks" to Dan and Amanda for never really using that room as I had initially intended. It turned out great for me!

Employment

I was enjoying the summer off with the kids, but I was getting a little nervous about finding a job. I had been sending resumes for various positions at various organizations but had yet to get one interview. I had been unemployed since April, and it was already the end of June.

Daryl and I continued shopping for homes but knew that making a purchase would not happen until I was employed. This weighed heavy on me because I wanted my family to set down some roots finally and have some stability for the kids.

In early July, I interviewed at a local hospital for a position as a Systems Analyst working not within the Information Technology Department but in the Cardiology Department. This setup was a little unusual, but it was a decent-paying job, and I did have the qualifications they were looking for.

After the interview, I felt I had a good shot at the job, but unfortunately, I was one of the early applicants, and they were weeks away from deciding.

In the first week of August, I had given up on the only job I had interviewed for. I was resigned to being unemployed for a more extended period when I received a phone call from the individual who had interviewed me asking if I was still available and interested in the position. Trying not to sound too excited, I made it known that I was available and interested. So, after a short conversation, I accepted the position!

With the employment search now over, it was time to find a daycare for the kids and ramp up our home search.

Home Sweet Home!

In September of 1991, Daryl and I had been through several homes for sale in the North Hills of Pittsburgh, and wouldn't you know it, we both agreed that the first home we had walked through back in June was the one we knew would suit us the best. It was in Ross Township in a plan named Kinvara.

The home was a "For Sale by Owner," so we got to deal directly with the owner rather than a real estate agent. As we progressed through the buying process for the home, I told the owner that I wanted my father to look at the house. My father's experience in the construction business would help provide insight into the home's bones. During this discussion, we discovered that my dad and the owner grew up in the same neighborhood in Pittsburgh and were childhood acquaintances.

When my father and the owner met, they recognized each other immediately. It also was revealed that my grandmother and the owner's mother were good friends. My grandmother, who had passed away a few years earlier, came to this home and had dinner with the owner's family. Knowing all this sealed the deal for us.

We bought the home, and at the closing, the owner gave me a picture he had of my grandmother sitting at their dining room table enjoying dinner with them. The gesture touched me; whenever I walked into our new home's dining room, I would think of my grandmother. It wasn't with sadness but with a fondness of knowing that she was at one time in this room amongst people who cared for her.

On Thanksgiving weekend in the fall of 1991, we moved into our new home and began 28 years of memory-making. Most were good memories, some were terrible, and some were straight from hell.

The Early Years in Kinvara

After we settled into our new home, we had a routine suburban lifestyle. Daryl and I would go to work, the kids would go to daycare, and towards the end of the day, we would all have dinner, watch TV, and get ready for the next day.

Kinvara was an excellent neighborhood for our kids. Our neighbors on each side of us and across the street all had children around the same age as ours. Since we had the most extended and most level driveway amongst our homes, the kids naturally used it to play basketball or street hockey. Due to errant street hockey pucks, I had to replace many windowpanes in my garage door!

The backyards for the homes on each side of us had no fences, so the kids would play ball in the yards during the summer and would sled ride down the hill behind us in the winter. We also had a covered back porch, so it was a great gathering point for getting some rest from the sun in between ball games.

Dan started kindergarten at the local elementary school while Amanda continued in daycare. Dan was always very cerebral as a child. When he was three months old, we could place him in front of the TV and have Sesame Street on, and he would watch it for hours, not making a sound. He began using words very early in his infancy. Most were words he learned on Sesame Street.

Amanda was a little different than Dan. She was very social as a child and could win people over with just her cuteness. She was a pass-around baby who was happy to be held by everybody and anybody. The staff at her daycare loved her because she was just so lovable.

Life was going great in our new home. We were very content as a family.

The Beginning

I've been setting the stage for what comes next in my story. I did it this way because I wanted you, as the reader, to try and determine if any of the early years of our family life could have affected the mid or later years. It's something I've done several times myself. I know I have my answer, which I'll reveal much later in this story. It's something I've learned on this journey.

To continue with the story, though, Dan and Amanda were both in elementary school, and while Dan excelled, Amanda struggled. Almost every parent-teacher meeting we had with Amanda's teachers would start by them telling us that they thought she could learn but that she was more interested in being social. I can't tell you how often Amanda was described as a "social butterfly."

Daryl and I worried, though, because we thought she might have a learning disability. Amanda would be doing homework and asking us for help. I recall sitting with her trying to explain the most basic math or spelling problems and being frustrated that she could not understand no matter how differently you described it.

We asked her elementary school to test her for a learning disability. They were very reluctant to do that, even though she was primarily a below-average student. After numerous requests, they tested her and told us she was borderline but did not "qualify" as having a learning disability. Daryl and I felt that borderline was close enough and that the school should treat her as if she had a learning disability. They disagreed. The school felt that Amanda was not applying herself to learning. I told them about my experiences with her when helping her with homework. We argued with the counselor, Amanda's teacher, and the principal. It did no good. They were firm that Amanda did not have what "qualified" her as having a learning disability. We felt abandoned by the school district. This was the first time we felt this way about the school district. Unfortunately, it wouldn't be the last time.

Anxiety

At around eight years old, Daryl and I noticed Amanda beginning to have an uncontrollable concern when Daryl and I traveled without her. There were several conventions that Daryl would go to that I would tag along on to have a brief couple of days off. Either my parents or Daryl's parents would stay with the kids at our home. Amanda's anxiety would be displayed mainly when we had to fly to our destination.

We don't know how it started, but Amanda would be so frightened that our plane would not reach its destination that we had to call her immediately when we landed so she could relax. While we were away, we would call frequently, but she was ok once she knew that we were on the ground and safe.

About a year after these incidents, Amanda began fearing bad weather. It wasn't all the time, but it would manifest itself whenever there was severe weather in the area. Even though we had never been through a tornado, she feared being hit by one.

At this time, we decided to take Amanda to a child psychiatrist. After a few sessions, she was diagnosed with anxiety. The psychiatrist told us there was pharmaceutical treatment and non-pharmaceutical treatment. We opted for non-pharmaceutical treatment. This involved Amanda learning how to anticipate her fear and to be able to calm herself by retreating to a calm space. The doctor told her to imagine herself as a turtle and pull herself into her shell whenever she felt threatened.

After a few sessions, Amanda didn't want to go any longer and said she knew what to do when she felt anxious because of the weather. I don't remember if she improved, but we must have seen improvement. Otherwise, we would have continued the sessions.

I think that her anxiety manifested itself in other parts of her life, as she would worry more about various other items that we could soothe by reassuring her that she was okay.

To this day, Amanda still suffers from anxiety and is on several meds to keep it somewhat under control.

Scoliosis

Amanda was heading into the sixth grade when we were notified by the school district that she was due for a physical exam. During this physical exam by Amanda's pediatrician, we were told that Amanda had a curvature of her spine. The pediatrician told us Amanda had scoliosis.

Scoliosis occurs most often during the growth spurt just before puberty. What causes scoliosis is unknown, but it is possible that it can be caused by muscular dystrophy. At the time, I did not know that my sister had scoliosis, and later in life, I found out I had a very mild case of it. We also found out in 2016 that Daryl had muscular dystrophy. It appears there was a genetic component from both sides of our families.

We set up a time with a spinal specialist and took Amanda in to be examined. After x-rays and the exam, the physician told us that Amanda's spinal curvature was more moderate than most. We were also told that because she hadn't reached puberty yet, the curvature could increase and lead to severe back pain, with a possible need for spinal surgery.

The only method that would stop the curvature from worsening was for Amanda to be fitted for a body brace. She would have to wear the brace continuously. The brace was made of plastic wrapped around her torso and propped her up against the curve's movement. It covered her from under her armpits to her hips. It wasn't heavy, but it was cumbersome.

Daryl and I were beside ourselves with apprehension. Putting a 12-year-old girl in a body brace like this and sending her to school would be a disaster for her. But we had no choice. We certainly didn't want the curvature to get worse and the need for spinal surgery to be explored. The spinal surgery itself was not without its drawbacks. Surgeons would have to make an incision the length of her spine and place hooks and rods along it to straighten it. She would probably have back pain for the rest of her life, and the rods and hooks could become dislodged, which would mean additional surgeries.

Amanda was fitted for a brace, and it arrived a few weeks later. All during this time, she was distraught by the prospect of having to wear the brace all the time for possibly 18 months or longer. Her anxiety was ramped up through the roof, but we couldn't focus on that now. The more significant concern was trying to stop her spine from curving more.

Amanda was always very concerned with her appearance. She had to have the right clothes and shoes to fit in with the other girls. She didn't do that to keep her friends. Remember, Amanda was the "social butterfly" and had plenty of girlfriends. She quickly made friends with most people and had both school friends and those in our neighborhood. But now she would have to wear loose-fitting clothes that fit over the brace. She was going to stick out like a sore thumb.

The first day she had to wear the brace to school was terrible. We tried to make her feel good about herself by telling her how proud we were of her, how this wasn't a long-term situation, and that someday we would all look back at this time and realize that we did the right thing at the right time. It isn't easy attempting to use adult reasoning with a child.

When she got on the school bus, my heart broke. I know that kids can be very hard on each other, but I was hoping that her friends would stand behind her and be kind, and for the most part, they did.

When Amanda came home from school that day, she was furious. The brace was uncomfortable for her. It applied pressure to her body, which she said hurt her, and the brace was hot. It trapped all her body heat and made her body sweat. We didn't have answers for most of her issues. We just kept trying to be supportive. We tried to stay positive with her. It was difficult for all of us.

At one point in the school year, a few months after she wore the brace, Amanda told us about a girl in her class that the other girls didn't like and how none of the girls would sit or talk to her. She told us how bad she felt for the girl. We discussed this with her and asked her what she thought should be done. I want to believe that she was feeling compassion for the girl because Daryl and I always stressed helping others who were physically or mentally bullied. Her kindness and empathy could have also come from recognizing her feelings due to her back brace.

In any case, Amanda went to school and befriended the girl in hopes of having her friends also accept her into their group. That didn't happen, however. Amanda's friends turned on her and excluded her. She was surprised by her friends. She really didn't think they would turn on her. Amanda and her new friend hung out together in and out of school, but we knew she was heartbroken about how it all turned out.

As her parents, we told her how true friendship works and how you can begin to distinguish between those who you *think* are your friends and those who *are* your friends. We all know this life lesson but asking a 12-year-old to understand and make some sense of it regarding her circumstances is unreasonable.

Goodbye Elementary School, Hello Middle School

Over the summer, Amanda was miserable having to wear her brace. Imagine, if you can, having to wear a piece of thick plastic that surrounds your torso from your hips to your arms and trying to be a 12-year-old who wants to play outside with her friends in sunny 80–90-degree weather but can't because it's too hot inside your plastic cocoon. Imagine sweating profusely whenever you run, jump, skip, and expend energy. Imagine having to wear a t-shirt under your brace to help absorb some of the moisture. Can you imagine what that must be like? I couldn't at the time and still can't imagine it. Every day of this period was heartbreaking for Daryl and me.

Now also imagine having to begin attending a new school and having to wear the same brace. The new school is a middle school that brings together children from several elementary schools. So, for Amanda, her first impression with these new students would be one of being "different". The last thing she wanted at that young age was to be different. She wanted to blend in. Not to stand out and not to stand out for the wrong reason.

Daryl and I worked hard all summer to bolster Amanda's self-esteem. It wasn't easy, but we tried to tell her that she needed people to get to know her personality and character. We also told her it was an excellent opportunity to make new friends since the girls in her elementary school had abandoned her.

By the beginning of the new school year, Amanda had been wearing her brace for about 11 months, so we made a deal with her that she wouldn't have to wear her brace on the first day of school. She was so happy. She could wear clothes that weren't baggy and were more appealing to her.

Pretty soon, that one day turned to two, and then to the first week of school to where it became just wearing the brace after school when she was home.

Amanda started making new friends, and her happiness at school was pretty good. She was still only a below-average student. We approached the middle school and asked to have her tested again for learning disabilities. Still, they would not because she was tested in elementary school, and the results indicated that she did not qualify. We were disappointed, but Amanda was glad because she was tired of being "different".

We met a couple of Amanda's new friends, some of whom had what I would call a "very rough edge". From what we could ascertain, they didn't come from very stable home environments. Daryl and I talked about this and knew we had to convey to Amanda our observations and how she needed to respond to her new friends.

We talked to Amanda about how she was at a point with her new friends where she could either become a follower and conform to their level of thinking, or she could become solid in knowing what she knew about coming from a loving, caring family and lead her friends to always making good choices when the opportunity arose.

Unfortunately, as Amanda progressed through middle school, she became a follower. She was tired of being unique and just wanted to blend in. After a few more months, the brace was not worn, and Daryl and I were tired of fighting with her. She had passed puberty, so we hoped her spine was done moving.

At her next doctor's appointment, Amanda's doctor told us her spine had not curved any further, so either we were successful in stopping it, or we were too late from the beginning, and it curved all it was going to curve before the brace. I hate to think that we put her through so much anguish for nothing, so I like to think we stopped it from curving more.

How's that for making yourself feel better about your decision-making?

Tylenol

Amanda suffered from body aches due to her scoliosis. They would lead to headaches, so she took over-the-counter Advil and Tylenol when needed. This was what her back doctor told us she could do. Unfortunately, Amanda would get these body aches and headaches at school, so she required Advil and Tylenol during the school day.

The school had a zero-tolerance policy toward drugs and alcohol. This was not something we disagreed with. We reached out to the school and communicated her need for Advil and Tylenol. Usually, when a student needed medication, that student had to go to the nurse to ensure the proper dosage was given and taken. In Amanda's case, since her meds were over the counter and we only gave her a couple to carry with her, she was exempt from going to the nurse to take them.

It was the middle of her third year in middle school when I received a call from the school to meet with the principal. When Daryl and I were in the principal's office, they brought Amanda in and told us that it was reported to them that Amanda was distributing pills to another student. We were thunderstruck! My daughter was distributing pills??!! We wanted details because we couldn't believe that she was leading a double life where she was a typical high school-aged girl to one where she was a drug dealer!

What had occurred was that a girlfriend of Amanda's told Amanda that she had a nasty headache. Amanda offered her a Tylenol which she gave to the girl. Another student saw the exchange of a pill and reported it to the school because they thought it might have been something illegal. When the school confronted Amanda and her friend, they told them what had occurred. This was a violation of the school's drug policy. The principal told us that Amanda must attend an alternative school program. This program started at 3 pm and finished at 6 pm on weekdays. It replaced her daytime classes, and she would be in this program for the rest of the school year. The school was treating her like a drug dealer for giving someone Tylenol!

Now Amanda was already having difficulty with her classes, and it was our understanding that the teachers in the alternative program were not interested in the student's success because the students in the program were all troublemakers and not interested in learning.

We begged the school district to please show some leniency. This was Tylenol and not a controlled substance. Their posture was that the rules were the rules and that they had no choice.

I contacted the school superintendent, who took the same position. I was flabbergasted! I couldn't believe they couldn't use common sense to give her detention rather than changing her to a different schedule and ostracizing her.

I couldn't let this happen, so in desperation, I contacted the host of a local radio talk show. I explained what was going on with my daughter, and he agreed that the discipline was overboard.

The radio host arranged a call-in interview with me and the school superintendent. The host interviewed me first, presenting the facts from my point of view. When I was finished, he then interviewed the school superintendent. The superintendent stuck to his guns as far as the policy was concerned but did drop a bombshell that my daughter's attendance in the program would only be for three weeks and not the remainder of the school year.

After the interview, I talked with my wife, and we decided that the shortened period was somewhat an admission that the policy was flawed. Still, we were concerned that they would withdraw the shortened time and enforce it to the end of the year if we continued to fight it.

Amanda was not happy about attending this program. She didn't want to be stigmatized as one of the "bad" students. We told her about our concerns about continuing to fight with the school board and what the repercussions may be. Reluctantly she agreed to attend. It was probably one of many bad decisions that Daryl and I made over the next five years.

Alternative School

Alternative school was a disaster for us. Amanda wasn't getting the same education, and we knew that when she returned to her old classes, she would be behind everybody else and struggle to pass.

Amanda was also exposed to students who were habitual troublemakers. The guys in the alternative program liked her. She was petite, blonde, and beautiful. She loved the attention they gave her, and while in the beginning, she hated the alternative program, by the time it came for her to leave, she was unhappy.

The teachers in the alternative program never really had a curriculum. They were so busy always addressing the unruliness of the classroom that teaching was not a priority. I don't believe that Amanda ever came home with an assignment.

When Amanda was integrated into her old regular classes, she suffered greatly. Daryl and I were still convinced she had a learning disability, and being three weeks behind everyone else was too much for her to overcome.

Thankfully, she passed her courses so she could move on to the next grade level, but all she learned was that the school district was less interested in her education and more interested in enforcing their policies at any cost.

This whole alternative school fiasco left a terrible taste in my mouth about the school district, and from that point on, I never believed they had my daughter's best interest at heart.

I felt they had labeled her, and that label would follow her throughout her high school experience.

Bad Boys and the Dentist

Even though Amanda met many boys in the Alternative program, there was one she met before going into the Alternative program that magically ended up in the Alternative program shortly after she started it.

I'm not sure if Amanda began experimenting with drugs and alcohol, but her character and attitude began changing around this time.

The summer after she was discharged from the Alternative program, Amanda needed to have her wisdom teeth removed. We had spent a fortune on braces for her, and we were not going to let the sprouting of wisdom teeth ruin her beautiful smile.

We removed the teeth, and she was given a two-week supply of Percocet to relieve her pain. This was the start of a 10-year odyssey into drug addiction.

Amanda began abusing the Percocet. You may ask how that could have happened or why didn't we give her the pain medication ourselves. The thing that needs to be remembered is that there was nothing known as the Opioid Epidemic when this occurred. We weren't aware of how addicting these meds could be. We were attempting to teach Amanda to be responsible for herself and told her to take the meds only when experiencing pain. Who knew a two-week supply could start an addiction? We were unaware of the dangers. I hate to use ignorance as an excuse, but in this case, we were.

Amanda had acquired a boyfriend, we'll call him Sam, who was becoming an undesirable influence on her. We weren't aware of this. Around us, he seemed such a personable and friendly guy. Amanda liked him and he treated her well, so we had no real concerns.

Amanda would like to go to his house because, according to her, a bunch of their friends lived around Sam's house, and everyone congregated there. We asked if Sam's mother was always there and if we could meet her. It was arranged, we met, and everything seemed on the up and up. So again, we never had any concerns.

We found out a few years later how concerned we should have been.

High School and Jobs

When Amanda was 15, and in the ninth grade, she got a job working at a nursing home as an aide. She would be in school until three and then go directly to the nursing home and work there until 7. She would then come home and do her schoolwork.

She loved working there and told us about the people she would help care for. She displayed compassion and empathy for the people she cared for and would always tell us how much they loved her. She talked about how she connected with some of the patients and how much she enjoyed sitting with them when she could and just listening to them talk about their lives and family.

I remember how one patient she enjoyed sitting with passed away while she was off work. When she entered the patient's room, not knowing that he had passed, she was so confused that he wasn't there. The room was clean and the bed was made. She just cried when she learned from one of the other staff members that he had passed the day before. She came home that evening and told us what had occurred. She felt so bad that she had no chance to say goodbye. It reminded her of how fragile life is and how it should never be taken for granted.

We didn't know Sam was also working at the nursing home until Amanda had been working for about six months. It somehow came out in conversation with Amanda, and we were surprised. She played it off like we should have already known, but we couldn't recall her ever mentioning this to us. But we thought maybe she did say something in passing, and we didn't pick up on it.

This was the beginning of a series of rationalizations with Amanda that would haunt us for years.

Amanda worked at the nursing home for almost a year before she lost that job for reasons I don't recall. This was the beginning of a series of jobs that Amanda would run through over the years. Sam continued to work at the nursing home for a bit longer until he quit. This also began a timeline of them doing anything they could to be together as much as possible.

Amanda's grades weren't excellent, but they were consistent, and it wasn't like she wasn't trying. So, if she kept her grades where they typically were, we didn't ride her too hard. Some people are just not college material, and we were beginning to face that Amanda may be shaped in that mold.

A Cell Phone and the Principal

Amanda was in her junior year at high school when Daryl and I received a phone call from the principal that we needed to come to the school for a meeting that day.

We arrived in the early afternoon to meet with the principal and were directed to her office. Once there, she told us that Amanda had been in a fight with another girl. Both girls were removed from class and taken to the administrative office suite. Because of this incident, their backpacks and cell phones were confiscated.

The principal told us she was scrolling through Amanda's text messages, and in her opinion, some of the texts looked very suspicious.

The first thing that went off in my mind was, what right did the principal have to go through my daughter's phone looking at texts and photos or anything else for that matter? I was furious. The principal tried telling us that she had every right to look at the contents of the phone, and the only reason she called us in was that it appeared the texts were describing the purchasing or selling of drugs.

We asked the principal if she had spoken with Amanda about the texts and what her explanation was. She told us she did not talk with Amanda and wanted to communicate with us first. Based on my experience with the school district, I felt this prophecy was being fulfilled. I believed that the Tylenol incident had labeled her as a problem student, and this was the school jumping straight to a conclusion without a reasonable investigation.

Amanda was eventually brought into the room with us, where she explained away all the suspicious texts, and my feeling was then one of "I hope you had your fun, but I've had enough of this school."

The school did nothing further. There was no discipline

given to either girl since the fight did not involve physical contact, and after a few days, the whole thing was forgotten.

I recall that a few days later, Amanda and I were in the car together, and I had what I thought was a meaningful conversation with her about how she needed to be very careful with what she stored on her phone or how she used it. That the phone could be a very incriminating device even when used innocently. I told her to make sure she deleted any texts or photos that she thought were inappropriate or could give the impression of inappropriateness.

I thought I was a good dad telling her this. I was nothing more than a fool.

Policed

During the summer after Amanda's Junior year of high school, I was picking her up from Sam's house one evening. Amanda and a girlfriend were in the back seat as I pulled away from Sam's home.

I had to go up the road about 150 feet to make a U-turn around a median so I could head back towards my home. As I turned, I noticed a police cruiser also make the turn behind me. I thought that maybe I had made an illegal U-turn, but I knew that was not the case.

We traveled about half a mile making a few turns along the way, and the police cruiser stayed right behind me. I knew at that point that I would be pulled over. Not soon after that thought, the lights went on the cruiser's overhead rack, and I pulled to the side of the road.

It was dusk, and the road was somewhat dark where I had pulled over. The officer approached my car and asked me for my license and registration with his flashlight. He asked where I was going and shone the light on my daughter and her friend in the back seat. I explained to the officer that I had just picked up my daughter and her friend and that I was driving her friend home and then heading home myself.

He took my license and registration back to his car and, after a few minutes, came back to my car and gave them back, and said to have a nice night. I asked why I was pulled over, and he said, "Do you know anything about the house where you picked your daughter up?" I was stunned, but I said, "No." He then said, "Well, just be careful." He then went back to his car. I sat there for a second and thought, "Did I just hear that right?"

The police cruiser was still behind me, so I got out of my car and went back to ask the officer what he meant by his comment. I know you should never approach a police cruiser during a traffic stop, but I felt like he had opened a door I needed to go through. I asked the officer what he meant by his comment about Sam's house, and he said something to the effect that he had said all he was going to say. I asked him if he was sure that he saw me picking up my daughter from the correct house. I could not recall him being behind me when I was picking her up, and I thought maybe he thought she was coming from a home she did not. He did not answer me. He just closed his window and directed me back to my car.

When I got back in the car, I told the girls what had happened, but they could not understand why the policeman would have said that about Sam's house. The girls were sure he must have thought they had come out of another house. The homes on Sam's street were built close to each other and with me not being sure the police were there when I picked them up, it easily could have been a mistake on the police officer's behalf.

On my way home, in my head, I was having this conversation about what had just transpired and trying to make some sense of it. The only thing that made sense was that the officer was mistaken about the house the girls came out of. The other alternative was one I did not want to face. When I got home, I told Daryl what had happened, and she agreed that the officer was probably mistaken. That made me feel somewhat better, but I was beginning to have uneasy doubts about my daughter's life.

Senior Year Disaster

As Amanda's senior year began, I was starting to have suspicions that she may have a drug problem. She was less and less at home. She was spending more time at Sam's house.

She did not have an after-school job but did not need money. Sam was buying her everything she wanted. She did not have a driver's license. We did not want her to drive until she was 18. She was not concerned with that because she always had a ride wherever she wanted. Amanda was extremely popular and had many friends who did drive.

On occasion, Amanda would tell us she wanted to sleep over at a girlfriend's house who lived close to school and was in a class with her. She said they would work on their homework together, helping each other out. About a third of the way into the school year, the school contacted us and told us that Amanda was tardy from some classes and had skipped school several times. The school would suspend her from school if she missed another day.

Daryl and I were furious. First, we were angry at the school for not contacting us when she skipped her first class, and more importantly, we were mad at her for violating our trust. I should have gone after the school and asked why they weren't contacting us sooner, but by then, I was so fed up with the school district that all I wanted to do was get Amanda through her senior year and put the school district behind us.

We grounded Amanda severely, and she was not happy. She insisted that she did not skip school. She was just late for her homeroom because it was across the campus from her where her locker was located, and she could not make it there in time. She said she explained this to her homeroom teacher but that the teacher would not give her any slack and told her that she would be marked absent from school if she continued to be late.

We told her we would make sure that she was no longer late. We started driving her to school so she would have plenty of time to get to her locker and homeroom. The absences and tardiness came to an end.

Amanda's senior year started poorly but worsened as the school year progressed.

Senior Picture Day

We had navigated through most of the school year but not without incident. Amanda's grades were an issue throughout her senior year, but she was getting enough done to pass her courses. We constantly fought with Amanda about her schoolwork. She would come home and tell us she had done all her homework in study hall, but then, when it came to her grades, they were just at a passing level. It was as if she was doing as little as possible to get by. I swear the school was doing all they could to ensure she passed because they were tired of dealing with her. I have nothing to prove that with, but it was undoubtedly strange how we would get contacted by the school that she was failing a course, and then a short time later, she would get a passing grade.

As spring approached, it was time for Senior pictures to be taken. We had scheduled a day with the photographer, and on that day, we were set to go. We had a late morning appointment. By 9 am, Amanda was still not awake in her room, and we knew she needed time to prepare. By 9:30 am, we began knocking on her door. It was locked, so we got the passkey and opened the door. She was still sleeping and looked like she had been through hell. We shook her until she woke up and reminded her that she had an appointment for her senior pictures. She told us she was up all night with menstrual cramps and asked if we could cancel and reschedule for another day.

What choice did we have? So, we rescheduled. I later found out that Amanda was suffering from withdrawal symptoms. We had no idea. We were so uneducated and so unprepared.

On the day of Amanda's new appointment, she was ready on time and looked great. Her photos were excellent. Several were displayed in my work office, wallet, and home. Little did Daryl and I know that she was high on Oxycontin when those pictures were taken.

It's hard to believe that Amanda got high before
her Senior pictures were taken. She looks so
good in this shot.

The Prom & The Breakup

The Prom was probably the highlight of Amanda's senior year. She was so excited about going to the prom with Sam. They had been together since her sophomore year.

On the day of the prom, Amanda looked radiant! Her hair was in an updo, and her makeup and dress made her look like a princess. Daryl and I were so happy for her. She went to the prom with several of her friends and their dates. She was going to attend an after-prom party, but we made her promise to come home first and change so we could see that she was safe. She and Sam returned to our house around midnight, and she said they would meet with their friends, have breakfast at a local diner, and then drive out to a state park where there were rapids and white-water rafting.

Everything went terrific for Amanda during the prom. She was just so happy. Then the bottom fell out.

About a month after the prom, Sam broke up with Amanda. She was devastated. She was inconsolable. She went into a personal spiral that had her acting irrationally. I thought Sam broke up with her because her drug habit was getting too expensive for him. I just had nothing to prove that she was using drugs.

We rarely gave Amanda any money. We believed that if she wanted money, she had to earn it. There were many months in her senior year when she had no job. We assumed Sam paid for everything they did because she had no money. Not that they did much. We thought Sam was still working at the nursing home because we did not know otherwise.

Amanda's broken heart threw her off. She kept reaching out to Sam, but he was not responding. Then she heard that he had a new girlfriend, which crushed her. She did not want to go to school because she did not want to be humiliated seeing him with his new girlfriend.

She started skipping school again. Her appearance was becoming more and more disheveled. She spent most of her time in her room. Daryl and I both thought a lot of this behavior was due to a broken heart, but in the back of my mind, I kept wondering if somehow drugs were involved.

I didn't grow up in a bad neighborhood as a kid, but it wasn't the best. There were things I learned as I grew up that stuck with me. One of those things was drug addiction. I had met a few people during my teenage years fighting drug addiction, and one of the things you observed quickly was that you didn't want to become addicted to drugs or alcohol, and those who did become addicted never found help until they asked for it.

I knew that if I ever began confronting my daughter with my fears that she was addicted, she would deny it and never ask for help from Daryl or me unless she was ready to admit to her addiction. I shared my thoughts only with Daryl, but she was in denial and did not see what I saw with Amanda. Her doubts had me questioning what I thought I was seeing.

We were about to board the "crazy train" of addiction without knowing where or when the train would stop.

The Invisible Graduation

Amanda was approaching the end of her senior year, and graduation was rapidly approaching. Again, the school contacted us to say that she was behind in three different subjects and would not graduate if she did not get the work done.

We pushed Amanda extremely hard to get the work done, and she was agitated and angry throughout the process. She felt that no matter what she did, the school would never graduate her and that they would hold back her diploma at all costs.

Daryl and I kept pushing her through the assignments, and they ended up getting done and turned in. About a week later and a couple of weeks before graduation, we found out that Amanda had passed all her courses and that she would graduate.

As graduation day approached, Amanda told us that she did not want to attend the ceremony. She did not want to be in the same ceremony as Sam. We pleaded with her to participate in the graduation ceremony. We told her that she was permitting Sam to control her even though he no longer wanted to be with her. We tried everything.

On the day the graduation ceremonies were held, Amanda was not there. We have no pictures, videos, or memories of her getting her diploma. We returned her cap and gown to the school a couple of days later and were given her diploma then.

We learned years later from Amanda that she was not permitted to attend graduation. She had gotten high, skipped all the graduation practices, and because she missed the practices, the school had barred her from walking with the rest of her class.

Beach Vacation?

Every year since we returned to Pittsburgh, Daryl and I would take Dan and Amanda and travel to a beach resort on the east coast for a week's long vacation. We would go with other family members and have a great time just relaxing on the beach or by the pool, playing shuffleboard or beach football with the kids, riding bikes on the boardwalk, or just swimming in the surf.

Before our vacation, Amanda was still sulking even though she had a new job and started making new girlfriends. The idea of going to the beach brightened her up, and she asked if she could bring a friend with her so she would not have to spend all her time with her mom and dad. We agreed to let her bring a friend.

My son also did not want to hang with mom and dad, so he got a bunch of his friends together and rented an apartment for the week down at the other end of the beach from where we were staying.

My son had just turned 21 so going to the bars with his buddies was something we would not deny him. He drove our second car with a couple of his friends while another drove the rest of their entourage down.

My son still wanted to be at the beach during the same time we were there so he could come to join us at his convenience and be with his family when he wanted. He also joined us for dinner a few times. It was a nice arrangement for him and us.

My daughter and her girlfriend (we will call her Eve) also thought it was a great arrangement. While they did spend most of their time with us, they liked being able to have the guys pick them up and let them hang out with them. I was not concerned with the girls being with my son's friends. My son was responsible and would not allow any harm to befall them. He had become very protective of his sister as he aged.

A little more than halfway through the week, Amanda and Eve told us they would take the bus down to the boy's apartment so they could all go to the boardwalk together. This was ok with us since we did not enjoy the large crowds at the boardwalk.

Our family had a lovely evening at our hotel. We went to dinner and then had a couple of drinks at the bar. We were walking back to the hotel when I got a call from the local police.

The police told us that Amanda and Eve had been arrested for being under the influence while driving and for possessing narcotics. You want to talk about the floor collapsing under you. I felt like I was in free fall. This vacation was so good for all of us. Daryl and I were relaxing after a year of strife with Amanda and the school; my son was having a great time with his friends, Amanda's spirits were good, and she had her shine back, and now this.

Amanda was in an ocean of hot water, and so was her friend Eve. I was responsible for Eve. I had promised her mother that I would care for her and keep her safe.

I remember the police telling me that the girls had to be processed, and then if they did not have any outstanding arrest warrants or priors, they would be released to us with a trial date set for a later time. My head was spinning. I tried to write this all down as quickly as possible, but it was impossible. Even as I write this, I cannot believe how much I can recall from that phone call. It is incredible how stress makes us each function differently.

I now had the unenviable task of calling Eve's mom and telling her what had happened with her daughter. It was close to midnight when I called Eve's mom to tell her that her daughter had been arrested for drug possession. The shock, disappointment, and anger came through the phone and grabbed me like a vice. She wanted to know what had happened, but I did not know. The police were not releasing any details. She was ready to jump in her car and post bail for her daughter, but I told her that Eve would be released to my custody and that I would pick them up at that time. I told her there would be a pending court date. She wanted her daughter to come home immediately. After talking with my family, I told her we decided to stay until our vacation was over, but if she wanted to come to our location and get her daughter, I could understand. I told her that I would bring her home if she could wait, and I also told her that her daughter and Amanda were not leaving my sight for the remainder of the vacation.

I do not know what made her change her mind about coming to get her daughter. Maybe it was the 12-hour roundtrip drive, or it was in the middle of a work week, and she could not miss work. No matter what the case, she let her daughter stay with us for the remainder of our vacation.

I finally got a call from the police at 2 am telling me the girls were being released to my custody and I needed to come down and sign some paperwork. I immediately went to the police station, and after all the necessary paperwork had been reviewed and signed, the girls were released. Of course, as soon as we got in the car, I asked what had happened. Their story was the following:

They had gone down to hang out with my son and his friends but got bored. My daughter asked my son if she could borrow the car so she and Eve could drive around and flirt with the boys. My son gave her the keys, and the two drove the strip, smoking weed and talking to guys in other cars and on the street. It just so happened that one of the cars they pulled up to was an unmarked police car with two young-looking male undercover cops inside. Eve rolled down her window and started flirting. They said the guys inside asked them if they knew where there were any good parties. Eve pulled out a joint, lit it, and said the party was in their car. That was it. They pulled them over and arrested them. In the cup holder of the front console were four Xanax tablets. Eve told us they were hers. Later we heard that Eve said they were Amanda's. We may never know the truth about that one.

The rest of the vacation was anything but relaxing. The girls were miserable, as were Daryl and I. Incredulously they wanted to go down and hang with my son and his friends. I could not believe that I had to remind them that was how their current problem began. My daughter called her brother and implored him to tell us that he would keep a close eye on them. When my son called me on his sister's behalf, he told me privately not to let her come down. She and Eve were out of control, and he did not want to be responsible for them. That was stunning to hear from my son. I asked why he felt that way, and he said he could not speak right then and that we could talk about it when we got back to Pittsburgh. Knowing that he might be around his friends, and it wasn't very comfortable to speak about this in front of them, I agreed.

The last three days of our vacation crawled by. My mind could not stop working. I could not help but feel that this was a dangerous path my daughter was on. Every time Amanda and Eve had to leave us to go to our apartment, I would follow them from a distance to ensure they did not try to get down to where my son was staying. I did not want them to put my son in a precarious situation.

When the vacation ended and we had to head back to Pittsburgh, I felt very somber. There was no conversation in the car. The girls were on their cell phones the entire time while Daryl and I were in the front seats, lost in our thoughts.

I will never forget dropping Eve off at her home and the look her mom gave me as she took Eve inside. It was the last time I ever saw Eve or her mom again.

Drug Court and The New Beau

Fall was arriving, and with it was Amanda's upcoming court date. We had to book a room in a hotel back in the city where she was arrested. It was not difficult since this was a summer destination, and the town was deserted in October.

Amanda had also found a new boyfriend. We'll call him Jack. Jack was her age but a graduate of a different high school. I don't know how they met, but he seemed like a good guy when we met him. Amanda was happy around Jack and vice versa.

A week after Amanda's arrest, we started getting flyers in the mail for defense attorneys. Being new to this, we called a couple, and they all promised the same thing. For the small price of $5000, they could get Amanda's arrest pled down to a misdemeanor for possession of marijuana. It would stay on her record for five years but could then be expunged with their help.

Five thousand dollars was an awful lot of money, so to ensure I explored every avenue, I called the public defender's office and spoke with a woman. She wasn't a public defender, but she looked up the details of my daughter's arrest and told me that the public defender's office could get the same deal for her.

There would be court costs and a fine involved of about $500. The other attorneys had told me not to use a public defender. They said you never knew who would represent you until the day of the trial, and it could be someone fresh out of law school. The public defender's office assured me that they would not be using someone new and that the public defenders they had on staff had all been with the office for several years. We decided to use the public defender and take our chances.

Amanda asked if Jack could come along with us to her hearing. They had been hanging around each other consistently, and this was the happiest we'd seen her since her breakup with Sam. Since we would all be staying in the same room at the hotel, we agreed. Amanda and Jack wanted to follow us to the hearing in his car so they could listen to their type of music. We were ok with that since their music was far different from ours.

When we got to the resort town, we unpacked for the night. We had traveled light because the hearing was in the morning, and we were leaving after the proceedings. Amanda and Jack went for a walk on the boardwalk while Daryl and I looked around for places for us to eat. The city was deserted because it was the off-season, so finding a restaurant proved to be somewhat of a challenge. Once we did locate one, we got Amanda and Jack, and all went to dinner.

I only mention these two events because Amanda and Jack got high during the walk on the boardwalk. They seemed perfectly normal at dinner, but later, as I became more educated on substance abuse, I discovered that when a user acts normal, it's because they are high on something.

The next day we went to the proceedings and met the public defender, who told us he had already talked to the prosecutor. They would drop the charges on the possession of a controlled substance, Xanax, and would prosecute for the use of marijuana as long as Amanda agreed to plead guilty. We were told the fine would be about $400 plus court costs.

We all agreed this was the best way to go. So, after the court formalities, an admonishment to Amanda from the court, and payment of the fines, we had this nightmare behind us. In five years, Amanda could petition the court to expunge her record, and if she had no further arrests, it would be granted.

I have one observation that I would like to make here. At the court proceedings that day, there were many young people in the court. I guess these arrests were frequent, and as quick as the whole process was, it is a great money maker for the county.

Jack did not last long after this. While he liked my daughter and would supply her with all the drugs she needed, she decided he was not her type. Thus, began a string of quickie boyfriends who, if they could satisfy my daughter's drug needs or money needs, would stick around until she got fed up with them or they got fed up with her.

To make it clear, we were unaware of anything concerning drugs until much later, when Amanda would enlighten us about what was going on during her drug use at different times in her life. My wife and I were so naive to my daughter's drug use and how it escalated over time with her. It wasn't until later, when we were far into her drug addiction, that we learned how we should have dealt with it.

This lack of knowledge leads me to speak publicly about my daughter's addiction and what we should have done to help her find a path to sobriety.

Moving Out

Amanda's behavior was getting out of hand. She would go out and not come back until the early morning hours on most nights of the week. She would sleep in late, and her appearance started to look bad. She had just broken up with another boyfriend. I lost count of which one this was.

Daryl and I were fed up with her. Money was missing, and we thought it was her taking it. She couldn't hold a job for more than a few months, but it wasn't her fault each time she was fired. At this point, Daryl and I were both in denial that she had a drug problem. It was far easier to do that than to confront her. Besides, engaging her would have led to her denying her drug problem.

She denied that she had taken anything that was missing around the house and always made us feel that we either misplaced whatever was missing or didn't have as much money as we thought we had.

Life at our house was getting very chaotic. My 18-year-old daughter could not stay employed, did not want to attend community college, and lived off her family without contributing anything.

It was around this time that Amanda met a girl about her age who was also a mother to an infant The girl and her baby lived in a house about 10 miles away, and the girl needed someone to watch the baby while she worked. Amanda announced that she would move in with the girl, watch the baby, and work in the evenings at a local bar.

We were thrilled. She was moving out and doing something productive. We felt that maybe she was finding her way. Little did we know that the girl Amanda was moving in with had a drug problem, and they met because of it.

Within six months, the girlfriend lost her job and was now on welfare. We weren't aware of this at the time. Amanda never told us anything.

Around this time, Daryl and I went away for a few days and left the house unattended. When we returned, the place looked the same, but somehow, I felt something was wrong.

We got a bill from a local department store for over a thousand dollars a few weeks later. We immediately checked to see if our credit cards had been stolen, but they were not. Most of the purchases were for clothes in the Young Ladies department. I called the department store to tell them we did not make the purchases. They said they would investigate and contact us if they found anything.

About a week later, the department store contacted us and told us they had videotaped two young ladies making the purchases. The descriptions they gave us fit our daughter and her friend. My heart sank. They asked if I still wanted to contest the charges, but I told them I knew who it was and would take care of it.

At this point, I knew that I was fighting a problem unlike any I had ever dealt with before, and I was extremely ill-equipped for this fight. I called my daughter and demanded to know what was going on. She admitted making the charges and said it was because she had no clothes for a new job she was starting and knew if she came to us, we would lecture her about her lack of saving money when working.

I could have pressed charges against her, but I did not want her to have a record. I was thinking that at some point, she would get out of this "phase," and having a record would cut out many opportunities for her. We paid the bill and told her never to do that again.

Daryl and I were a mess. We were not rationally dealing with the situation. We were reacting to what Amanda was throwing at us instead of anticipating what she would do and having a plan to solve it.

I was not sleeping well and not finding any joy in life. My daughter was at the forefront of my mind constantly. I have no idea how I functioned at my job. I know I must not have been at my best.

Cutting Off the Cash

Amanda was turning into a cash drain for us. Even though she would get a job, she always ran out of money before her next payday and then either did not have money to put gas in the car or could not buy lunch for herself. There was always a reason she needed money, and my wife and I always gave it to her. We didn't give it without question, but it was at a point where the answers were always the same, and the solutions we provided her were never used.

Amanda and the girl she was living with had a falling out, and she moved back home but only under the stipulation that she finds a job and pays her own expenses. Of course, her paycheck was gone as soon as she got paid. She would go out with her girlfriends and always complained that they would do expensive things, and she made the least out of all of them, so by the end of the night, she was extremely low on money.

We took a stand and told her that if she could not afford to go out with her friends, she had to find a better job or get herself educated so she could get a better job. She would get mad at us and storm off, and then by the middle of the week, she would be out of money and need $25 to put gas in the car so she could get to work. It was like we were stuck in a "Catch-22". Our perception was that Amanda did not make enough to travel to and from work; if she lost her job, we would give her money while she tried to find another. She was still depressed when her girlfriends called her to go out with them. She would have to turn them down because she had no money.

We got so tired of her moping around that we would give her money to go with her friends or pay for gas in her car to go to work. We just kept hoping that she would grow up and begin to take her job seriously and climb the pay scale or decide to go to college or trade school to get an education or skill set.

None of these things were happening, and we kept giving her cash. Daryl and I often talked about how she went through her money quickly. It was something we did not understand. Daryl even sat down with her to list her expenses and income so she could teach her how to budget. Amanda claimed to understand, but then she would run out of cash and come up with some excuse for spending more than she had anticipated.

The whole time this happened, I had little voices in my head telling me something was up. Was she spending the money on drugs? I was hoping that wasn't the case, so I convinced myself it wasn't drugs. I wanted this not to be the reason so badly that I convinced myself she wasn't addicted.

After almost nine months of this, I decided enough was enough. I was not going to give her any more cash. So, I told Daryl about this plan. I told Daryl that If Amanda came to her asking for money, she should send her to me. When Amanda did come to me for money, I told her she was no longer getting any more cash from us. She was furious. She begged me. She told me it was her girlfriend's birthday and she needed to get her a gift. I held my ground. This is when things escalated and went to a new level.

Check Mate

Amanda was becoming unmanageable. Her begging for money so that she could go out was never-ending. But somehow, a girlfriend would pick her up at the house, and off they would go. When she ran out of money to go to work, she would have to find alternative means.

Daryl and I were usually out of the house by 7 am to go to our jobs, and since Amanda's job did not start until 9 am, she was still in bed when we left. She worked part-time and never worked more than 4 or 5 hours daily. There were quite a few days when we would get home where she would be in bed. Some days we did not want to bother her because we did not want to deal with her and her moods. On other days, we would knock on her door, it sounded like she had just woken up, and she would tell us she was either sick or didn't sleep well the night before and was catching up.

I cannot recall why I called her work phone number, but when I asked to speak to Amanda, they told me she no longer worked for them. When I asked about her last day, they told me it was two weeks prior. I was numb. How could she have kept this from us? I knew it had to be bad because of all the secrecy. I called Daryl, and we both decided that we needed to get to the bottom of this.

When we got home, we knocked on her bedroom door. She again sounded like she was getting up. We asked her how her day at work had been. It was a hard day, she said. She was exhausted and just wanted a couple of hours of sleep.

We then told her that we knew she was fired. She initially tried to make it sound like she just got fired, but I told her I knew she was fired two weeks ago. She said that wasn't true. So, we asked what had happened.

The story went something like this. There was money missing from the cash register on mistaken ring-ups. Instead of $10 being rung up, a $1 would be rung. Amanda claimed that she would sign into the cash register every morning, but during the day, when she would take a break, other people would work at her cash register, and that was when the false ring-ups would occur. We asked why she didn't sign out of the cash register when she took her break, and she told us that most of the time, she did, but there would be days she would forget, which was when this occurred. We asked her if she had let her boss know, but she told us the boss did not like her and was looking for a reason to fire her. She was ashamed to tell us because she didn't want us to be disappointed in her and that she was already looking for a new job.

We fell for it and felt so bad for her. We told her we would help her find a new job and give her some cash to help her through this period.

Please don't judge Daryl or me for our response. It's all a part of what was happening to Daryl and me. We were slowly but surely becoming codependent on our daughter's addiction. I'll explain codependency in a later chapter, but you'll be able to see it happening as you read. I can tell you that unless you live through something like this with your child, it is challenging to see through the fog of codependency.

About a week after this incident, I was balancing my checkbook online when I saw a check for $200 come through. It was made out to "Cash." I brought the check up on the computer screen and immediately recognized Amanda's writing and signature. She had taken the last check from our stack of checks and used it to get money.

Again, I was furious. What the hell was this girl doing?!! I called her to my office and asked her how she got around in the car when she had no money. She told me she had her last paycheck and was stretching it out until she had a new job. This is the same girl who blew through her pay two days after she got it. I then showed her the check on my computer screen. She looked defeated. She told me she was desperate. She did not want us to know she was fired and needed money to look for a job, so she borrowed it from us. Daryl and I were livid. We were sick of being lied to, and quite frankly, we could no longer tell when she was being honest or not.

She told us that she would pay us back as soon as she got a job. We told her that was definitely going to be the case.

We're still waiting for that payback.

Admission

Amanda was out one evening with her girlfriends when she met a guy at a local bar. She liked this guy and brought him to our house for us to meet. He was a nice guy who had a job in the trades. We'll call him Roger.

One summer day, shortly after we met Roger, Daryl, Amanda, Roger, and I were talking on our back porch. Amanda seemed happy and engaged in the conversation. It was so good to see her this way. This was the Amanda that we knew. Amanda excused herself to get ready so they could go out, and Daryl went inside, leaving Roger and me on the porch. We talked about all kinds of things, but somehow, we got around to Amanda. He told me he thought she was a great girl, but sometimes she "partied" too hard. I asked him what he meant by that, and he indicated that she sometimes took pills, and he was not too fond of that.

At that moment, I wanted to hit the "pause" button and go back and review that piece of the conversation. But then Amanda came out, and they went off on their date.

I sat there and contemplated what I had just heard. Amanda's boyfriend of two weeks told me my daughter was taking pills, leading to "partying" too hard! I knew then that Amanda's drug problem was genuine, but I still did not know how bad it was.

At that point, I started taking a different approach to her. I sat her down one day and told her how much she meant to us and that if she had any problem or issue that she wanted our help with, her mom and I would always support her. She was a little surprised. I'm not sure she knew how to handle that. We had been at such odds with each other for what seemed like forever, and now we were reaching out with a fig leaf. But the conversation ended well, and I hoped she would reach out to us for help.

About a month later, she was again begging me for money.

I told her I was done funding her, but she should let me know if she was in trouble. She hung up angry, but about 10 minutes later, she called me back and said she had something she needed to tell me.

I was in my office at work, so I got up and closed my door to talk privately with her. I was agitated. I could feel my heart rate increasing. She told me that she had a drug problem and wanted to quit but could not. She liked Roger; he did not use drugs, and she was envious of how happy he was in his life. She wanted that also but knew the drugs were getting in the way. We talked about what kind of drugs she was using, and she told me that it was primarily pills, but she was also smoking weed. She was using Xanax, Oxycontin, and barbiturates.

I told her we were there to help and needed to get her into a rehab facility. She told me she didn't want to go into an inpatient program because she didn't want to be away from Roger. That was the least of my concerns. I told her we should get in touch with a rehab program so they could let us know the best way to address this.

I called a rehab and told them about my daughter's drug problem. The person on the other side of the line said the rehab center needed her to call because that would show them she wanted their help. Amanda was very apprehensive about this, but after we kept on her, she relented and called the rehab.

They had her come into an outpatient location so they could assess her. Since Amanda was over 18 years of age, they told us we could not be a part of her assessment. They said that when families sat in on the evaluation, the truth never came out about how severe the usage was.

Daryl, Roger, and I drove Amanda to the assessment, and we waited outside while she was evaluated. She came out after about 90 minutes and told us she would attend the outpatient program. We were thrilled. We thought that, finally, this nightmare might be coming to an end. Once again, we didn't know how naive we were.

Suboxone Success

The outpatient program the rehab had was not a good fit for Amanda. She had found yet another job, and her work hours and the outpatient program didn't work out. We knew about a new solution for people with opioid substance abuse. The answer was a medication called Suboxone, which we found curbed the desire to use opioids by blocking the pleasure receptors in the brain. If a user who took suboxone took opioids such as Oxycontin, they could not get high.

We investigated Suboxone clinics and luckily found a physician licensed to prescribe Suboxone and offered one-on-one counseling. This physician also referred Amanda to a psychiatrist who could help her with her anxiety problems.

Amanda was gung-ho about this program. She wanted to put the drugs behind her and work on living a sober life. Daryl and I were thrilled. It looked like the crazy train we were on was stopping.

The problem with Suboxone clinics at the time was that they were not covered by insurance, and neither was the prescription. It was all out of pocket, and the clinic would only take cash. Checks or credit cards were a hazard based on the clientele they had to work with.

To monitor Amanda on this program, I would drive her to all her appointments, pick up her prescriptions, and provide her with the daily dose. They started her out with four Suboxone tablets a day. I remember the exact dosage because Daryl and I thought it was a little high.

We had a family member who was addicted to opioids and was taking Suboxone. He was 6"4", weighed close to 225 pounds, and took only two tablets per dose. We didn't want to cause any issues with Amanda's treatment, so we kept our thoughts to ourselves.

After about a week of taking the Suboxone, Amanda told us

she thought she was taking too much. She said it was making her feel weird all day. We had her talk to her doctor, who reinforced that she needed that amount based on her prior opioid usage. This was the first time that Daryl and I became aware of just how bad her addiction to opioids was. We were just thrilled that she never turned to heroin.

Amanda was at the beginning of the opioid epidemic. You could not help but watch the local news and hear about another series of heroin overdoses. One of our biggest fears was her getting involved with heroin.

Amanda and Roger were incredibly happy together. Amanda was taking her Suboxone as prescribed, Roger had obtained jobs doing home remodeling and repairs, Amanda was holding onto her current job, and she applied to go to community college.

We were finally able to take a deep breath and relax. We kept an eye on Amanda, but as she progressed in the right direction, we started to relax.

Once again, we found out how little we knew.

The Slow Pace of Relapse

Amanda had started community college, and it was determined by her placement tests that she needed to take some college-level remedial classes before taking college-level courses. Amanda barely got through high school, so this was not surprising to us.

She worked a job and went to school at the same time. She worked hard in her classes and got support from Daryl, me, and Roger. She made it through her first semester, but the second one was exceedingly difficult. She put forth a ton of effort but could not comprehend the material. She dropped out in the middle of the semester after not doing well on her mid-term tests.

She was disappointed but got more hours at her job and decided that maybe a trade school would better suit her. We knew that community college would be challenging for her, so it was not surprising that she quit.

Amanda and Roger had been together for several months and were incredibly happy. Roger was so pleased that he came to me and told me he would like to marry her. I told him that he needed to slow down a little. I told him I thought he was very good to her but was not ready to support her. His odd jobs that put money in his pocket and were consistent did not provide him enough to provide for her adequately. He told me he wanted to start his own business. I told him to get that all in place and then come back and talk to me. He was disappointed, but he seemed ok with everything, and I felt we parted with a good understanding.

Amanda was still taking her Suboxone daily, but she asked if she could manage it herself because it wasn't always convenient to get up early to get her dosage from us before we left for work. Since she was doing so well and appeared to be very vested in her sobriety, we told her that would be ok but that if we saw anything that concerned us, we would return to the current method.

The Suboxone physician still had her prescription level at four tablets once a day, which was somewhat concerning. Still, Amanda told us she was only taking three at a time because it affected her work performance. Her boss commented that she seemed "a little off." She did not want to lose her job, so she took less, which did not seem to bother her.

We asked her what she was doing with the extra pills, and she showed us that she was holding on to them and would skip filling a prescription when she had enough. We did not know that Amanda had actually cut down to only two pills a day, and we only saw a portion of what she was storing.

While Roger did not use any drugs, he did drink. He was not an alcoholic, but he occasionally got drunk. Amanda was never a big drinker, so she told us that it never bothered her that he would drink. Roger also had friends that smoked weed and did harder drugs.

Amanda and Roger were visiting a couple's home who were friends of Roger's. This couple knew Amanda took Suboxone, so when Roger was out of the room, they asked her if she was interested in selling any of her Suboxone. Suboxone has an excellent street value since opioid abusers love to take it when they cannot get their fix. Taking suboxone stops them from getting "dope sick." Dope sick is when abusers cannot get their fix and then start getting nauseous, having the chills, then the sweats, and throwing up. From my understanding of talking to recovering users, it is like having the worst case of the flu that you can imagine. It lasts for days and drains you physically and mentally.

She started selling her stockpile of Suboxone and was making a nice chunk of change on the side. Roger had no idea she was doing this. Her staying sober was essential to him. He did not want to be involved with anyone who had an addiction.

No one knew that Amanda started trading her suboxone for

Xanax and other pills a short time later. She was still selling some, but her relapse had begun.

The Crazy Train Leaves the Station Again

Just when we thought we could breathe again. Just when we thought we could relax and begin to enjoy life. Just when we thought that Amanda was doing so well, that she was using her suboxone, going to her counseling, holding her job, and looking to get into a beauty school, Roger came to us and said he thought that Amanda was using again. Of course, we asked him why he thought this, and he said that she had been acting strange lately. He said she was acting like she did when he first met her when she was using pills.

Daryl and I did not want to believe him. We told him that he might be seeing things. We told him we did not see any differences, and besides, how could she possibly be getting high while she was using Suboxone? We told him not to worry. It was probably nothing. I don't know about Daryl, but I hoped that none of this was true.

I kept a close eye on Amanda for the next couple of weeks and didn't see any difference in her behavior. I did notice a difference in Roger's behavior, however. He was more cautious with her, and that kind of unnerved me. I kept thinking, "I hope he doesn't drive her to use drugs because of his suspicious behavior." I look back at it now and realize how wrong I was to blame him. He was the smart one. He trusted his gut. He believed what the voices in his head were saying to him. I chose to live in an alternate reality. I decided not to see what he was seeing. I did not listen to the voice warning me that something wasn't right with Amanda.

A few weeks after Roger told us of his suspicions, he came to Daryl and me again. But this time, he came with proof. He said he went through Amanda's purse while she was in the shower and found six pills. He took them to show to us. We went on the internet and found out they were Vicodin.

When Amanda finished her shower and joined us, we

confronted her with the evidence that was found in her purse. She looked at the pills and said those were Vicodin. She asked Roger what purse he found them in and when he told her, she said that she had just started using that purse again. Amanda said she hadn't used the purse for over a year and she forgot they were in the purse. This explanation seemed very plausible. Well, that was a relief! Mystery solved! We had our answer! It all made so much sense.

I asked Amanda if she would have a problem with Roger flushing them down the drain, and she responded that she was ok with that. That made it even more believable that the pills were old and had been misplaced in her old purse.

Roger flushed the pills, and we all left feeling all was good in the world. I couldn't explain to myself the uneasiness I was feeling.

The Volcano Erupts

A couple of months after the pill discovery, Daryl and I were away for the weekend when we got a call from Amanda in the wee hours of the morning. She was crying and babbling, and we had difficulty understanding her. She was so distraught that I had to yell into the phone to calm down because I couldn't help her if I didn't know what was happening.

She calmed enough to tell us that Roger was breaking up with her. We asked her why, but I couldn't get a straight answer. She just kept crying. She was a total wreck.

I called Roger, and he was also crying but composed himself and told me that he was breaking up with her because he was sure she was using drugs again. I asked him how he knew that, and he said he had friends who told him Amanda was trading her Suboxone for other pills to get high. He said one told him he had dealt with her that night. He also said to me that when he fell in love with Amanda, he told her he would not stay with her if she started using drugs again. He was moving out and taking their dog with him because he didn't trust her with the dog.

I called Amanda back and told her everything that Roger had told me. She said she asked Roger to search her purse and told us that the "friends" who were talking to Roger were all jealous of him because he had such a good life with Amanda.

Amanda begged us to come home. She was so distraught and needed us to be with her. We packed up and headed back home at 3 am. We were about an hour away, and when we got home, we consoled her and let her know that we believed her and that, hopefully, after some time to reflect, Roger would also come to believe her.

But Roger did not believe her. He was not getting back together with her. He was moving on. He loved her but didn't want to watch her destroy herself. He was so much more intelligent than us.

I saw Roger a few days after this all went down, and we talked about that night and how strongly he felt about Amanda not using for them to stay together. I told him I couldn't blame him for leaving her. I told him it's hard to have a relationship if there isn't any trust. I told him that if he believed she was using drugs again, I could understand how living with someone with a drug problem would be very challenging. What I didn't realize at the time I was saying this was that I was facing this challenge and how frightened I was.

I kept hoping that Amanda was honest with us and that Roger's friends had told him a lie.

Gone to the Dogs

A couple of days after the breakup, Amanda was still distraught. She was sad, quiet, and withdrawn. When we tried to talk with her about the separation, she would start crying again. She was broken. She missed Roger, their dog, and she was upset that her future life with him was nonexistent.

We couldn't get Roger back for her, so Daryl and I thought we could get her a new furry friend to brighten up her spirits. We told Amanda about this idea, and she thought it might work. She thought having a new dog to love would be a big help.

We already had two small dogs, so our only stipulation was that the new dog would also have to be small. The dog she owned with Roger was a boxer and was extremely large. We didn't want something that big again.

Amanda and Daryl scoured the newspapers and online for people selling small-breed dogs. They found a couple of local breeders, and we went to see their pups. None of the puppies Amanda saw made a connection with her.

We were running out of stops when Daryl found another breeder we hadn't called yet. The breeder was located about 90 minutes away, so off we went to see what they had. We met in a mall parking lot, and they showed us a box of pups in the back of their SUV. There was a little black and brown pup that Amanda liked, so we gave the breeder $450, and off we went hoping that this little fur guy would get Amanda out of her funk.

A couple of days later, Amanda told us she wasn't feeling a connection to her new puppy. While he spent every minute with her, she missed her big boxer. This feeling never changed for her, and when an acquaintance showed an interest in buying the puppy from Amanda, Amanda jumped at it.

The kicker was that Amanda sold the dog for $450 and kept the money since, in her mind, the dog was a gift from us. We were glad the dog would go to a good home with someone who loved the little guy. Within a matter of a few days, the $450 was gone. I'm sure Amanda spent it on drugs, but I was so tired of trying to chase down what she did and why she did it that I didn't even bother this time.

If you're starting to notice something here, it should be how Amanda controlled our lives and how easily we gave up that control. It should also be noted how Daryl and I started giving up rational thinking to bring some calm to the family. It only got worse as time moved on.

Stages

Substance Abuse Disorder (SUD) is an American Medical Association (AMA) defined mental disorder. One of the things you learn from living with a loved one with SUD is that the disease progresses in stages. These stages are not easy to identify because the characteristics of each stage do not occur in a fashion that permits you to keep track of them.

These characteristics occur slowly over time as the disease progresses. There may be months that pass between individual traits. This passage of time makes them easy to forget, so by the time a new set appears, you don't recall the previous ones. It also makes the characteristics easy to deny.

Denial is SUD's best friend. It permits the person with the disease the opportunity to either justify or ignore the consequences that it is causing in their life. Denial also enables the family and friends of the abuser to rationalize or disregard what they are seeing or hearing.

We were now in a new stage of Amanda's SUD. She was now in the stage of not wanting to feel anything any longer. Her heart had been broken, and she was angry at Roger for that. She didn't recognize that her behavior caused the breakup. She took no responsibility or ownership for her actions. This was all on him, and Daryl and I didn't do much to alter that perception; we may have reinforced it by telling her that his breaking up with her was his loss.

So she wouldn't have to deal with her feelings for Roger, Amanda turned more to taking Xanax and Vicodin. At the time, we didn't know she was taking these pills. She was still going to the Suboxone clinic, being drug tested by them, and still went to the counseling sessions. In our eyes, she couldn't have been on anything but Suboxone.

What we didn't know was that she was gaming the system. She was passing her drug tests by cheating. I'm not going to list the ways that can be done. There are far too many. She was selling or trading her Suboxone for the other pills or cash.

Amanda started to get some new girlfriends. Most of them were charming girls. She would go out to bars and clubs and hang out with them when she wasn't sleeping or feeling ill.

She was still on the hunt for a boyfriend because a boyfriend provided her an opportunity to get cash or gifts that she could later sell for money. I know what that sounds like, and it makes me ill just putting the words in this book. She will tell you how she liked all her boyfriends and how she had feelings for each one, but as I reflect on this period, I now must confront what she was doing.

At the time, it was again easy to deny. To do otherwise would mean that I would have to start confronting the disease, slowly tearing our family apart. I was so worn down by all the drama and chaos swirling around us that facing the illness seemed insurmountable.

New Reality

As Amanda's addiction worsened, the lines of the accurate perception of reality began to blur. This is one case in point.

One day, Amanda wanted to go out with her girlfriends in the worst way. I can't recall what Amanda did, but we told her she couldn't have the car to go out. None of her girlfriends had transportation either. She was relentless. She kept coming at Daryl and me for all kinds of reasons why she had to go out that evening. I was sure it was just an excuse to get out and get high, but I never vocalized that. It was already bad enough that night that I didn't want to escalate the situation any further.

I was mentally exhausted from all the drama Amanda delivered to us daily. There was always some disaster that had occurred or would occur if things didn't fall out the way she wanted them to.

After Amanda broke up with Roger, we told her to take a break from having a steady boyfriend and focus on hanging out with her girlfriends. So, what does Amanda do? She tells us that we were the ones who wanted her to hang out with her girlfriends, and now we were denying her the ability to do that. She told us how lonely she was and that she just needed to be with friends to whom she could talk.

I'm going into all this detail to show how messed up my thought process was. I told her I wasn't happy with her running out to bars with her friends and not coming back until the early morning hours. Amanda stormed off angry again but came back a short time later to tell me that one of her girlfriends asked her to come over to the girlfriend's house and that Amanda would get a ride home later and would be back before midnight. All the parameters I had set for her were now met so that I couldn't say "No." I would be accused of moving the goalposts.

I agreed to drive her to the girlfriend's house. On our way

there, Amanda got a call on her cellphone, and I could hear that it was another girlfriend and there was some issue. Amanda told me the girl who called her could not get a ride to the girl's house that I was taking Amanda to and asked if we could stop by and pick her up. I didn't want to sound unreasonable, so I said that would be fine.

Amanda was directing me to this girl's house, which certainly wasn't on the way. I was angry that she had taken us so far away. When we got to this girl's house, Amanda called the girl, and after a brief conversation, this girl came, but she was not alone. She has two other girls with her. What could I say? You can go, but the other two are out! I just kept my mouth shut and started heading to our original destination.

No sooner did I start driving, but one of the girls asked if I could stop up the block at her friend's house so she could run in and grab something she left there earlier in the day.

She pointed out the house, which was very beaten up. I try not to judge people on where they live or how they take care of their property. Some people can't take care of things the way I would for various reasons, but the front steps of this house looked like they would fall off at any moment. As soon as I stopped the car, the car doors flew open, and all the girls, including Amanda, got out. I opened the window and yelled at Amanda about why they were all going in, but she turned and said they'd be back in a minute.

The girls ran up the rickety front steps like they had done it a million times. They didn't even bother to knock. They just opened the front door and went in. I thought this was weird, but I sat there and waited. After 10 minutes, I started calling Amanda's cell. I was tired and wanted to go home to spend an evening with Daryl, watch TV, and relax. She never answered, but after 20 minutes, the front door flew open, and they all came running out and jumped back in the car. The girl who claimed she needed something from inside apologized for making me wait. She couldn't find what she was looking for. I never asked what it was she wanted so badly. I just wanted to get rid of these girls and go home.

While the girls all talked, I sat there and stewed. I finally got them to where they wanted to go, and out of the car they went. Happy as could be.

As I drove home, I had the sickening feeling that I just took the girls to get drugs for their night together. I was furious at myself. I felt used. I remember going home and not enjoying my night at all. I never relaxed and stayed awake until I heard Amanda come home at 1:30 am.

Disintegration

For a family unit to be successful, you need some essential human traits. You need love, trust, honesty, compassion, and empathy. When those traits begin to erode, the unity of the family becomes very fragile.

Addiction has a way of slowly breaking down the family unit. First, it separates the family members. It separates the family by eroding trust. When someone lies to you daily, even about the most inconsequential matters, it causes you to no longer trust them. You can no longer count on them to do anything productive for the family. The disease of addiction needs the victim to feed it constantly, and if being trustworthy or honest gets in the way, those traits need to be compromised.

An old saying goes, "How do you know when an addict is lying? Their lips are moving." That was how it was with Amanda. We couldn't tell when she was telling the truth any longer. It got to the point where we assumed everything she said was a lie.

Even though Amanda was still going to the Suboxone clinic, we doubted that she was taking it consistently. She was not holding a job for more than 3 or 4 months. She was constantly sleeping past her alarm. She lost interest in going to a trade school. She was drifting through life.

She had reasons for all these items, and never once was it her fault for anything occurring in her life. What did we do? While Daryl and I would try and talk to her about how she was affecting her life, she would be angry at us for not understanding her thinking. How could we? It had no rationality to it.

Amanda lost all compassion for what she was doing to the family. I don't even know if she recognized that or not. Addiction is such a selfish disease that all the user can do is focus on the needs of the disease. It makes the user a complete narcissist.

When we would ask her to do the simplest things, like cleaning her room, she would tell us that she was busy and had to go shopping or visit a friend before she went to work. She always had an excuse for every situation. It was almost as if she would prepare for various scenarios so she could have a reason or lie available. It must have been exhausting for her to have an excuse always ready to be used. I know I was exhausted!

My son, Dan (you remember him from earlier in this story), had become invisible. He was doing so well in life while he was living with us. We just took it for granted that he was ok. We were so focused on Amanda that having not to be concerned with Dan was a blessing. I hope you're keeping score because this family unit is falling apart.

I didn't realize how bad this was for Dan because I never asked. But I knew Dan disapproved of how we were handling Amanda. He was frustrated from watching her break us down and his mom and dad not doing much to stop it. Dan moved out shortly after he hit his twenties, and I think some of his reason was to escape the chaos. I tried to tell myself that he was moving because it was the natural progression in life, but somehow, I was to blame for not talking with him more or giving him the time he needed from me. I was envious of him and wished I could have moved out with him.

I love my daughter, but she was slowly destroying all the other people I loved, and it was becoming difficult to have any compassion or empathy for her. I felt she certainly had none for any of us.

While Daryl and I disagreed about what to do to help Amanda, we continued to talk and find time to be with each other. I have seen many marriages broken because of addiction, and I'm always so grateful that ours survived

A moment when Dan and Amanda seemed to be in tune as siblings.

A New Kind of Shopping

Once Roger was no longer in Amanda's life, and we thought she had moved on, we started to have a new set of issues being introduced to us. Amanda told us she was released from her suboxone clinic. She told us that she missed a couple of her counseling sessions because her job had her work later than expected.

We were all panicked. The Suboxone clinic only gave a person enough suboxone to last until the next visit. If the program dropped you, then you were out of suboxone. This is not particularly good because it is perilous for someone taking a regular dosage of suboxone to be cut off. A patient has to be slowly weaned off suboxone, not cut off. But the clinics are dealing with a very unreliable clientele. The clinic's goal is to help those serious about recovering.

We immediately started looking for a new clinic Amanda could use. At the time, there were few clinics in Western Pennsylvania, and some were only there for the money. There's a ton of money made at Suboxone clinics, and it's usually an all-cash transaction. No credit cards or checks are accepted.

We found a clinic a little further away for Amanda, and they had her undergo a drug screening. It was the same setup. You had to attend several weekly counseling sessions, pass a drug screening, and then meet with a physician for about 5 minutes before you came away with your suboxone prescription. I know this because I took Amanda to several of her clinic visits. What always concerned me, though, was that her dosage never decreased. She was at the exact dosage almost two years after she started. Suboxone is purportedly a transition treatment from using opioids to a sober life without nasty withdrawal symptoms. Amanda and I talked about her being weaned from Suboxone, but she always told me that when she brought it up to the physician, they would say that she wasn't ready yet. She was probably lying, but I had no way to prove that. Patient confidentiality stood in the way.

After about six or so months at a clinic, Amanda would violate a stipulation, and we would have to go shopping for a new clinic. This happened more times than I can remember. But I remember that, according to Amanda, none of the dismissals were her fault. It was either an inaccurate drug screening, a miscommunication, or an unreasonable physician. There would be panic and a massive frenzy to find another clinic each time this occurred. It was usually Daryl or me that had to find a new clinic. We were more worried about Amanda not having Suboxone than she was. Again, this was another sign that she had other means of not withdrawing that we weren't aware of.

At Home Screenings

With all the issues concerning the dismissals from the suboxone clinics, Daryl and I decided that we were going to buy some drug screening tests for us to use at home. We told Amanda we were going to start screening her on a random basis. Our random basis wasn't so random, however.

We usually screened her when we thought she might be high or wanted to borrow the car or go out. We never screened her before we went to work because she was always sleeping, and we didn't usually screen her right after work because we were preparing dinner. Screenings were done around 7 pm and 11 pm on weeknights and were more scattered on weekends.

I can't tell you the number of screenings she failed because she would test positive for opioids or THC. She would always argue that the tests were inaccurate because if they were correct, she would not be able to get Suboxone from the clinic. It made sense to us.

If the test showed THC only, she would tell us that wherever she was the night before, someone was smoking weed in the house; she must have picked some up via secondhand smoke. There was always an excuse for THC; quite frankly, we weren't as concerned about the THC as we were with the opioids. We had never heard of anyone overdosing on THC. This is the kind of perverse thinking that we had adapted to. Because of all the chaos and confusion addiction causes to the family, addiction distorts the family's perception of reality. It permits us to adapt to a reality that helps it to thrive.

After months of at-home screenings and numerous arguments, accusations, and denials, we cut back the screenings to once every now and then. It was expensive to do and was not providing us with the results we had hoped for. I don't know what results we expected. We were doing all these preventive measures by the seat of our pants. We were so uneducated about what to do; the worst part was that we didn't even know how to get educated.

Monopoly Money

It was decided that Amanda needed a checking account during this same period. We thought it was time for her to understand the value of a dollar. This again shows how out of touch with reality we were. While my daughter was struggling to find sobriety, Daryl and I were concerned that she wasn't learning life skills. We set up a checking account with our bank and had it attached to our accounts so we could keep an eye on it.

After we opened the account, we sat down with Amanda to explain how to use the account to make deposits and withdrawals and record each transaction in her checkbook register. We told her how to use the ATM and debit card.

We thought we were empowering her to manage her money. What we didn't know was that we were opening a can of worms that would destroy her credit rating for years.

After the first month, we sat with Amanda to show her how to balance her checkbook. While we noticed that she had recorded some transactions, a few were missing from the statement. She explained them as gas purchases or stuff she bought at a convenience store where it wasn't always easy to enter the transaction into her checkbook register. We explained the importance of keeping receipts so that they would help her reconcile these types of transactions when her statement arrived.

After a few months, we got a notice from the bank for overdraft fees. I knew this couldn't be from my and Daryl's accounts. We had never had an overdraft fee. We talked to Amanda, and she said she wasn't sure how much money she had in the account, so she went to the ATM and withdrew $100. She figured if she didn't have that in her account, the ATM wouldn't give it to her. We chalked that up to a lesson learned, and we paid the overdraft fee. I know, another SMH moment.

The following month there was another overdraft fee. Amanda said she looked at her checkbook and thought she had $30, so she took out $25. When we examined her bank statement, it showed she had $5 in it when she took out the $25. She again missed entering transactions in her register. I was becoming apprehensive about her having an account attached to ours. Again, we paid the overdraft fees. Logically it made sense to pay the fees. If we had tried to make her pay the fees, then she would have had no money left to put gas in the car so she could get to work. So, I had to pay the fees or put gas in her car. It was more important to me to keep things with the bank in good standing.

After the third overdraft, I closed Amanda's account. It was apparent she wasn't using it correctly or interested in learning. I told her that if she wanted a bank account, she would need to open one on her own.

She went to another bank and opened a checking account with her next paycheck. I took a big step back and let her manage it. Within a couple of months, she had overdrawn on her account again and what she didn't realize was that when she deposited her next check, the bank deducted the overdraft amount. She was shocked that the bank could do that! I felt like I was dealing with a 10-year-old. How could she possibly think otherwise? She was distraught. She owed some money to one of her friends, and when she paid her back, she would have very little left from her check. I couldn't understand why she had to borrow money from someone else!

This continued for a few months until the bank closed the account for unpaid overdraft fees.

This didn't stop Amanda, however. She went to another bank and opened another checking account which they promptly closed three months later for the same reasons.

This whole time Amanda was using the banks to fund her drug usage that her paycheck couldn't cover. We believed she was still on suboxone, so we didn't think (or maybe not want to consider) that Amanda was using it for drug purchases.

After that, Amanda had to use check cashing services to cash her paychecks, or she would go to the bank where it was created and cash it there.

In any case, she had begun the destruction of her credit rating and had frustrated and angered Daryl and me to the extent that we were ready to let her deal with all her money problems without our help. This was when the stealing kicked in, and she was almost arrested.

Search and Rescue

I had been uneasy with Amanda's honesty about using Suboxone for quite some time. That little voice in my head telling me something was wrong was getting louder and louder, but I still had earplugs in.

Amanda's continuing erratic behavior didn't help quiet the voice, and I knew I had to do something to find out if she was using pills again. I remembered how easily Roger found out Amanda had drugs by searching her purse. I thought this would turn up nothing because she had to be smart enough not to hide them in her purse again.

When Amanda was in the shower, I went into her room and searched her purse. I found six pills. I looked up all the pills on the internet and found that two were Vicodin, three were Xanax, and one was oxycontin. I knew Amanda had a prescription for Xanax from her current psychiatrist, who was doing her counseling for the Suboxone clinic, and was taking these for her anxiety; so, I left those behind and took the rest. Later I flushed them. I didn't realize how big of a mistake that was until quite some time after.

I waited to see if Amanda would react to the missing pills. It didn't take long. After Amanda had dressed and was ready to leave, I heard her go to the garage and open the car doors. She was down there for about 15 minutes until she returned to her room. I was in the kitchen making dinner and pretended I didn't know what she was doing. She closed her bedroom door, and I could hear her talking to someone on her cell phone. I couldn't hear very well and didn't want Amanda to discover that I was attempting to eavesdrop on her conversation, so I just worked in the kitchen. After another 30 minutes, Amanda came downstairs and said she was leaving. She had a friend picking her up, and she would be back in a little bit.

She didn't come back home until almost midnight. She said

she was exhausted and was going to bed. She looked like she was high. I knew better than to try and engage her when she was this way. Nothing ever progressed from it other than to escalate into an argument ending in slamming doors and a ton of stress.

I searched her purse a couple more times until she stopped carrying pills in it. I kept thinking that if I took the pills from her, she would have to take her suboxone to prevent getting "dope sick." I justified my search for her drugs as an attempt to rescue my daughter. I didn't know what else to do.

I searched her room when she wasn't home but rarely found anything. She had wised up and taken her "stash" with her wherever she would go.

Arrested Development

During the pill search period, Amanda worked as a liquor store clerk for the State of Pennsylvania. She wanted this job because she felt that working for the state would allow her to advance within the State system and offer her a good wage and benefits. The clerk position that she had was a part-time entry-level position. She was making just a little more than minimum wage. She was thrilled about that. All her past jobs were for minimum wage.

She worked at a state liquor store not far from our home and was doing very well. She would tell us how much her boss loved her and how much she loved working. She never missed her shift. There were some close calls where we had to wake her up about 30 minutes before her shift started so she could get there on time.

It was amazing how quickly she could go from looking thoroughly hung over to being presentable. Her at-home behavior was still erratic, and we hoped she wasn't taking that behavior to work. Daryl and I talked about not waking her in time to go to work, but we saw how much she liked this job, and we were hoping this job would set her straight and she would quit all the pill nonsense.

After three or four months of Amanda working at the store closest to our home, she was transferred to a different store about 30 minutes away. She was unhappy about this. Her boss told her it had nothing to do with her performance and that this was how the employment process went with the State.

Her next boss also thought Amanda was a good worker, but she was transferred further away after a month. I was beginning to believe that the State was making it difficult on her in hopes she would quit. She didn't, however.

At the new store, she kept pestering her boss to have her transferred to a store closer to home because driving so far was becoming a burden. They ended up moving her again. This store was closer to home but in an unbelievably lousy section of town where there was a ton of crime. The store itself was in an ancient building and extremely small. The windows and door had bars around them. They always had two people working there.

A couple of months later, a letter came from the State. It looked official, so I opened it. The letter said that the State had conducted an audit and found that Amanda had been falsely ringing up incorrect sales. The missing amount for her registers totaled $650, and she should consider her temporary leave a final termination and that the State would contact her again with the ramifications of this theft.

Again, we were stunned! We had no idea Amanda was no longer employed. Where was she going on the days she told us she was working? How could she do this to the State and not think she would get caught? Why was she so desperate for cash?

We showed her the letter when Amanda got home from "work" that day. Her first reaction was to be angry at us for opening her mail. I was angry right back at her for losing such a good job and for losing it because she was stealing. I remember telling her that if she didn't like the things we did, like opening her mail, she could move. She then proceeded to say to us that the false sales rings were done in error. She thought the procedure for working at the register was that if the store opened and she was signed into a cash register, she had to stay signed in for the day. I said, "What??!! Are you kidding me?!!" Who in their right mind would think this was how it should have been done? Anyone with common sense would know this would not be the correct procedure. But rather than tell Amanda, I didn't believe her. I told her that this was her problem and that she needed to solve it. I also told her she should get another job because she needed to pay back the State.

I was angry, stressed, and frustrated! I was watching my little girl slowly destroy her life. This was the little girl that I always took care of and defended. This was the little girl I could always talk to and know that she trusted me and trusted what I told her.

I didn't know this girl that was in front of me. My little girl was gone, and some other girl had replaced her. I didn't like this new girl and was starting to wish she was not a part of my life. The love I had for her was starting to dissolve. That's what the chaos of this disease does.

Breaking Point

When Amanda was still in high school, Daryl and I bought a trailer in a large campground about an hour from our home. Friends of ours owned a place in this campground, and we would go there occasionally and stay the weekend with them in their trailer. The campground was a charming, family-oriented place with a lake stocked with fish. There was an adult pool along with a kiddie pool, a miniature golf course, numerous playgrounds, and adult and family-themed social activities. After visiting our friends a few times, we decided to purchase a place.

Amanda loved our place up there and would come up with a friend as often as she could. We had several people whom we had developed friendships with, and most nights, someone would host a campfire where everyone would show up with their drinks and sit around the campfire playing music, talking, and having lots of laughs.

Around the time Amanda lost her job at the state liquor store, and before we received the letter from the State saying she was terminated, Amanda came up for the weekend with a girlfriend of hers. We went to a campfire at my neighbor's lot. There were about twenty people there, and we were all having a good time.

We had been there for about an hour when Amanda asked the host if she could use the bathroom in their trailer. I didn't think much of this as Amanda went inside, but suddenly, I felt uneasy. I got up and went inside my neighbor's trailer, only to see Amanda bent over and going through a purse on the floor, which I knew wasn't hers. I surprised her and asked just what she thought she was doing. She tried to make an excuse, but I cut her off and told her to put the cash back and get out. I was so angry and ashamed of her!

I went back out to the fire and just sat there. I was noticeably quiet after that. Daryl asked what was wrong, but I couldn't tell her right then. Amanda got up from her chair and went back to our trailer. I feigned a headache and said I was going to my trailer to get some aspirin. When I got inside the trailer with Amanda, I told her I was never more ashamed of her in my entire life than I was right then. I told her I no longer trusted her and did not want her to come to our trailer again.

Daryl knew something was up because she came over to the trailer and saw that Amanda and I were having it out. I told Daryl what I saw, and I swear I could see a little piece of her die right in front of me. It was one thing to steal from us but to steal from my friends was unforgivable. Amanda's resolution to this whole thing was for me to take her and her girlfriend home. I told her that was not going to happen. She said it was apparent that neither of us wanted her there so that she would get a ride home. I told her to be my guest. I could have cared less whether she stayed or left. She stayed.

I didn't sleep well that night, and at 5 am, I got up to go to the bathroom. Amanda's purse was on the floor next to the foldout bed in our main room. I grabbed it and took it into the bathroom with me. I searched it and found six OxyContin. I flushed them down the toilet and then sat there and cried. I realized that I was losing my daughter to her addiction. I became overwhelmed with the belief that she would not live much longer. That her addiction was going to consume her.

As I came out of the bathroom and put her purse back, I sat on Amanda's bed and watched her sleep. I thought back to all my years with her before this addiction and tried to figure out how we got where we were now. I don't know if I woke her, but she must have felt my presence because she opened her eyes and looked at me. I don't know if she was coming off a high or was shaking off the sleep, but it took her a couple of seconds to get the cobwebs out before she asked me what I was doing and why I was crying.

I told her I felt like I was losing her. I said that I knew she had an addiction problem, was not using her Suboxone the way she should, was on the road to overdosing, and was afraid I would be left having to bury her. I told her I was looking forward to walking her down the aisle at her wedding and to doing the Father-Daughter dance with her, but that I was coming to the acceptance that those things were never going to happen. I asked her if there was an outfit she wanted to be buried in and where she wanted to be buried because I knew I would not be able to do any of those things when that time came, and with the track she was on, her death was imminent.

Amanda was crying at this point. She told me that she was not going to die. That I was going to walk down the aisle with her and that I was going to dance with her. She said she loved me so much and felt terrible about my hurt.

Not once did she say that she was going to quit using. Not once did she deny being an addict. Not once did she say, "Please help me."

I got up from her bed, and without looking at her, I told her I found her Oxycontin and that I flushed them down the toilet. I walked back into my bedroom, laid down next to Daryl, and waited for the sun to come up before I finally got out of bed and started packing the car so we could return home as soon as everyone woke up.

I had hit my bottom.

Demolition Derby

Like all teenagers learning to drive, Amanda had her minor dings and nicks in the car we let her use. The car she drove was a Hyundai Elantra. It was tiny and tinny, but it was a good car and ran well. We bought it purposely because we knew Amanda would start driving at some point and wanted a smaller car for her to handle.

I'm not sure if I mentioned this earlier, but Amanda is not significant in stature. She was 5'1" and weighed right around 105 pounds. So, you can see why we went with a smaller vehicle. Watching Amanda drive the car was always funny because she had to sit on the edge of the seat to see over the dash. She looked like a little old lady driving that car.

Like most teenage drivers, Amanda would not wear a seatbelt unless we were in the car. We would always yell at her to put on her seat belt, and she would tell us she would, but we knew that as soon as she was out of sight, she would take the seat belt off.

It was the beginning of summer in 2009. I was at work, when my cell phone rang. The caller ID said it was Amanda. I would get these calls from Amanda consistently to see if I could give her some money. I contemplated not answering the call. I was just so beyond wanting to deal with her any longer. Somehow, I felt this call was different. I had spoken to Amanda earlier in the day, and she told me she was going to a local wave pool with some friends. Maybe that had something to do with me answering her call.

In any case, I answered her call, and all I heard was sobbing. This wasn't the first time Amanda called me crying. She was the biggest drama queen I had ever known. I told her to take a deep breath and start over, speaking slowly, so I could understand her.

She told me she was in a car accident, and it was terrible. I asked if she was ok, and she told me she didn't know. She thought so, but that the paramedics were on the way so they could check her out.

Paramedics! "How bad was this accident? Was there anyone else involved? Was anyone else injured?" These questions were coming out of my mouth faster than I could finish.

I learned from her that the accident occurred just before the entrance to the freeway not far from our home. I told her I was on my way and hung up. I called Daryl and told her what I knew, which wasn't much. Daryl and I carpooled to work, so she had to come to pick me up. We had to take the freeway to get to where Amanda was, and when we exited the highway, we could see police cars, an ambulance, and a fire truck. All had their lights flashing. As we got closer, I saw the vehicle facing the concrete median. The front end was crushed into the windshield.

We had to make a U-turn to return to the accident scene, and when we did, we found Amanda sitting on the curb and she appeared to be in a state of shock. When she saw us, she ran over to us and started crying again. Getting details from her was challenging, but a police officer came over to us and gave us the facts they knew. There was an eyewitness to the accident who told the police what he had seen.

He was about 100 yards behind Amanda when he said a car from a road to the right ran a stop sign, forced Amanda to swerve severely, hit a concrete barrier to her right, which deflected the vehicle to the left, and plow head-on into the concrete median strip. He said the car that ran the stop sign never stopped and just left the scene.

He said he stopped and ran to Amanda's car to help get her out because he feared the car might catch fire. Within minutes the police were on the scene. The witness gave his statement and left because he had to go to work.

The police and paramedics told us they couldn't believe she had walked away from this crash with nothing more than a black eye. She got a black eye from the airbag deployment.

They wanted Amanda to go to the ER to get checked out for a concussion, but her anxiety was sky-high, and she did not want to go to the ER.

The police officer told us that if she didn't have her seatbelt on, she probably would have gone through the windshield and would probably not have survived. What!!?? She was wearing her seatbelt! I couldn't believe what I was hearing! A few minutes later when I was alone with Amanda, I said to her that I knew she drove around without her seatbelt and wanted to know why she had it on this time. She told me that she didn't know. She admitted that she never drives with it on but for some reason, that day, she decided to use it.

I remember looking at her and telling her that she should not be here right now. That God just saved her life. I told her that there must be a purpose for her that she hadn't fulfilled yet and that she should take this opportunity to look at her life and decide how she wanted to live it. I was hoping for the accident and her survival to act like an intervention. That it might be a life changer for her.

I went back over to the police and asked if I could look at the car and take out any valuables from the vehicle before it got towed. They said they had already looked through the car and I could take whatever I needed. When I got close to the car, I couldn't believe the destruction. The front of the car was pushed back to within a foot of the windshield. The windshield was shattered but still in place. The inside of the car was pretty much intact. The airbag was out and deflated, and the steering column was bent upwards. I don't know where the engine went. It wasn't inside the car. I walked away thinking, "How did she survive this?"

I asked the police officer if I could have the name and contact information of the eyewitness. I wanted to call him and thank him for helping my daughter. The officer completely understood and gave me his name and phone number.

Amanda's current boyfriend showed up at the accident scene and said he would drive her home if we wanted to return to work. There was nothing more to do there, so we returned to our jobs and finished the day.

I did call the man who had witnessed the accident and thanked him profusely for helping my daughter and staying to talk to the police. We talked about the accident, and he told me what he had seen. It was exactly as the police had told me.

My daughter, somehow, had survived and cheated Death. It wouldn't be the last time she did that.

Number 1

The Insurance company totaled the car due to the extensive damage. The salvage yard that now had the vehicle asked me to come in and take everything we wanted out of the vehicle. I went through the car from top to bottom. I pulled out umbrellas, pens, some rags, and other items from the glove box. I decided to look under the seats to see if there was anything I had missed. I didn't have a flashlight, so I stuck my hand under the seat and fished around. I pulled out a couple of coins and some business cards. There was something lodged in one of the seat rails. It was hard to get, but I finally freed it and saw that it was a brown prescription pill bottle. It was a bottle for Amanda's anxiety medication. I opened the bottle to see if there were any pills in it. There were no pills, but there was liquid in it.

I thought that was strange, but knowing that Amanda's addiction could be involved, I slowly brought the bottle up to my nose. It was urine! My daughter kept a bottle of urine in the car. I knew immediately what she was using it for. She was passing her drug screenings at the Suboxone clinic with it.

When I brought the bottle home, I debated showing it to Amanda. I thought about what my purpose was. What was I hoping to accomplish? I didn't think she would admit it was hers. She would say someone had left it in her car by mistake. There would be some excuse she would give me.

I decided to show it to her. When I showed her what I had found, without missing a beat, she said it was hers. I thought she must be slipping up or suffering from a moment of honesty. I asked her why she carried around a bottle of urine. I wasn't expecting what she would tell me next. She said the urine in the bottle was hers and that she was giving it to another girl in her suboxone program who screwed up and used drugs once and needed the urine so she could pass the drug screening and get her suboxone prescription.

She told me this without a hitch in the story. She said it so convincingly that I didn't know whether to believe it. As you read this, you're saying to yourself, "Really?! Is this guy that blind?!" This disease called Addiction will do this to you. It makes you doubt everything you know you should question. It bends reality and perception. You know what you hear is a lie, but thinking and accepting what you know is the truth is much worse.

I poured the bottle's contents onto the ground and said to her, "I don't believe you." As I was walking away, she replied, "Whatever."

Grand AM

Since the insurance company totaled the Hyundai, we had to buy another car with the dollar amount they provided. This came out to about $6000.

I looked on the internet for a car for around that amount and was not happy with what I could get. After weeks of looking, I thought I would have to pay additional out-of-pocket money to replace the car.

I then saw a Grand AM with low mileage, was only six years old, and was right at our price point. It was for sale by a private owner, so Daryl and I went to see the car. It was owned by a mechanic and his son, who found cars that needed work that they could easily restore and quickly sell. They kept their price low so they could sell them fast.

The car was sitting outside the garage, where they did auto repairs. It had a fresh coat of paint, and the engine sounded great. We did a test drive with it and thought this could be a suitable replacement. The interior showed some wear, but for the price, I was willing to overlook this. We haggled a little, so I could get the price where I needed it to be and bought the car.

When we got home with the car, I told Amanda to come down and see what we got to replace the Hyundai. She couldn't believe that she had a sports car to drive. She was elated! Before I gave her the keys, I made her promise to always wear her seatbelt while driving or as a passenger. She gladly agreed, took the keys, and went for a short drive.

As I write this, I'm shaking my head over this. Why would I give a car to a girl I believed was addicted to pills? One of the things I can point out to you is that when you are so deep in the chaos and havoc that addiction causes, you will do all you can to avoid that chaos and mayhem. The user's happiness is your happiness. The user's anger is your anger. The user's drama becomes your drama. In other words, you become a puppet to the user. They control your emotions; the worst part is that you never realize how you relinquished that control. Like a puppeteer, as they pull the strings, you raise an arm or a leg, but, in this case, they control your feelings.

Within one month, Amanda was in another car accident. She was out with her latest boyfriend. We'll name him Craig. Amanda and Craig were at a red light. When the light turned green, they proceeded to be hit in the passenger side front fender by a pickup truck running the red light.

The pickup stopped for a moment but took off. A car behind Amanda saw what had occurred, went around Amanda's car, and chased the truck. The guy returned a few minutes later and said he lost the truck but gave Amanda his name and phone number and said she should call the police. He couldn't stay, but if the police needed to speak with him, he would tell them exactly what he saw.

Instead of calling the police, Amanda took Craig home and then came home to show me the damage.

Before I saw the car, Amanda told me that she had been in another accident, but again it wasn't by any fault of hers. She gave me all the details, including the eyewitness information. I went down to the garage and looked at the damage. It was extensive. I called the eyewitness, spoke with him, and he corroborated Amanda's version.

I next called the insurance company. They spoke with Amanda and told us to get the car fixed. They said they would contact the witness and get a statement. We fixed the car, and the insurance company treated it like a hit-and-run.

I don't know the odds of being involved in two hit-and-run accidents within months where you are the victim, but I think they would be high.

The car was fixed and looked new again, but I was beginning to have bad feelings about Amanda being behind the wheel of a vehicle.

The Invisible Tattoo

One of the elements of having a loved one who suffers from either alcoholism or substance abuse is the stigma it brings along. Growing up, I recall my mom telling me that I shouldn't drink or do harmful drugs because I could end up like the people you see sleeping on the streets or under a bridge. She told me that you would disgrace yourself and the family. I know that's a harsh assessment, but I was raised in the 60s before the internet and when the world viewed mental illness, such as alcoholism or substance abuse, as a character defect. Having that image embedded within you and within society brings baggage you hope you never have to carry.

I raised my children not to drink until they were legally old enough and to say no to drugs. If one of my children failed at honoring those values, what kind of job did I do as a parent? You hide the disease so you will not be judged by others or so you will not to have your loved one exposed so their opportunities are diminished. You hide it from your family, friends, neighbors, and strangers. You don't realize this is precisely what the disease wants you to do. When exposed, the disease has an exceedingly difficult time surviving. The disease depends on the family members' fear to help sustain it.

The stigma of the disease hinders the ability to seek help from everyone you know or anyone you don't know. Stigma enabled Amanda to feed her addiction and let it progress to a life-threatening level. It was as if Daryl and I had a tattoo that we wanted no one to see.

Daryl and I are friends of a couple with a son who was also struggling with addiction. We'll call them Frank and Peggy. When Peggy shared with Daryl that her son was battling addiction, that opened the door for Daryl to share about Amanda and this allowed the four of us to talk about our situations and fears.

Peggy and Frank started to go to Nar-Anon meetings. These meetings are attended by people with loved ones who suffer from the disease of addiction. Daryl and I weren't comfortable attending a forum like this. Neither of us was ready to discuss our family life and expose our misgivings.

That would change by the early fall of 2009.

The Straw

In late September 2009, Amanda was involved in a third car accident. This was a minor fender bender, but she was the one who initiated the contact. When she came home with the car that night, she never mentioned the accident to me. I found it while I was in the garage looking for something.

I saw the damage and immediately asked Amanda about it. She claimed someone side-swiped her when she parked on a busy street. I called the insurance company and reported the accident. They wanted a statement from Amanda, but she told me she wasn't feeling well and would speak to them the next day.

About a week later, the insurance company contacted me and said they still hadn't spoken to Amanda. They also told me that the insurance company of the other vehicle involved in the accident contacted them and claimed that it was Amanda who side-swiped the other car. I wasn't surprised. They needed to get a statement from Amanda to get the claim moving.

I tried calling Amanda, but she wasn't answering my calls. When I got home from work, the Grand Am was missing, and so was Amanda. I had told her she could not have the Grand Am without running it by me first. When she finally came home, she had Craig with her. I told her she needed to talk to the insurance company. I didn't say anything about who was at fault. I wanted to make sure she would speak with the insurance company to get the claim moving so I could fix the car.

She told me she had to take Craig home and would call them when she got home. She didn't come home until 3 am. The next day I went down to the Grand Am to get something out of the car. While there, I saw something in the center console that I didn't recognize at first. When I picked it up and looked more closely at it, I saw it was a hypodermic needle!

I felt the blood rush from my face. My worst fears were now right in front of me. My daughter was using heroin. I took the needle up to her room and woke her up. She was irritated, and when I showed her the syringe and asked her what it was, she just rolled her eyes at me and said it was an insulin needle. She said Craig was diabetic and needed an insulin shot last night. He dropped the syringe in the car after he was finished. She couldn't find it last night, but she said her intentions were to look for it later that day.

I didn't know whether to believe her or not. She was very convincing, but I had the voices in my head telling me otherwise. I decided right then and there that I would figure this out. If she was using heroin, we were now playing a game of Russian Roulette. She could overdose at any time.

One of the things I noticed was that our kitchen spoons started decreasing in number about a month before this. This wasn't too unusual. I know Amanda would make food in the middle of the night and take it to her room to eat. I would find bowls, plates, and silverware in her room. I decided to do a silverware search in her room when she wasn't there. I looked in all the usual places but couldn't find the missing spoons. I got a feeling of dread. I know what heroin users used spoons for. I decided I needed to expand my search. I entered the bathroom Amanda used and looked through all the drawers and cabinets. I found a belt of hers in one of the drawers. This was another piece of evidence that she was shooting heroin. She could be using the belt as a tourniquet. I looked in the cabinet under the sink. I started pulling everything out and found two spoons. They were bent, and the bottom of each spoon had burn marks. The picture was complete. She was cooking heroin in her bathroom and shooting it into her veins.

I showed all of this to Daryl. We were utterly depressed. Our daughter was a heroin addict, and we could not stop it. We knew we had to stop her somehow. Our first thought was to get her into an inpatient rehab program, but we knew from experience that she had to call the rehab and request to be admitted. We knew she wouldn't do that.

When Amanda came home, we showed her our evidence and told her she needed to go to rehab. We told her how frightened we were that she would overdose and die. She told us we were crazy. That she wasn't shooting heroin, I asked her to show me her arms. At first, she said no, but as we got angrier and told her she was never leaving the house again, she gave in and showed us her arms. There wasn't a mark on them. We didn't know that heroin users would inject the drug into veins in less conspicuous locations on the body so as not to be discovered by law enforcement.

She told us she didn't know where those spoons came from or how they got under her sink. She said maybe one of her friends had shot up in our house. She had an answer for everything.

Daryl and I were not convinced but knew we were tired of fighting with her. We knew we had to take another track with Amanda, and we needed to figure out quickly what that track should be.

The Track We Chose

Daryl and I knew we needed to try something different, and we recalled that Peggy and Frank had been going to Nar-Anon meetings for a few months. We reached out to Peggy and Frank to see if they could provide us more details about these meetings.

They first told us that the meetings were strictly confidential. All introductions were on a first-name basis only. The attendees were loved ones of someone with a substance use disorder (SUD). They would go around the room asking folks to introduce themselves and, if they desired, to share why they were there. Peggy and Frank said it was very informal and helpful. Peggy and Frank went to meetings close to their home and told us that we could find a meeting close to our home by just going on the internet and searching.

Daryl and I decided to give it a try. We had nothing to lose and everything to gain. We found a meeting that was close to our home. We drove to the meeting, located in the basement of a church. We arrived early so we could park and see how many people would be there. There were already a handful of cars in the lot, and as we sat there, about ten cars arrived. As the start time of the meeting approached, I was feeling uncomfortable. I knew if I walked through that entry door, our family's secret would be exposed, and things would never be the same.

When we got to the door, I pushed it open and stared into a room with about 30 people around our age sitting at a set of tables. I felt like all eyes were on Daryl and me. Thankfully, someone at the door welcomed us and told us to come in and relax. They said that we could feel safe here. Daryl and I found some seats at the table and joined the group.

The meeting started, and the rules for the group were explained. After that, the meeting leader gave his story about being in the group. After he was done, the person next to him did the same and continued around the table. When it was our turn, I gave my first name and told them how we were struggling with what to do with our daughter, whom we believed was mainlining heroin. I told them we were looking for some wisdom and guidance. The leader looked at me and said we were in the right place. What a relief I felt. Hopefully, these folks could tell us what to do.

As the meeting progressed, anyone who wanted to share their latest experiences with their user could. I didn't say much after that. I just wanted to listen and see if I could get enough information to help me and Daryl plot a course of action.

The one thing we found interesting was that the people who saw the most success with getting their users to sobriety were the ones who put in place some harsh parameters. They called it "setting boundaries." If the boundaries were violated, the user had to face whatever consequences were established. For many people, the most severe consequence was removing the user from the home.

When I found the needle in the car, I had been advocating with Daryl that I thought we needed to tell Amanda that she either had to check herself into rehab or move out of our home. My biggest fear was that either Daryl or I would find Amanda dead from an overdose in our home. I knew that would scar us, and our home would never be the same. I reconciled with myself that I would rather receive a phone call from the police than be the one to discover her death. Daryl was not in agreement with this. She did not want her daughter living on the streets.

When the meeting was ending, one of the members told our group that at a different group called "The Bridge to Hope", there was going to be a physician speaker at their next meeting to talk about the pros and cons of Suboxone. I thought that sounded interesting.

After the meeting, when Daryl and I were sitting in the car, Daryl said we must ask Amanda to leave if she won't go to rehab. I was shocked! My wife had done a complete 180-degree turn. I wondered what had changed her mind, and she told me that everyone in the meeting whose user was now practicing sobriety had removed the user from their homes. Daryl was still worried that Amanda would have to live on the streets, but I reminded her that Amanda was a princess that would never let herself experience those harsh conditions. I was sure she would check herself into rehab.

So, we had the endpoint of our new plan. Now we had to figure out how to put the other pieces in place to reach the endpoint.

B2H

As Daryl and I continued to put our plan in place to get Amanda to rehab, the meeting at the Bridge to Hope, where a physician was going to discuss Suboxone and its place in the Opioid Epidemic, arrived. I told Daryl it probably wouldn't hurt to attend this. Amanda had been using Suboxone for about three years, and maybe we could get some information to help us.

The Bridge to Hope Support Group met in a large conference room within a senior living complex. The building was newly constructed, and the conference room was bright and well-furnished. The tables in the room were set up to form a large square, and about 25 people were already there.

No one greeted us at the door as they did at the Nar-Anon meeting, but the meeting started, and the format was somewhat the same. The only difference is that if you didn't want to speak, you didn't have to. When it came to our turn to introduce ourselves, I gave our first names and said we were there to hear the speaker. That was it. That's all I said.

They had some additional announcements, and then the physician spoke about Suboxone. We didn't learn much more than we already knew except that usually, within six months to one year of good suboxone usage and going to the counseling sessions, most people have begun the process of being weaned off Suboxone. Amanda had three years of Suboxone usage and was still at the same dose. She also was changing clinics and physicians almost monthly, so we knew she was scamming everyone trying to help her.

At the meeting's end, one of the members (we'll name her Karen) approached us and asked how we liked the meeting and the speaker. We gave her our opinions, sat, and talked with her for a while. Karen was genuinely friendly and spoke to us with compassion and kindness about our daughter. She also had a daughter who suffered from SUD, but her daughter had found sobriety about five years prior and was doing very well.

We told Karen about our plan to have Amanda check herself into rehab or move out of our home. Karen told us she could not advise us on what to do. She said that our choices were our choices. Karen said the only thing you must be is comfortable with your choice and with either outcome.

We left that meeting, and Daryl and I decided that this support group was the one we would use to help us going forward. We both felt very comfortable there and enjoyed our one-on-one experience with Karen.

Now we had to tackle "being comfortable with either outcome."

Execution

Daryl and I knew that a couple of items needed to be in place before our ultimatum. Amanda still had to talk with the insurance company about the sideswiping accident she was involved in; after that, we had to get the keys to our house and car from her.

Amanda's 21st birthday was rapidly approaching, and we knew she wanted to celebrate with her girlfriends. For her birthday, she had asked for cash so she would have spending money for her girl's night out. I told her I was not giving her any cash until she talked with the insurance company about her accident. I knew she didn't want to because she would probably lie about the accident, and she and I had already discussed committing insurance fraud.

After much drama, she relented, went into her room, and called the insurance company. I told her I wanted to talk to the agent after she was done. I don't know if Amanda thought her room was soundproof, but I could hear her side of the conversation perfectly. I heard her tell a different story to the agent on the phone than what she told me. She told the agent that the other driver was parked on a narrow side street and that the other driver pulled out of the space as my daughter passed her, and they sideswiped. My daughter told the agent she was unfamiliar with the area where she was and that it had a lot of one-way streets. Amanda said to the other driver that she couldn't block the roadway, so she was going to find a place to park and then return to exchange information. Amanda claimed she had difficulty finding someplace to park, and when she did find a spot, she couldn't remember how to get back to where the other car was. She walked around for about 30 minutes before she left.

Amanda came out of her room and gave me the phone. I asked the agent if she had all she needed to process the claim, and she said she did.

Amanda then stuck out her hand and asked for her cash. I asked her if I could borrow her keys to the Grand Am to run out to the ATM and get the money. She was reluctant and kept asking me where my keys were and why didn't I take the other car we owned, but I told her I misplaced my keys and I wanted to listen to the Grand Am as I drove it because I thought I heard it making a funny noise the other day. She gave me the keys.

Now we had all that we needed to execute the next phase of the plan. We were going to deliver the ultimatum to her. We were going to give her 48 hours to decide if she wanted to go to in-patient rehab or move out of our house. I got Daryl, and we made our way up to her room.

Down the Drain

It was the middle of the day. Amanda was on the phone talking to her girlfriends about their girl's night out to celebrate her 21st birthday. Daryl and I went to her room and told her we needed to talk to her. We told her we loved her very much and that we were concerned for her. We told her that we knew she was using heroin and wanted to help her get sober. We told her we wanted her to check herself into an in-patient rehab. She had to move out if she didn't want to do that. We told her we loved her too much to watch her kill herself.

She flipped out. She went into an instant rage. She thought we were terrible for wanting to ruin her 21st birthday. We told her we didn't care about her 21st birthday. We wanted her to see all her upcoming birthdays. She told us that was absolutely nuts. She said she wasn't using heroin and that all we wanted to do was to ruin her life. We told her she was wasting her life and we were trying to save it.

She then asked me if I had her money for tonight. I told her I was not giving her any money. I couldn't trust what she would buy with it, and I didn't want to be the person who gave her the money that she could overdose on.

That just ramped her anger up. I had never seen her like this. She was crying. She was screaming. Her arms were flailing. She told us that she couldn't stand us any longer. She ran to the kitchen, and I could hear her rummaging through one of the drawers.

Daryl was crying. I was stressed to the max and not anywhere close to being calm. She came back upstairs with a large butcher's knife. She held it up to her throat and said if I didn't give her the money I promised her, she would die right in front of us.

I don't know what happened. I snapped. I was outraged. Probably angrier than at any other time in my life. I grabbed her by the wrist and pulled her into her bathroom. I told her if she was going to cut her throat, then to get in the bathtub and do it! At least all her blood would go down the drain and not ruin our carpeting!

Amanda was stunned. She just stood there looking at me. I could see the simmering anger that she had. She threw the knife down, went back into her room, and slammed the door. I told her she had 48 hours to check herself into rehab or move out, and the clock was ticking.

I looked at Daryl and, hoping to lighten the mood, said something to the effect of "That went well." We went downstairs and waited to see what would happen next.

A couple of hours later, Amanda came out of her room dressed for her big night. She went out the front door, got in a car I didn't recognize, and left.

Daryl and I did what we had to do. We set up a boundary, and now it was up to Amanda to decide what she would do. We were at peace with our decision.

Times Up

The following 48 hours were not relaxing at all. We were all walking on eggshells. Amanda wasn't talking to us, and we avoided her at all costs. She didn't come home from her birthday night out until the next morning. She slept most of that day, and when she did emerge from her room, she looked like hell.

We kept waiting for Amanda to tell us she would check into rehab. I knew my daughter. She was a princess, and this princess would not live in the streets. With time running out, we told her she had a decision to make soon. Amanda didn't answer. I could hear her on the phone talking to someone, but I couldn't hear exactly what they were saying.

As the 48th hour approached, I could hear Amanda rustling around in her room. I was beginning to think that she was going to leave.

The 48th hour arrived, and Daryl and I knocked on Amanda's door. We asked her if she had decided. She told us she was leaving and asked if we could give her a ride to a friend's house. I told her that would not be a problem. She had a bag ready, and we went down to the car.

This is the stranglehold that heroin had on my daughter. Rather than go into rehab and want to begin living a life that she would enjoy, she decided that the streets would be better for her. That was when I knew that her drug problem was larger than life, and she didn't understand how to live without the drugs.

Amanda was high. Her speech was slurred, and her eyelids were drooping. She gave me the address to where she wanted to go, and we drove her there. The house we took her to wasn't in the best part of town. On the way, we told Amanda how much we loved her and hoped she would find her path to sobriety. She didn't answer much. She was so high that she couldn't understand what we were saying. We watched her leave the car and climb the steps to the front porch. The front door opened, and Craig came out and helped her with her bag. I just shook my head. I should have known she would go to his house.

What I didn't know and would only find out later was that Craig was Amanda's supplier of heroin.

We drove back home, and I hate to admit this, but I felt relief. I was going home and knew no drama would be waiting for me. I admonished myself for feeling this way. How could I be relieved when my baby girl was now away from us with the possibility that she could die? I slept soundly that night, but it was probably the last sound sleep I would have for a long time.

Villains

I will pause this story to clarify a few items that need to be understood. Throughout this story, I may have given the perception that either Daryl or I had lost our love for our daughter. To set things straight, neither of us EVER stopped loving Amanda. She may have made loving her difficult, but we always loved her.

A family caught in the grasp of addiction doesn't alter their reality or logic because they dislike their user. It's quite the opposite. You do outrageous things because you love the user and want to protect them from their dangerous behaviors. You want them to have all the opportunities for a good life and hope that by assisting them in their endeavors, they will find sobriety and still have those opportunities available.

My descriptions of events and conversations paint Amanda as an unloving, selfish human who only cared about getting her next fix. While that may be the perception of her behavior, the one thing I do not want to do is to label Amanda as some villain.

What needs to be understood is that opioids had hijacked Amanda's brain. Once a user is hooked on opioids, the brain demands that you give it more. Opioids release endorphins into the body. The pleasure receptors in the brain become so overwhelmed with opioids that to achieve the new levels of endorphins, more opioids must be introduced.

Just let me clarify that I am not a doctor. I have no degrees in any field of medicine. I only know what has been explained to me by others. If you want to understand how opioids affect the brain, I suggest using the internet and finding a reputable website.

I think of a craving for opioids as the same as a craving for food, water, warmth, shelter, and sleep. If you are deprived of any of these essentials, your body lets you know it craves something by your stomach growling for food, your lips and mouth getting dry, your body shivering or sweating, and your brain's inability to keep your eyes open. When a user does not get the appropriate amount of opioids in a timely fashion, the body will start responding by making the user "Dope sick." Once the user's body begins to detoxify, they will get chills and shakes. They will vomit and have diarrhea. They will sweat, and their body will hurt all over. These symptoms can last for days. A user who has experienced these symptoms will do all they can not to experience them again.

When explaining this to others, I use the following analogy. Say, for instance, you are dropped off in the middle of the desert. Before you are left to fend for yourself, you are told that if you walk for three days in a specific direction, you will come to an oasis where there will be food, water, and shelter. If you go in any other direction, you will perish. As the temperature rises, you walk in the direction you are told. Since you were not given food or water and the desert has no shelter, you begin to sweat as you trudge along.

By the end of the first day, you are incredibly thirsty and hungry. Your body demands rest, so you lay down to sleep. You awake when the hot sun hits you, and off you go. You notice that your steps are becoming more challenging as you walk. Your mouth, lips, and throat are dry. Your stomach hurts because you have not eaten in over 24 hours. You only know that if you keep going in the right direction, you will get to the oasis. Late into the second day, your mind is telling you to slow down and that you need to conserve energy so you can survive, but if you do that, you will only prolong getting to the oasis, so you ignore your brain and keep going until you are overcome by exhaustion.

You are awakened on the third day by the same hot sun, but moving is much more challenging. Your mouth, lips, and throat feel like they are coated in sand. Your stomach stops hurting, but you realize how weak you've become. You are no longer perspiring and are sunburned. You are crawling in the same direction you've been told to follow. Your brain says stop moving; you need to rest, but your other cravings keep you moving.

At last, on the horizon, you see the oasis. It's as if you got a sudden jolt of energy. You try to walk, then crawl toward the oasis. As you get closer, you notice something surrounding the oasis. It is a four-foot-high, ten yards wide thicket of 2-inch-long thorns. You can see the water well on the other side of the thorns. There are fruits and vegetables inside a tent where you can also see bedding and a two-way radio. Your brain is telling you not to go through those thorns; you will undoubtedly get cut and injured, but the part of your brain that says you need that food, water, and to get out of the hot sun takes control, and you plunge yourself into the thorns and claw your way through them getting cut and injured as you go. You make it through the thorns and get to the well and drink as much as possible, then you crawl to the tent and eat as much as possible. You fall asleep on the comfortable bedding in the cool tent and only awaken to deal with your injuries later.

That is an addict's journey every day in between fixes. They will do whatever they have to to fill that craving that is as essential to them as food, water, sleep, and shelter.

Would you deny someone who hadn't had a drink of water in three days from taking a sip from your garden hose without asking you first? Would you deny someone who hadn't eaten in a week for taking some fruit from your tree without asking you first? It's the same with opioid addiction. The user's body is demanding what it believes is an essential item to keep it alive, and the user is only providing it with what it requires, and that user will crawl through a four-foot-high, ten-yard-wide thicket of two-inch thorns to get it what it needs.

Amanda was never a villain in my eyes. There may have been times when I disliked what she did or said, but it wasn't her doing those things. It was the disease of addiction that compelled her to do those things. So, I villainize the disease, never the user.

3 Days

Amanda had been gone for three days, and as much as Daryl and I wanted to reach out to her and call her to see how she was, we held back from doing that. We knew we had to take control of this process. We knew that having Amanda as an active addict in our home was toxic. It was negatively affecting us both mentally and physically.

I had counted on Amanda's comfortable upbringing and niceties to drive her from living as a homeless addict. At the three-day mark, I was beginning to have my doubts.

I was leaving my place of employment when my cell phone rang. The caller ID showed it was Amanda. I was anticipating this call, but what kind of call was this going to be? Was it going to be a call for help, a call for money, or worse, a call from someone telling me Amanda was in trouble?

When I answered, it was Amanda on the other end. She told me that she was ready to go to rehab. She said that she had been sleeping on the couches at different friends' homes over the past few days and had plenty of time to reflect. She said several friends contacted her and told her that she needed to go to rehab because they feared for her life. I told her I would not come and get her until she called the rehab facility, and they told her she would be admitted to their inpatient program. I told her I would pick her up and drive her to the rehab facility whenever they were ready to take her.

She called me back a few hours later and told me the rehab couldn't take her for a few days. They told her to call every morning to see if they had an opening. She asked me if she could come home until this occurred because she had no place to stay. Please don't ask me why I trusted her, but I agreed to pick her up.

I picked her up, and Amanda told me she wasn't feeling well on the way home. I knew she was starting to detox and figured that must be one of the reasons she contacted me.

She couldn't get her next fix, and in rehab, she could detox easier. I told her to hang on, and hopefully, there would be a bed for her the following day.

The following day Amanda called the rehab as soon as they started taking calls. She was not looking good at all. Her face was ashen. She was sweating, and she had chills. The rehab told her they still had no room for her. I asked to speak to the rehab, and after getting Amanda's permission for them to talk to me, I told them how sick she was feeling and what I was to do to stop it. The rehab person told me to let her use heroin until a bed was available. Did I hear right??!! I was to let her use heroin while waiting for a detox bed!? That was the thing we were hoping to stop! I was never more dumbfounded. The only other recourse was to let her detox.

After we got off the phone, I asked Amanda if she had any Suboxone. She said no, but she knew where she could get some. I was not too fond of this option, but I agreed to get it for her. She made a couple of phone calls and then told me where we could get it and how much it would be. We got in the car, and I told her that when she got the suboxone, she would have to take it in front of me. If you do heroin immediately before taking Suboxone, I know it will throw you directly into withdrawal. I was afraid that when she went in to get the suboxone that she might also do heroin. Amanda was appalled that I didn't trust her. I asked if we switched places would she trust me? Case closed.

Rehab

The rehab finally had an opening after three days of waiting. It was about 30 miles from our home. We drove her out there, got her admitted, and then went home. Daryl and I were feeling very relieved. Amanda was now trying to find sobriety; she was in a safe location and wasn't getting out for 28 days. We could finally sleep peacefully without fear of a middle-of-the-night phone call from the police or the morgue.

This rehab had a family day every Saturday where you came in for a presentation, followed by a discussion group and visitation with your loved one for a couple of hours. When we got to the rehab, we were escorted to an auditorium with about 75 other people. The presentation was done by one of the counselors who talked to us about addiction and how our loved one was on a lifelong journey to sobriety. They also told us not to be overly concerned if our loved ones relapsed. They said to us that relapse was a part of recovery. That was not something I wasn't expecting to hear. I thought the purpose of rehab was to give the users the tools to stay sober. Over time I found out how wrong that was.

After the meeting, we were brought to a large sitting area with many tables and chairs. Amanda was there. She looked radiant. Her makeup and hair were amazing. Her skin glowed from the life back in it, and she was as happy to see us as we were to see her. I couldn't believe what ten days had done to her. She told me she was learning so much in the counseling sessions. She said that she didn't take the counseling sessions seriously after she got out of detox. But the other people in the counseling sessions started calling her out, and she had no choice but to share her story. She introduced us to a couple of her counselors. They said that Amanda was doing very well and that if she stayed on that track, she had a good chance at long-term sobriety. That was the first time I had heard of "long-term sobriety."

We spent an hour or so with Amanda, where she

introduced us to some of the other girls she had met over the last ten days and took us on a mini tour of the outdoor area. I couldn't believe the number of young men and women in this rehab that were all such good-looking young people. If you had passed them on the street, you would have never guessed they all suffered from the disease of addiction.

We said our goodbyes to Amanda and her new girlfriends, and as we left, I looked back to see her talking with them as if she had known them her entire life. Daryl and I drove home optimistic about our daughter. It was the first time we had felt that way in an exceedingly long time.

A Pain in My...

In my early twenties, when I lived in Miami, I had a period where I experienced some personal and professional challenges. I tried navigating through these challenges as best as I knew how. I started to experience headaches that increased in severity and frequency over this period. It finally culminated in what was diagnosed as migraine headaches. I only went to a physician when they were so severe that over-the-counter medications did nothing to relieve them from affecting my vision and hearing.

My doctor informed me that I was experiencing migraines and asked if anything had recently changed in my life. I answered that nothing had changed. He wondered if anything in my life was causing me stress. Again, I told him that there was no stress. I didn't want to admit that I was experiencing stress because I should not have been letting my problems get the better of me. My pride stopped me from being honest.

My doctor prescribed me medication to assist me with the migraines. Later, I decided to see a therapist to help me understand how to handle my personal and professional life. After many sessions with a therapist, I understood how to manage my stress, and my migraines dissipated. I would still get headaches throughout my life, but they rarely met the migraine level.

When we moved back to Pittsburgh, I acquired a new physician I would see for yearly physicals. He knew of my migraine history, but I never had an office visit because of a migraine. That changed when the discovery that Amanda was using heroin occurred. The migraines returned with a vengeance and became so unbearable that I went to see my physician.

My physician also questioned me about changes in my life. I hesitated in my answer. The stigma of my daughter's drug addiction was keeping me silent. I had at this time not admitted it to anyone except Peggy and Frank. Thankfully, my physician waited for me to gather my strength and tell him about my daughter's addiction and our recent discovery that she had graduated from pills to heroin.

My physician was sympathetic and compassionate and displayed great empathy by patiently listening to me and spending much more time than he probably allocated to handle my migraine issue. He wanted to prescribe me some medication, but I was so anti-pharma by that time that I told him pills were out of the question. As far as I was concerned, drugs started destroying my daughter, and I was adamant that I would not be adding to "big pharma's" revenue stream.

This put my doctor in a corner. But he had another course of action for me. He said that my headaches were induced by stress, so he wanted me to see a psychiatrist specializing in hypnosis. He thought hypnosis could help me train my brain to better process stress. I thought hypnosis sounded kooky, but I was desperate, so I made an appointment to be hypnotized.

When I went to my first appointment, I went into a small waiting room where I was instructed to fill out a questionnaire. The topics on this form were all about family members, professional acquaintances, and work. It was apparent to me that the psychiatrist was going to see from the information on the form that I had a conflict with my daughter.

When my appointment time arrived, I was directed into his office, where he looked at my questionnaire and started asking me about the relationship that I was having with my daughter. I didn't hold back and told him all about her, her addiction, and how it affected my family. He told me he had minimal experience with addiction but said he could help me deal with the stress of the situation so I could learn how to perform self-hypnosis when I felt migraines coming on.

I did two sessions with the doctor attempting to hypnotize me, but it wasn't working. I didn't say anything to him because I thought maybe it was something that took time to take effect. Halfway through the third session, I stopped him and told him that the hypnosis was not working, and I asked if we could talk about what was going on in my life and my thoughts surrounding it. He again reiterated that he was not an addiction specialist but he agreed to discuss it with me and offer his analysis. I began telling him about what it was like to live with someone you love that has an addiction.

After many sessions, he determined a few things that I did not. He first pointed out that I was not losing my mind because of all the illogical and unreasonable stuff I had done during the height of Amanda's addiction. Second, I blamed myself for not seeing Amanda's addiction coming on earlier, so I could have intervened earlier. He told me that without a crystal ball, there was no way for me to know that there was a problem on the horizon, especially when it comes to our children. He told me that we always see the best in our children and believe they will always make the best choices since we instill the values they are to follow. Third, he thought I was spending too much time and energy hiding the addiction, which he pointed out I wasn't doing a good job of.

These three things, and some others he made clear, started me on my way to being honest with myself and others. It made me open my life to others and ask for help. It made me begin retaking control of my life.

I also started attending the Bridge to Hope Support Group every week halfway through my psychiatric sessions. Between the two, I reduced my stress to the point where I could function better at work and at home.

I will be forever grateful to my psychiatrist for starting me on a new journey that helped me to discover who I was and not fear sharing that with others. When I shared my experiences about my daughter's addiction with friends, neighbors, or co-workers, I found that they also had someone struggling with alcohol or drugs in their lives. This sharing helped us both to find comfort and compassion with each other.

Who Me???

Amanda was still in rehab when Daryl and I attended our third meeting at the Bridge to Hope (B2H). B2H was founded by a group of women and men who had children suffering from the disease of addiction. This small group of people started meeting in the living rooms of their homes because, at the time, support groups were limited. This group of people met to share their good and bad experiences about their addicted loved ones. They educated each other on various addiction topics and worked hard to have guest speakers who were experts in the addiction arena. Some long-term members were still actively involved with B2H even though many of their children had found long-term sobriety.

At our third meeting, after the introductions, the group was broken into smaller groups where the task was to discuss a specific characteristic of addiction. Each small group contained one long-term member who led the discussion. I recall sharing my feelings concerning boundaries with our group and how I struggled with setting boundaries for Amanda and sticking with them. I explained how I believed setting boundaries was just one more thing that would cause arguments, anxiety, and stress. They would cause Amanda to get upset, leading to me getting upset. My group leader approached me towards the end of the meeting and said I have a book I think you need to read. It was titled "Codependent No More" and written by Melody Beattie.

Not knowing what codependency was, I assumed it was a book about people with multiple dependencies spawned from addiction. I thought I would educate myself on what my daughter was dealing with.

As I read the book's early pages, I realized that this was not a book describing my daughter. It was a book describing my addiction to my daughter's addiction. If that sounds confusing, believe me, I was. As I continued reading through the book, I kept seeing myself and how the behaviors of codependency were my behaviors with my daughter.

My daughter's moods were my moods. If she had a good day, so did I. If she was having a bad day, my day was terrible. Her wishes became mine to fulfill. Her needs were needs that I had to deal with. My daughter's addiction was controlling me, and I let that happen. It wasn't that I decided to do that one day. It was a very gradual process that occurred over the years. It was so subtle that I didn't even realize this had happened to me until I began to read the book.

This revelation began my recovery process. I knew I had to regain control of my life, emotions, and decision-making. I knew this was not going to be a quick recovery process. It had taken me years to become codependent, and it would take my entire life to suppress it.

At the next B2H meeting I attended, after my introduction, I told the group about my discovery and how stunned I was by it. It had never occurred to me that I was suffering from an addiction not caused by consuming alcohol or a narcotic. I told them that later as I read through the book, I became relieved that I could now understand why I did all those illogical and unreasonable things that enabled my daughter to stay in her addiction.

After the meeting, I approached the woman who gave me the codependency book and hugged her, telling her how grateful I was to her that she recognized what I was going through and for helping me to discover it. If she had said that I was codependent at the initial meeting, I might have become offended and not returned to the group. I remembered this lesson from this wise woman and knew that in the future, with this group, it would be my responsibility to make sure I helped others discover their issues without making them feel attacked, blamed, or shamed.

To this day, I still work on my codependency. I can easily fall back into it if I don't stay diligent. This whole process has helped me to be open with people. I don't hide who I am and the weaknesses I have. I work hard to have no fear of my flaws. I work harder to own them. They are a part of me. They are not something to be ashamed of.

Two and a Half Weeks

My daughter called us from the rehab after she was there for two weeks and told us that she would be released in a couple of days and wanted us to come to the rehab facility and pick her up. Daryl and I were caught by surprise. We thought she would be there for at least 28 days and questioned her about that. She told us that she felt she was ready to leave rehab and try living a life of sobriety. She said her counselors agreed to her release if she agreed to attend daily outpatient rehab sessions. These were not mandatory, but they were strongly suggested.

Our mistake was that we never talked to the counselors. They would have never discussed any of the details of their conversations with Amanda, and we knew that. But we could have told them about our concerns about her coming home. She had used heroin in our house. We had already learned that addiction was triggered by people, places, and things. All those items were at our home.

Daryl and I were very apprehensive about Amanda coming home, but we didn't know of any other choice. We were confident that if she came home to live eventually, she would relapse, and everything would be lost.

When we picked Amanda up at the rehab, she was so happy to be with us. She was so enthused about her sobriety. She told us about the daily outpatient rehab sessions. We were surprised to hear that they were about 6-8 hours per day. We had no idea how she would attend those sessions and work. We were determined not to give her any money. It wouldn't be from the money we gave her if she relapsed. She was so happy and healthy looking that we didn't want to say anything that would burst her bubble. Maybe two and a half weeks of rehab had given her the tools to stay sober. We were cautiously optimistic but very ignorant about how staying sober works.

When we got home with Amanda, she went to her room and unpacked her clothes while Daryl and I gave her some space to readjust. Later that evening, I noticed she wasn't so happy and bubbly. I didn't want to ask her if anything was wrong. I was afraid of hearing the answer.

In the middle of the night, I awoke because I heard Amanda going down the stairs of our house. This was a trigger for me. It was a reminder of the night walks she would take when she was getting high. I admonished myself for not searching her room to see if she had hidden any drugs there that she could use. The next day when she was at her first outpatient rehab session, I did a complete and thorough search of her room, including going through all her clothes and pulling out all the drawers in her dresser to see if anything was taped to the bottom. I was genuinely concerned about getting stuck with a used needle. I didn't want the possibility of contracting Hepatitis C. The only thing I found was the missing spoons from our silverware set. All were bent with burn marks on the bottom of them.

When Amanda came back home after her session, she was very subdued. This was concerning. I asked her if she was ok. She said she wasn't and wanted us to take her to a Narcotics Anonymous (NA) meeting.

Since Amanda wanted Daryl and me to go with her, we had to find what was defined as an "open" meeting. "Open" meetings were for the users and anyone who wanted to attend. We got on the internet and could not find an "open" NA meeting in our area. We did find an 'open' Alcoholics Anonymous meeting close by.

When we got there, we were greeted warmly at the door. We found a seat, and the meeting began. Without going into specific details, I found the forum to be very moving. I saw that this was a genuinely caring and empathetic group of people. It was inspiring to see many people who had found long-term recovery and many who were very early in the recovery process.

As the meeting concluded, several women who had long-term recovery stopped to speak with Amanda. They offered their contact information in case she needed someone to talk to. It was very refreshing to see that someday this could be Amanda offering her contact information to someone in need.

When we returned to our house, Amanda went to her room and called someone on her cell phone. I hoped she was calling one of the women she had met that night.

Sober Living

Daryl and I could tell that Amanda was struggling with being in her old bedroom. We were fearful that she would relapse, but we didn't know what recourse we had. The next day Amanda came to us and told us that she couldn't stay in her bedroom. It was a trigger for her. She told us that last night she called one of the girls she had met in rehab and knew she had moved into a sober living home right from the rehab facility. Amanda told us that the house her friend lived in was located in Carrick, a neighborhood within the Pittsburgh city limits.

Daryl and I had no idea what a sober living home was. Amanda said it was a privately owned home where the owner was typically an addict with long-term recovery. The owner would buy older homes that had many bedrooms. The house would be refurbished and rented to people in recovery who needed a sober residence. The rent was relatively minor for a month. Everyone who lived at the house had to find employment within two weeks.

The house was gender specific, all females or all males. You could not have guests from the opposite sex visit you at the house. There was usually a house manager who would assign housekeeping tasks to those living within the home. If you didn't complete your housekeeping tasks, that could lead to removal from the house. Everyone at the house was subject to random drug tests that the house manager gave. If you failed a drug test, you had to leave the house immediately. You would be given two hours to pack your stuff and leave. You would forfeit your monthly rent even if you had just paid it.

There were strict curfews for new residents. Violating the curfew could lead to removal from the house. If you were removed from the home, you could ask to move back in after two weeks and with a negative drug test. You would have to pay the total monthly rent regardless of when you paid it last.

Residents fresh out of rehab were required to attend NA meetings daily. At the end of a session, a resident must get a signed slip indicating that they had attended the meeting. The idea of the sober living house was to promote a sober lifestyle and prepare the resident to maintain a sobriety they could manage when they eventually felt the need to move out. There was no time limit on how long you could stay at a sober living house.

We drove Amanda to the house she wanted to move into and met with the house manager, who told us all the house rules. We paid Amanda's first month's rent and helped her move in. We hoped this would be the environment Amanda needed to keep her on the road to sobriety.

Disease or Choice

One of the topics at a Bridge to Hope meeting was whether someone with a substance or alcohol addiction had a disease or if the addiction was caused by a lack of morals, bad character flaws, or wrong choices.

I struggled with this topic. Was it a disease or a choice? I did some research on the topic to help me find an answer. I found it was both.

Amanda chose to abuse her pain meds, but within a brief period, that choice became for her a disease of no choice. As I described earlier in layperson's terms, opioids alter the chemistry within the brain. They latch on to the brain's pleasure receptors and change the body's pleasure feelings. Continued use of opioids continues the alteration where the brain requires an increased dosage of opioids to satisfy the pleasure receptors.

This is what makes addiction a brain disease that has been recognized as such by the American Medical Association since the 1950s. The proper term for the illness is substance use disorder (SUD). It's a term that people who work in the field of substance use would rather have everyone else use. This helps identify it as a disease and has a much softer tone than the word "addiction" and all the baggage that word carries.

Focusing on SUD as a disease allows you to view your user differently. It helps you not to villainize your loved one. It will enable you to better understand why your user is doing so many illogical and unreasonable things. It allows you to remove the stigma of blame and shame from the user and center you on helping the user find long-term sobriety.

If you view your loved one as having bad morals or making bad choices, you allow this view to affect you negatively. The bad feelings you harbor for the user will physically and mentally hurt you.

When I accepted Amanda as having a brain disease, it lifted a giant weight off me. I viewed her no differently than someone afflicted with diabetes or heart disease. I was able to help her see that she had a brain disease that, unfortunately, is a lifelong disease. Helping her understand she had a disease allowed her to release the blame and shame she carried.

This was the most important item that helped me in my recovery.

Grieving the Undead

I believe that one of the things that those of us who have a loved one suffering from a SUD experience, is that even though they are alive and breathing, we grieve for them.

Grief is a powerful emotion and is usually associated with a loved one who has died. Grief is different for everyone in how intense it can be or how long it can last. There are five stages to grief: Denial and Isolation, Anger, Bargaining, Depression, and Acceptance.

I went through the stages of grief with Amanda while she was actively using. I didn't know I was going through these stages of grief because I saw a living, breathing Amanda almost every day while she was actively using. I didn't associate what I was feeling with grief.

Even though Amanda was alive, I was grieving for all the lost opportunities and potential I saw for her. I saw her chance to go to college, find a career, find someone she would love enough to spend the rest of her life with, have children if she desired, buy a home, and live a long and happy life as all disappearing.

Denial was very evident. In the beginning, denial was my tool for coping with Amanda. If I could deny or rationalize away some of the bad traits that Amanda was displaying, then I could move on with my life. If I stopped denying them, I would have to confront them, and life would become complicated.

Isolation was something I had to do. Seeing friends and family and listening to them talk about all their children's successes would make me long for those same successes for Amanda. Staying away from others was another coping mechanism for me. I couldn't imagine telling anyone of my friends or family that my daughter was using drugs. To clarify, I didn't stop seeing my family or interacting with friends. I wasn't being honest with them regarding how Amanda was doing.

As you read in previous chapters, I experienced Anger. Anger was easy. I was angry at Amanda for letting this happen to her. I was mad at myself for not acting sooner when my inner voice told me something was wrong. Anger is what almost tore my family apart at the seams. Anger is destructive.

I can't tell you how much bargaining I did while Amanda was actively using. It was immense. I bargained with her almost daily to do more productive things with herself. I would promise her cash or gifts if she completed specific tasks. Most of the time, I would reward her before she did the job. I wasn't a great bargainer. I also would bargain spiritually. I would ask God to help my daughter, and if that happened, I would do something in return. This bargaining I would make out of desperation.

Depression hit me hard, and I had no idea I was depressed. The depression came when Amanda was totally out of control. I was losing her and could do nothing to stop it. I was in over my head and had no answers. I was suffering from migraines, and I was questioning my sanity. I was doing things I thought were helping Amanda, no matter how questionable. I felt my perception of reality was distorted, but necessary to save my daughter. I didn't like who I was or what I had become.

Finally, Acceptance arrived. Acceptance came upon me gradually. It started with reaching out to my family doctor and asking for help with my migraines. It gained momentum when I began getting therapeutic help from my psychiatrist, who helped me to understand that I wasn't going crazy. It picked up more speed when I went to my B2H family support meetings and was educated about SUD. It took firm hold of me when I accepted that my daughter had a brain disease and she wasn't some evil entity that brought with her nothing but sadness.

Acceptance helped me to forgive my daughter and myself for all the missteps, harsh words, and slamming doors. Forgiveness brought me peace. Peace let me see life from a new perspective. Acceptance helped me to start my recovery.

I was very quick with explaining my process through these steps of grief, but to be clear, long periods passed through and between these steps. It is so easy in hindsight to reflect and document how each of these steps of grief progressed, but time makes it difficult to see them as they occur.

Recovery Romance

Amanda was doing well living at the sober living home. She looked good, her attitude was good, she had a minimum wage job, she attended NA meetings regularly, and her house manager gave a good report about her. They even started giving Amanda some additional freedoms and loosened her curfew.

About three months later, Amanda told us about a boy she met in one of the recovery meetings. He lived about 30 miles south of Pittsburgh but liked coming up to the Pittsburgh NA meetings for a change of pace. He would be the next significant love in Amanda's life. We'll call him Jake.

We got to meet Jake a few weeks later. He had two years of sobriety under his belt and was very active in NA. He helped run NA meetings in his town and attended meetings daily. We had lunch with Amanda and Jake at our house, and afterward, they left to participate in a meeting before Jake had to head back home.

Jake and Amanda became quite an item over the next few weeks, with them seeing each other consistently. Jake could not visit Amanda at the sober living home due to the house rules, so they only saw each other for short dates or at NA meetings, where they would go out for a bite to eat afterward.

A few weeks after we first met Jake, when they visited us at our house, Jake and Amanda told us they wanted to rent an apartment and move in together in the town Jake lived in. Amanda said it was better for her because it took her away from Pittsburgh and the possibility of her being triggered into relapse. Pittsburgh provided too many opportunities for that to occur. Jake assured us that he had a strong presence in the recovery community where he lived and would do nothing to jeopardize his or Amanda's sobriety.

There wasn't much we could do or say to stop them. They were both adults, and their points were valid. About a week later, they came by with a small moving van, grabbed Amanda's bedroom furniture, and moved into their new apartment.

Since they were much further away, Daryl and I would only visit once every couple of weeks and take Jake and Amanda to dinner. They both appeared to be doing well. Jake was a server at a chain restaurant and brought home some nice money in tips. Amanda was having a little more difficulty finding work. The town was small compared to Pittsburgh, so employment opportunities were limited. But her spirits were good, and they both were happy.

The Other Shoe

It was late fall, and Daryl and I met my sister Mary Jo and her husband Alan for dinner. We all arrived early and were directed to the bar while we waited for our table to be ready. My cell phone rang. It was Amanda.

Right away, I could tell this wasn't going to be a pleasant call by the seriousness of her voice. Amanda told me she and Jake were low on money because Jake had his hours cut at his job because business was down. The voice in my head told me to be alert. I asked Amanda what they needed the money for, and she said they needed food. I offered to drive down the next day and help her grocery shop, but she said they needed the money immediately. The voice in my head got louder. She told me that if I couldn't get the money to her tonight, they would sell their flat-panel TV to a neighbor.

So now my inner voice is yelling at me. I told her that I was not bringing her cash tonight. That I was out at dinner and then heading home afterward. I reiterated that I would come down the next day and take her grocery shopping. She said that wasn't good enough and I was forcing her to sell the TV. I told her to do what she felt like she had to do.

A few days later, Daryl and I visited Amanda and Jake. Jake was at work, and the TV was missing and replaced by an old small color TV. She had sold her TV. At that point, I knew things were not good with her. We took her to dinner, bought her some groceries, and then left.

A couple of days went by when I got another call from Amanda. She called to say they needed rent money. I reminded Amanda that when she and Jake decided to move in together, they would have to manage their finances. I was not going to pay her rent. She thanked me for nothing and hung up.

A couple of weeks after that, Amanda called me again. She was very subdued. She told me she needed to check herself back into rehab. I wasn't surprised. I asked her if she had made the call to the rehab, and she said she did. She said they were going to call her back when a bed was going to be available later in the day.

It was about 9 pm when I called Amanda and asked her if the rehab had called her yet, and she said they had and that a bed would be ready soon. I was beginning to doubt this scenario when she called me about an hour later and told me the bed would be ready at midnight.

At 10:30 pm, I drove to Amanda's apartment to pick her up. The apartment had only a few pieces of furniture left in it. I asked her where all the furniture was, and she said they had sold it. She told me she and Jake had started using drugs again about two months prior and were behind on their rent. They were going to be evicted the next day. Jake was nowhere to be seen. I never did see him again.

I drove Amanda to the rehab in silence. I knew she was going to rehab because she had nowhere else to live. When we arrived at the entrance to the rehab facility, I didn't even park. I pulled up to the door, helped her with her stuff, kissed her goodbye, and told her I loved her and would pray for her. She was crying as she pushed the button to enter the building. I drove home, knowing I had handled this episode correctly.

Family Day Part 2

With Amanda back in rehab, I had a couple of weeks to reflect on her eight months of sobriety and what went wrong. Daryl and I did everything we could to help her be successful at staying sober, but somehow, I thought we didn't do enough.

At my next support meeting, I mentioned that Amanda had relapsed and that I couldn't understand what more I could have done to prevent it. Someone in the group said maybe I did too much. That was it. Just a passing comment until someone else spoke next. At the end of the meeting, one of the long-term members approached me and said, "We can't want recovery for our loved ones more than they do and sometimes the best thing we can do is just get out of their way."

How do you get out of the way of someone afflicted with a disease that wants them to destroy themselves? How do you not try to step in and stop it? The answer to these questions comes with a short little saying I read on the internet while searching for ways to help an individual stay sober.

It read: "I didn't cause it, I can't control it, and I can't cure it."

When I read this little sentence, it launched an opportunity for me to reflect and understand the power of this sentence. Of course, I didn't cause this disease to overtake my daughter. She had a genetic predisposition for the disease. There is a history of alcoholism in my family tree. She also didn't intentionally decide to become an addict. No one with a history of alcohol or drug abuse ever sat down one day and said to themselves, "I want to become addicted to drugs or alcohol."

I certainly can't cure the disease. No one can. If there is to be a cure someday, it will come from someone far more intelligent than me.

I had been learning over the last year that I couldn't control this disease, but I also learned that I couldn't control the person afflicted. I tried to control my daughter during her addiction, and I was trying to manage her recovery. Based on the results, I would say it was an abject failure.

Family day at the rehab arrived, and Daryl and I visited Amanda. I had already decided that I would not talk much when we were with Amanda. I wanted to focus more on listening. I wanted to hear how she was going to help herself.

Just like the last time, Amanda looked good when she came to greet us. Her hair was clean and beautiful, her skin color was great, and her clothes were clean and neat. She was happy and bubbly. Daryl and Amanda did most of the talking. I was listening. I wanted to hear from her what would be different about her second shot at sobriety. I was hearing nothing different.

After a few minutes, Amanda asked me why I was so quiet, and I told her that I wanted to listen to what she had to say about her newly found sobriety and what she would do to sustain it. She said she would return to living in a sober home, get a job, and attend NA meetings. I reminded her that those were all the things she did the last time and to look where it got her. She asked me what I thought she should do then. I told her it wasn't up to me to tell her how to manage her disease. She had to figure out the best way to gain a sobriety that would be long-lasting. I told her I would no longer help her manage her sobriety. I was going to get out of her way, just as my support group told me. I told her she had to manage her life from now on.

She wanted to know why I was being so hostile toward her. I told her I wasn't hostile but that I was facing reality. I pointed out all the things we did for her while she was attempting to achieve sobriety. I asked her to tell me what the outcome was. I told her to look where it got us. We were back where we started nine months ago.

I told her she needed to direct her recovery. I pointed out that she should set goals and try to attain them. I let her know she had complete control of her life and how it would turn out. I told her I loved her and would support her recovery.

My daughter left the rehab after 14 days and moved into a sober living home. She was starting her second attempt at sobriety.

180 Degree Love

While Amanda was working on her latest recovery, Daryl and I would see her occasionally and talk with her whenever she would call us or we would call her. When speaking with Amanda, she often asked us to do something for her or pay for something she needed. The criteria for whether we would do anything for our daughter was "Is this helping our daughter with her recovery?"

Sometimes, we would deny her request for something, and she would become distraught and attempt to manipulate us into giving in. We couldn't get mad at this behavior because we unintentionally encouraged it early in her addiction. But now we had a new weapon to battle manipulation.

We would start each reply with, "We love you so much that we can't...". One of our support group members had told us about this method. It was amazingly effective. It was difficult for Amanda to argue with us whenever we used this method. What could she say? "Please don't love me!"

We also learned that we had to understand how to love Amanda differently. Let me explain this. As a parent, you love your baby the moment you hold it for the first time. You vow to protect it and care for it as long as you take a breath. As life progresses, we bandage all the boo-boos, nurse all the illnesses, and solve all the problems. We ensure that our children's lives are as comfortable and problem-free as possible. This is one of the ways that we show our love to our children.

When you are initially confronted with a child in addiction, your parental instincts are to protect the child and help solve all the problems that addiction causes. You don't realize that while you believe you are helping your child, you are enabling the disease to grow and flourish. You are doing these sometimes illogical and unreasonable things out of love, but in essence, they are helping to destroy the one you are trying to help.

This is where my term "180 Degree Love" comes from. How it works is that you must train yourself to demonstrate your love for your addicted child differently than your parental instincts tell you. The disease of substance abuse brings consequences with it. In other words, for the disease to flourish, it will cause the victim to make many bad decisions. Those bad decisions carry consequences with them. It is these consequences that parents try to take care of or cover up in order for them to believe they are helping the user.

180 Degree Love requires that the parent let the natural consequences of addiction occur. Doing this exposes the disease much earlier in the addiction process and may stop more severe consequences.

180 Degree Love makes you start each sentence with the words "I love you so much…". By creating your portion of the conversation this way, it sets a gentler tone. It gives you your reason for the denial right at the beginning of the conversation. It is the one thing you can fall back on as much as you need to during the conversation. It makes it difficult for the other party to argue with you when you tell your user that you love them.

To be clear, I didn't invent this process of starting each sentence with "I Love you so much…". I called it "180 Degree Love" because it best portrays how someone unfamiliar with this concept could remember how to use it and why. It has been very effective for me.

Random Moves

Amanda moved into a sober home in the small town where she and Jake lived. She told us this was the best location because she could surround herself with women who had obtained long-term recovery. She felt she could learn from them and work a more robust recovery there. I told her she oversaw her recovery and that if she thought this was best for her, she should do it.

Three months later, Amanda announced she was moving back to Pittsburgh into a sober living home in Mount Washington. This community was only 20 minutes from our home. Having her around so close to us was a little concerning to me. But I told myself that she would only become a problem if we let her become a problem, and we were determined not to let her do that.

Amanda said she was moving back because this new sober living home did not require roommates. Amanda would have a bedroom all to herself. She said this would cut down on the drama that a roommate always seemed to bring with them. Again, our message to her was to do what she felt was best to strengthen her recovery.

With Amanda being so close, we would see her at least once a week to take her out for dinner. The conversation was usually about how she was doing and her new living arrangements. She always seemed to be finding a new job, but I didn't try to pry or judge her for how she was managing her life. We would tell her how proud we were that she was sober.

About three months later, Amanda moved to another sober living home in the Carrick area of Pittsburgh. It wasn't very far from the first sober living house she lived within. This new home was owned by a woman who lived in another home across the street. If any situations required the owner's attention, she was there immediately and would resolve them quickly.

Amanda had us come and visit her at her new location about two weeks after she had moved in, and she seemed to have a different attitude. She seemed more at peace with herself. She was talking about a job interview she was going to the next day and how she would have to take a couple of buses to get there. She told us she was applying for a job as a server at a bar/restaurant where she would work in the dueling piano bar area on the weekends. She told us a girlfriend of hers worked at this place and said the tips from the piano bar were great. Amanda told us her goal was to save enough money to buy a car.

I didn't know what happened between the last place she lived and this place, but for the first time in years, I thought she might be on the road to her long-term recovery.

A few months later, Amanda told me what had occurred to put her on this new road to sobriety. Keep reading to find out.

Baby Steps

Over the next few months, Amanda would accomplish small goals without even realizing it. When she and I talked, and she told me about something happening in her life, I would point out the little things she achieved.

For instance, she once told me how she had to take two buses to work and what a pain it was because they were scheduled so close together, and if she were a minute late, she would miss the bus and be late for work. I asked her if she had been late for work yet, and she told me she had not, but she was so fearful that she would leave her house 15 minutes earlier than needed.

I asked her if she saw how she was becoming a responsible employee. She was setting her alarm clock and getting up on time. She was making sure that her work clothes were clean and neat looking. Her makeup and hair were well-groomed. She was not late for work, and she now had held the same job for the most extended period of her young life. These were all goals that she subconsciously had set for herself, and she accomplished them daily. I told her that this is what sobriety looks and feels like.

I could see she had not considered this and was thinking about it. Moments like this gave me hope that Amanda was seriously working on her sobriety.

Amanda became more involved in her home NA group. She became one of the members who would help set up and conduct meetings. She surrounded herself with a group of women actively pursuing sobriety. She began enjoying life and the ability to sit with friends, talk, laugh, and be sober.

When someone is in active addiction, they live life in a fog. They miss the subtle little moments that life gives us to show us how precious and beautiful living life can be. Amanda was gaining clarity. Her fog was disappearing, and she was enjoying what she was experiencing. This was all accomplished via the baby steps of sobriety. The need to live one day at a time. One hour at a time. One minute at a time.

Accountability

I was attending a B2H meeting when the meeting facilitator had an announcement. There was a request from a local television station. The opioid epidemic was raging across the country, and they were looking to interview an active opioid addict to gain a perspective that wasn't being reported.

Our B2H group discussed this, and we all agreed that finding an active addict who would go on camera to discuss their plight would be extremely difficult. We also thought that even if we could find an addict willing to do this, they would be very unreliable and would probably want compensation in return. Active addiction is like that.

The discussion then turned to how we could help put a face on the opioid epidemic. The group thought it was essential to bring a voice to the media table to hopefully shine a brighter light on this dark disease. The question went out to the group if there was anyone in the group who would be willing to go before the camera with their addicted loved one and be interviewed.

No one was stepping forward to volunteer. I knew why no one wanted to do this. Exposing something like this could destroy the addict's personal life.

I was also hesitant to volunteer. Stepping out into the public circle and announcing that my daughter was a heroin addict could damage my daughter and me, but I also felt that this opportunity could not fall by the wayside.

After the meeting, I approached the facilitator and told her I would speak to my daughter about this and see if she was willing to expose her disease to the world. If she dared to do it, I would also step up and help. I told the facilitator I would have an answer for her at the following week's meeting.

A couple of days later, when I was driving Amanda to her job, I told her about the project the TV station was going to do.

She listened attentively and was silent when I explained what I knew. I could see she was thinking about it and was probably struggling with the same fear of exposure that I was. Amanda looked at me and asked me what I thought about going on TV. I told her that there were concerns. She would be opening herself up to the public. Her disease would become known to everyone, and some viewers do not believe that addiction is a disease. She might face ridicule and discrimination. These are all the traits that exist with the stigmatization of addiction.

I also told her that this was an opportunity to change the narrative. We had a chance to put a face to this epidemic and the disease and hopefully educate the public through our story. I reminded her about our short prayer before our NA and B2H meetings. "God grant me the serenity to accept the things I cannot change, the courage to change the things I can, and the wisdom to know the difference." I said, "We just have to find the courage to change the perception about addiction."

I told Amanda to think about this before she gave me an answer. I told her to take a couple of days and then let me know. Amanda didn't hesitate. She said, "Dad, let's do this. Let's find the courage."

I was so proud of her, but I had to make sure this was what she wanted to do. I pressed her about her decision. Amanda told me that the message at her NA meetings is about helping each other to stay sober or find sobriety. She felt she could get this news out to a larger audience. She felt obligated to do it.

At my next B2H meeting, I told the facilitator that my daughter Amanda agreed to be interviewed. But first, I wanted to meet the interviewer and discuss their storyline for an addict in recovery. A meeting was arranged, and I met with Katherine Amenta of WPXI. We talked about the storyline's direction, and she wanted to know where we would like to conduct the interview. We discussed a couple of locations until Katherine mentioned performing it at our home. I thought that was an excellent idea. I felt that people who saw the story had to see how Amanda was raised in an average ordinary neighborhood and that the heroin epidemic was not just an urban problem.

Katherine wanted to meet with Amanda before the interview to see how she felt about being interviewed and being on TV. I picked up Amanda a few days later, and she and Katherine had a terrific conversation. Afterward, it was scheduled for Katherine to come out to our home with a videographer. She interviewed Amanda and me about how Amanda fell into addiction and her journey to finding sobriety. We gave her a tour of Amanda's room and the bathroom where Amanda used to shoot heroin. I told Katherine how naive Daryl and I were to what Amanda was doing under our noses.

After the interview, I was extremely nervous. I hoped I was doing the right thing. I wasn't sure how people at work or whom I knew as acquaintances would react. I knew one thing, though by doing this interview, Amanda now felt accountability for staying sober for those who saw the story and were struggling with sobriety. I felt that whatever ramifications came from this, her feeling accountable made it all worth it.

A few weeks later, the interview aired, and we watched with anticipation. When the story ended, I was so relieved. Katherine did a fantastic job of presenting our story. It was professional and informative, but it was mostly human. I was so appreciative of how she put it together. We recorded it and played it repeatedly. My opinion never changed.

The next day at work, my co-workers and boss, who had no idea I was doing this interview and about my daughter's plight, were so kind and supportive. I was touched.

The funny thing, though, for days and weeks after that, I had people I knew remotely and people I didn't know at my office door who wanted to talk to me about someone in their family struggling with addiction. During this time, I began to realize how far this epidemic was reaching and how many innocent people were exposed to the chaotic lifestyle that came with it.

Setting the Date Straight

Amanda was doing great with staying sober. She was already eight months clean and quickly approaching her first year of sobriety. She had learned how to avoid the people, places, and things that could jeopardize her sobriety.

The owner of the sober living home Amanda lived in had put Amanda in charge. She was the house manager. She performed that function until the owner had a vacancy in her home across the street from the sober living home. She asked Amanda if she wanted to move into her house and rent a room from her.

Amanda called to tell us this bit of news. We were thrilled. We were so proud of her. To have the owner of a sober living house ask one of its inhabitants to move into her home was an indication of how she felt Amanda was progressing in her sobriety. We again pointed out that this happens when you achieve clarity through sobriety. Good things happen to those who do good things.

Shortly after this occurred, I drove Amanda to her job so she wouldn't have to take the bus. I was talking to her about how her life had made a big turn, how she was responsible for it, and how I couldn't wait for her one-year sober date.

Amanda paused and said to me that she had to tell me something. She said her clean date was not in January like I thought it was. It was in May. She then proceeded to tell me how this occurred. She said that when she lived in her previous sober living home in Mount Washington, she began using again and went downhill fast.

It became so bad that the house owner asked her to leave. She didn't want to call us because she didn't want us to know that she was using again. She was desperate, so she called her NA sponsor to see if she could go to her place. She didn't tell her sponsor that she was using again. Amanda just told her she was struggling. Amanda's sponsor agreed to pick her up and return to her place.

Once Amanda was at her sponsor's home, Amanda asked to use the restroom. Her sponsor became suspicious and entered the bathroom a few minutes later to see Amanda injecting herself with heroin. Her sponsor immediately told Amanda that she could not stay in her home and had to leave. She told Amanda she was taking her to a local hospital so she could check into their detox unit.

When they arrived at the hospital, Amanda asked to be dropped off outside the entrance to the Emergency Room. Her sponsor dropped her off, wished her well, and left. Amanda never went into the E.R. It was late at night, and she lay on a bench outside the hospital and fell asleep. When she awoke the following day, she realized that she was now homeless, and the possibility of this being her life was becoming a part of her reality. She called her sponsor and asked for help. Amanda was ready to do whatever she had to do to get clean.

Amanda's sponsor called a friend who owned a sober living home in Carrick and asked if she could bring Amanda to the house to detox. The owner agreed to take Amanda in and let her detox at the sober living home, on a couch, over three days. From that point, Amanda became a home resident and found her current long-term sobriety.

She told me her clean date was May 24th. I was so moved that she had the courage to tell me her story. I knew she trusted me not to give her grief over the date change. I could have cared less what her clean date was. I was just so touched that she had been honest with me. That was the day I knew my daughter would keep her sobriety.

When May 24th comes around every year, we celebrate it like her birthday. In my eyes, it's her re-birthday.

Single Life

One of the things that Amanda shared with me early in her latest sobriety was that all her past failures had been while she was in a relationship with a boy. She decided that for this run at sobriety to have any success, she was not going to get into a relationship. She wanted to try single life for a while.

She continued working at the piano bar on weekend nights and made great money in tips.

She also worked a few weekdays in the restaurant, which left her time to attend NA meetings regularly.

Amanda had reduced the distractions in her life so she could better focus on her sobriety. She also attended meetings in other areas of Allegheny county to be with her girlfriends, who had also found sobriety. Amanda had surrounded herself with a solid circle of women who all had the same desire. That desire was to stay sober and stay true to themselves.

Amanda had also changed sponsors. Amanda's original sponsor had found sobriety on her first attempt, so she didn't understand the relapse phase as well as she should. They both agreed that it was time for Amanda to find a new sponsor who could better advise her on her sobriety.

Amanda introduced Daryl and me to her new sponsor. We'll call her Kay. Kay was very friendly, had an incredibly positive outlook, and made us love her the minute we met her. Kay was an essential part of all our lives, and I owe her so much for helping my daughter discover who she was and what she was made of. I will always hold a special place in my heart for her.

All the girls Amanda was close with were single and not in relationships, which worked for them all. They all realized that having a solid base of sobriety would help them retain it as time progressed. I was very impressed with them and was happy that my daughter had found these young women who were supporting each other.

Amanda had turned her life around. She had walked through the hell of addiction and had come out on the other side a confident, compassionate, kind, empathetic, and loving woman. My daughter had survived this nightmare, and I couldn't be happier. But I could never truly relax because I had learned relapse is a part of the journey, and it could rear its ugly head even with those who had decades of sobriety behind them.

It's an ugly disease that never dies, but my daughter's words and actions gave me so much hope that she was on the sober side of her journey and that the more steps she took in this direction, the more the disease quieted within her.

Romanelli Genesis

At the end of each year, the Bridge to Hope would host a Holiday Celebration where the members were permitted to bring their active or in-recovery loved ones. There was a guest speaker who would be someone in long-term recovery and would tell the story of their journey from active addiction to sobriety and how they maintained their recovery.

I had been attending this event for a few years and would invite Amanda to come. Sometimes she would, and other times, she would not. Since Amanda was in a good place with her sobriety, I asked again for her to attend the upcoming celebration. I told her to bring her sponsor and any others she thought might benefit.

A woman, Deb Romanelli, started attending B2H meetings just before me. She had a son named Mario, who had found recovery and had about a year more sobriety than Amanda. I would envy her when she told me her son had just passed one month of recovery, then six months, and then a year while I struggled with Amanda to begin a recovery.

According to Deb's stories about him and without me going into details, he was many times worse than Amanda. When Deb would do her introduction and say how he had another month of recovery under his belt, had a good job, was attending NA meetings regularly, and was providing for himself, I could only hope that someday I could say the same about Amanda.

Amanda came with her sponsor to this holiday celebration, and Deb brought her son Mario. We sat at separate tables for the proceedings and afterward talked about how Mario and Amanda were both doing well in their recoveries.

A table near the back wall had coffee, water, cookies, and other snacks for the attendees. At one point, I glanced up and saw Amanda and Mario talking. I was a little concerned since my daughter was doing so well with her recovery while not being in a relationship. They didn't speak for long and went back to their respective tables.

Amanda did not mention her conversation with Mario; I had learned long ago not to pry into that part of my daughter's life. I did ask her if she knew Mario, and she told me that she had seen him at some of the NA meetings, but this was the first time she had spoken with him.

Free Meal

Just after New Year's Day, all the family gathered at my niece's house to watch a football game. This holiday season was one of the best we had in some time. Amanda was still doing well, and that cut down on the apprehension and drama that came with previous holiday seasons when she was actively using.

At one point, I was in the kitchen when Amanda approached me and said that Mario had asked her out on a date. She wanted to know what she should do. I asked her if she was ready to start dating again and reminded her of the success she was having with her recovery. I remember she was going to say something in response, but before she could, I reminded her that she oversaw her recovery and only she could decide if dating would be a detriment or not.

Her concern was that he also had the same background as her and that maybe that could screw things up. All I could tell her was that I knew his mother and from my perspective, Mario came from a large, united family. He had a good job that he had held for the last three years. He was involved in NA, and he seemed like a nice guy. I also told her he might decide that he wasn't ready to go down that road after a date with her.

I clearly remember telling Amanda, "Look, even if the date doesn't work out for either of you, at least you got a free dinner out of the deal."

She didn't tell me then if she was going to accept his offer or not. She said she had to think about it.

A few days later, Amanda told me that she had gone out with Mario, and they enjoyed being together. I was concerned. They both had active addictions in their past, but then I also thought that it could be a good thing that they both have active addictions in their history. They could support each other and recognize when that support was needed far better than anyone who had never dealt with addiction.

Mario and Amanda became an item, and the members of the B2H all knew about their dating. Debbie, Mario's mom, and I didn't try to dwell on it too much. We were taking it one day at a time.

Recovery and Romance

Amanda and Mario continued dating throughout the year. They would come to our home for dinner or visit us at our campground and stay for a weekend.

I got to know Mario better through our interactions. We both loved golf, so when I could arrange to play a round with him, I did. It was always an excellent way to see a person's character and learn more about them. I wasn't studying him so I could approve or disapprove of Mario. I knew that wasn't for me to do. But it helped ease my mind when he would talk about his job, how much he loved it and his family, and how tight they were. It showed me that Mario was thinking about staying stable in life.

Mario and Amanda also spent time with Mario's family. Mario came from a large Italian family, and get-togethers were always joyful events filled with good food, good talk, and mostly good feelings for each other.

Daryl and I spent a couple of Christmas Eves with Mario and his extended family and witnessed their special bond. It was a joy to see.

As time passed, it became apparent that Mario and Amanda had no plans to separate. They had found each other, and neither was willing to let go. It was a beautiful thing to watch as they progressed through their relationship.

I couldn't help but think that through all the most difficult times with addiction, something like their finding each other was one of the byproducts. I gave up trying to figure out what God's master plan was for Amanda. I guess it's one of those things that when looking back, you can sometimes see how it all fit together and how perfect it was.

The Ask

Mario's job had taken him to Columbus, Ohio. He had been there for about two months but was coming back to Pittsburgh to see Amanda on the weekend. The end of the year was rapidly approaching when Mario called my cell phone and asked if he could come to my house. He said he had something to talk to me about.

It was a Saturday night, so I assumed he was in Pittsburgh and would be over in a relatively short period. He then said he would be there around 10 pm. He was driving in from Columbus.

I got off the phone with Mario and told Daryl that Mario was coming over to talk about something. We both had a pretty good idea what that something was. Daryl wanted to know what I was going to say to him. I told her I didn't know. I didn't have a game plan. I had always imagined someone coming to ask for Amanda's hand, but I wasn't expecting it now.

I don't know why I wasn't expecting it. Amanda and Mario had been dating exclusively for quite some time. Before asking for her hand, I thought he would be done with the Columbus job and back in Pittsburgh.

In any case, Mario arrived, and he and I went down to the man-cave in my basement. We talked about numerous things before he came out and asked me for my blessing so he could marry Amanda. I told him that marriage was a big step in life and carried immense responsibility. I asked about his job in Columbus, how long he would be working there, or if Columbus would become home.

I told him that the one thing that impressed me about him was the strength of his family. He needed to understand the value I placed on taking a vow to be with someone for a lifetime and committing to that. I pointed out to him how, with all the chaos and tumultuousness that he and Amanda caused our families, Daryl and I were still together, and so were his parents. To me, that just emphasized that no matter how big or complex a problem may be, a married couple will stay together and work their way through it no matter what.

I asked him if he understood that and if he was ready to marry my daughter and care for her for the rest of her life. He said he did. So, I told him I would be honored to have him as my son and welcomed him to the family.

We went upstairs to tell Daryl, and after many hugs and kisses, he said he was going to Amanda's work to propose. That took me by surprise. He was dressed in his construction work clothes, had just driven 5 hours from Columbus, and Amanda's shift ended at 2 am. We told him to get going then and to make sure that he got a video of the proposal if he could.

Amanda was still working at the dueling piano bar, so Mario snuck in and arranged to have Amanda called up to the stage so he could propose in front of all her friends and co-workers. It went off without a hitch, and she was genuinely surprised. One of the co-workers got a video of the proposal, and you could see her put her hands to her face and then shake her head "yes" and give Mario a big hug and kiss. This was a fairy tale come true.

An Unforgettable Day

On September 15, 2017, my daughter Amanda married Mario Romanelli in a late afternoon ceremony. The wedding service and reception were held at the same place. It was a restaurant in Latrobe, PA, called DiSalvo's Station.

DiSalvo's Station was a refurbished train station, so the theme throughout the establishment was around trains and the railroad. The front entrance to the restaurant was a tunnel that passed under the railroad tracks overhead. The train tracks were active, and often, you would hear a train pass by now and then.

Amanda, her bridesmaids, and groomsmen decorated the tunnel with soft white string lights that made it look magical. This was the way Amanda was going to make her entrance. She and I were going to walk down the tunnel under the twinkling lights as I gave her away to the new, most important man in her life.

Daryl, I, and most of the wedding party arrived early so that we could help with last-minute decorations and setup so the bridal party could dress Amanda in her gown and take photographs.

Amanda was nervous all day. Her sponsor Kay was her maid of honor and was conducting everything. The reception and ceremony areas were decorated beautifully.

When the time came, I waited with Amanda at the tunnel's beginning, where the guests couldn't see us. We were waiting for our cue from the disc jockey. At that time, Amanda looked at me and said, "Dad, please make sure I don't fall." I looked into her eyes and said, "In your whole life, have I ever let you fall?" She smiled and started to tear up. She almost got me tearing up also, but I said to her, "We can't let your makeup run, so let's take a deep breath and smile as big as we can because this going to be the happiest day of our lives."

We walked down that aisle, and I handed my daughter over to the man who would now take care of her. They said their vows, professed their love for each other and were announced as man and wife.

The reception was a great time. I gave a "Father of the Bride" speech, and I took the time to thank everybody for helping us celebrate Mario and Amanda's marriage. The cake was cut, toasts were made, and then came the time for the father-daughter dance.

This was the dance that, at one time, I was sure that I would never get to experience. This was the dance that I told my daughter we would never be able to do because she was slowly killing herself. This dance symbolized how far she had come and how much she had overcome.

Amanda looked at me as we danced and said, "I told you I would dance with you at my wedding." I looked back at her and said, "Yes, you did, and I love you for keeping your word."

Walking Amanda down the aisle and the Father-Daughter dance on her wedding day. Two things I never thought I would do during Amanda's active addiction years. We were both so grateful to have these moments.

Happy Beginnings

Amanda and Mario decided to open their home remodeling and design business. They were confident they could build a company that would sustain them for a lifetime.

They started getting jobs from friends and family, and soon, through social media, they began to build a following. The job opportunities would come in, and Mario and Amanda would price them based on the homeowner's vision and with Amanda's design input.

They would post before and after photos on their company's Facebook page, which also helped drive business to them. They were doing well for themselves and decided it was time to start a family.

They had difficulty conceiving, but there were plenty of avenues to try, so they began going to fertility doctors in hopes that they could have the family they desired.

Life was going well for Amanda and Mario. They had a good business, were saving money to buy a house, and were trying to have a baby. They could go out whenever they wanted, get whatever they needed, and live life to the fullest. They were a happy, successful young couple with so much in front of them.

They had surrounded themselves with good friends who were all in sobriety. They would hang out together, watch movies, and share meals.

They were spending and celebrating holidays with their families. They were loving, laughing, and enjoying just being part of a life that just six years prior was not even a light at the end of a tunnel.

For Daryl and me, it was incredibly wonderful when they would invite us over to their home for dinner or a cookout. Most people take it for granted, but for us, it was a miracle that both survived the addiction lifestyle and could function like that part of their lives never existed.

I had to pinch myself whenever I saw them enjoying themselves, laughing with each other and others, and running a business that was doing so well.

Everything was going so well. I thought these kids would make it together and have the best life.

I was finding my peace.

Curves in the Road

When Daryl and I reached our mid-fifties, I noticed that Daryl struggled to climb steps and had trouble with her balance. Daryl went to her physician, who told her that she needed to exercise more and build strength in her legs. I thought he was right. Daryl was becoming more sedentary, and it was concerning.

As she was getting worse, one of Daryl's friends suggested she go to a neurologist. Her thinking was that Daryl might have a pinched nerve in her spine, causing her leg weakness. We thought, "What did we have to lose." Daryl made an appointment with a neurologist. The neurologist did a muscle biopsy as a part of the examination, and when Daryl returned a couple of weeks later, she informed Daryl that she had muscular dystrophy. It was a slow-acting version of Muscular Dystrophy. We were not expecting that. Life was throwing us another curve.

Daryl was already unemployed. She began having trouble remembering things. She filed for disability, and it was soon granted.

At this time, I decided that if it were financially possible, I would retire as early as possible. I ran the idea past our financial advisor, who ran some scenarios on his computer, and he said if I worked until I was 62, we would have an excellent chance to retire and live comfortably. So, knowing that, the goal became to retire at 62 so Daryl and I could travel and spend winter in the warmth of Florida while traveling for her was possible.

On January 4, 2019, I officially retired from my job. It was bittersweet for me. I had worked for 28 years at the same hospital and enjoyed the people I worked with and my work. I remember walking out of the building that day and thinking I was starting a new chapter in my life.

My sister and her husband gave me two tickets to a

University of Pittsburgh basketball game as a Christmas gift. The game started at noon on a Saturday in January. My son-in-law Mario went with me, and we went to a driving range after the game. When we returned to my house, I walked up the stairs from my garage and was greeted by all my friends and family. It was a surprise retirement party for me!

I was caught off guard. I wasn't expecting anything like this. I knew Daryl couldn't have put this all together, so I asked who planned this. I should have known it was Amanda. It's this kind of thing that touches me the most. To think that just a short time ago, I didn't expect her to be alive, and now here she was, putting together a party for me. I thanked God repeatedly in my mind. I felt so blessed.

About an hour into the party, Amanda grabbed Daryl and me, and Mario grabbed his parents, Debbie and Joe, and said they had special gifts for us that they wanted to give us in private.

We went upstairs to one of the bedrooms, and they handed us gift bags. When we opened the gift bags, there were gifts inside for Grandma and Grandpa! Amanda was pregnant! We were going to be grandparents! We were all so elated! We hugged, shook hands, slapped backs, and smiled until our cheeks hurt.

The kids told us we couldn't tell anybody yet because it was still too early to make that announcement, but they just wanted to share the joy with us so we could feel as much happiness as they were. I can't tell you how difficult it was not being able to say anything to anyone at the party. I felt like I was going to burst. I'm sure all my guests thought I was happy because of my retirement party, which I was, but what they didn't know was that there was going to be a new addition to our family that we couldn't wait to see!

Later after everyone had left the party, I again got to tell God how thankful I was for all the beautiful feelings that came my way on this day. My daughter gave me another gift I thought I would never see. She was giving us a grandchild.

This day was one of those days that when you recall all your blessings, this would be right at the front of the list.

Sun N' Fun

On February 1, 2019, Daryl and I packed up the car and our dogs and headed for Florida. We had rented a two-bedroom condo in a resort community in Orlando. Our resort location put us less than four miles from Disney World.

Our resort had a beautiful pool area with a beach entrance, so Daryl didn't have to climb any ladders or steps to get in or out of the pool. Every day we would go to the pool and spend the afternoon. I golfed at different courses in the area several times a week. We would cook dinners in our kitchen, and on nights that we didn't feel like cooking, we would go out to one of the many restaurants in the area.

There were many attractions we could go to on days the weather wasn't cooperating, so there was never a dull day for us. Family and friends visited and stayed with us, making the vacation that much more enjoyable.

While in Florida, Amanda called us one evening and said she had to tell us some news. She paused and then said, "I'm pregnant with twins!" How could this get any better?! We were over the moon with joy! We were going to be grandparents two times over! We couldn't believe it!

Amanda and Mario came to Florida to stay with us for a week in March. It was so good to have them there. Mario and I went out golfing a few times, then went to the pool in the afternoon. Amanda was getting big, carrying twins. She looked like she was six months pregnant, but she still had six months to go before the twins were born.

Amanda's back was hurting terribly. Her scoliosis was acting up. When Amanda was first diagnosed with scoliosis, I remember her doctor telling us that when Amanda was going through hormonal changes such as puberty or pregnancy, there was a good chance her scoliosis might worsen. I know that was always in the back of my mind.

When Daryl was diagnosed with Muscular Dystrophy, the neurologist told her the type she had was hereditary. When we found that out, we told Dan and Amanda that they could be predisposed to this disease. The only way to tell was to have a DNA test done. Dan said he wasn't getting tested. He said knowing if he had it wouldn't change anything, so he would live his life as if it didn't exist.

Amanda, on the other hand, had to know. I think her anxiety forced her to find out. She was tested, and it came back positive. She had the genetic makeup for Muscular Dystrophy. Of course, that ramped up her anxiety, and she was fearful that her babies would also be born with MD. It was hard to keep her calm, but we did our best. We kept telling her not to worry because it wasn't affecting her right now, and it didn't start showing up in her mom until she was in her fifties. We told her that the possibility of a treatment or cure was a real possibility by the time her children were in their fifties.

While they were with us in Orlando, we went to Disney World's Magic Kingdom. We talked about how Daryl and I were going to vacation in Orlando every winter, and we couldn't wait until Amanda and Mario's babies were old enough to enjoy it.

Daryl and I remembered bringing Dan and Amanda to the Magic Kingdom when they were five and three, and the looks on their faces at all the Disney magic around them was worth whatever Disney wanted to charge.

Life was going well for all of us. We were in Florida, where it was beautiful and warm, we had our daughter and son-in-law with us, and we were going to be grandparents to twins. I didn't know how much better it could get. Life stopped throwing us curves at last.

Amanda, pregnant with twins, and Mario with us at the Magic Kingdom.

Pregnancy and Anxiety

Amanda is the kind of person whose anxiety can sometimes take over her life. When she was pregnant, I'm not sure what was causing her anxiety to ramp up, but it was at a high level. She was worried about everything, and it seemed like she was constantly concerned about something or other about her pregnancy.

This is not to say she was making up scenarios in her mind to be anxious. She had been at an exam where the physician told her she could have a test to see if either of the babies were genetically predisposed to have Down's Syndrome. She agreed to the test, and the results showed a possibility for Down's, but the test couldn't tell if it was for one of the twins or both. Amanda was freaked out by this and was worrying about it every moment she was awake.

Daryl and I told Amanda and Mario that they should decline other tests that weren't required. We told them we never did any of these tests when we had Dan and Amanda. Primarily because they weren't available to us, but as we told them, what difference would it make even if they were? We would always love our babies if they had Down's or other complications.

Another test was more specific for finding Downs but more invasive, so Amanda and Mario declined. They also decided that no matter what happened with the twins, they would love them to the moon and back. Life was going to go on no matter what the circumstances were.

The Big Reveal

It was April 14, 2019, and Mario and Amanda were having their reveal party at Mario's Uncle Steve and Aunt Robin's house. All the family and friends were there. It was a full house.

Mario's cousin Alicia had planned the festivities with Amanda and her friends. The house was decorated, and the food was prepared and ready to be eaten. There were two big boxes filled with either pink or blue balloons.

There was a board for placing your vote for a boy and girl, two boys or two girls. I remember picking two girls. Baby girls were always so precious. If they were to be anything like Amanda, they would immediately melt my heart and have me wrapped around their fingers. It's not that I don't love baby boys. Dan was my "little guy" right from the start. He was the cutest, most precious baby boy of all time. Of course, that is my unbiased opinion.

In all actuality, I didn't care what the genders of the babies were. I just wanted two happy, healthy babies that would be best friends as they grew up.

The time came for the boxes to be opened. I knew Amanda wanted a girl and Mario wanted a boy, so the first opened box would make one immediately happy and put the other wishing for a different result. I don't believe either of them cared about the genders. They were looking forward to having a happy family.

Amanda and Mario began opening the first box. I know I was watching Amanda, so I could see the look on her face when the balloons came out. The package was unwrapped, the lid was lifted, and out came pink balloons! Amanda was jumping up and down and clapping her hands. She was so excited and happy to have a little girl that she could dress up and do her hair and take shopping with her and make her into a diva like her.

Mario was happy but was hoping that blue balloons would come out so he could relax, knowing he would have a son he could raise in his likeness.

They moved to the second box. Again, Mario and Amanda began unwrapping the box, and the crowd was teasing Mario about having two girls. They got to the lid and paused. I could see the apprehension on Mario's face as they lifted the lid. Out came blue balloons! That was perfect! Mario let out a cheer, and everyone applauded.

This couldn't have worked out any better. A boy and a girl! What more could you ask for?!

Nursery and Names

Amanda and Mario spared no expense on the nursery. They bought two cribs, the best twin baby stroller, and redecorated the nursery. Amanda was telling us about the room, but we hadn't seen it yet.

She invited us over to her house so we could see the nursery, and we were surprised when we saw the babies' names hanging above their cribs. The boy's name was Vincenzo, and Mila was the girl's name. Vinny and Mila. It was perfect! We were so excited and couldn't wait to meet the two little ones.

Amanda had put her decorator's eye to work on the nursery. It was beautiful with all the baby decorations and signs on the walls. Mario had removed the door and replaced it with a sliding barn door.

This young couple was so excited about their new family becoming a reality. I was so happy for them. For all their problems through their teenage years, to be at the point where they were about to raise a little family made me appreciate all their work to improve their lives. I was so grateful that they were experiencing so much happiness.

These were the things I thought Amanda would never experience, and she was about to embark on the most fantastic adventure she could have. She was going to be a mother! She and Mario ran a successful business and were saving to buy a home. It was all coming together for them. The pieces were falling into place.

Little did I know then that this feeling of immense happiness was probably the last time I would feel this way for a long time.

An Unthinkable Decision

Since Amanda was pregnant with twins, she had appointments more frequently than a single birth. During one of these visits, she was informed that her blood pressure was elevated to a level that concerned the physician and her feet and ankles were extremely bloated. Amanda was complaining about pain in her feet and ankles.

The doctor was concerned about her having preeclampsia. Preeclampsia is a condition in pregnancy characterized by high blood pressure, sometimes with fluid retention, and proteinuria. Proteinuria is the finding of protein in urine samples. This can be an indication of kidney disease.

The doctor wanted Amanda to come into the hospital, where her OB/Gyn practice was located, so that she could be monitored for a few hours. During this ultrasound monitoring session, they noticed that Vinnie's heart rate would sometimes drop significantly but rebound quickly back to normal. They wanted to monitor Amanda longer to see if this occurred again.

It did occur again, so the doctors decided they needed to keep Amanda overnight and continue to monitor her and the babies. That overnight stay continued for several days as the doctors became more concerned as they saw continuous drops in Vinny's heart rate, only to rebound back to normal very quickly.

Mario stayed with Amanda every minute of every day as she was terrified throughout this ordeal. The doctors suspected that Vinnie's umbilical cord was only functioning intermittently. They feared that Vinny could go into fetal distress, and they may have to remove him. Amanda and Mario had already been at the hospital for five days and as the weekend approached, they were feeling incredibly stressed over the whole ordeal.

The concern on the weekend was that Vinny might get to a

point where his survival would rest on removing him via cesarean section. The drawback was that they would also have to remove Mila. She was doing well. Her heart rate was regular and intense. At 25 weeks, removing Mila would be a risk to her survival. If Vinny could hang on until 28 weeks, his and Mila's chances of survival would be better.

Throughout this ordeal, Amanda wasn't permitted to eat because if she was possibly going to have a C-section, she needed an empty stomach. Mario and Amanda were left with making an exceedingly difficult decision, and her being miserable and uncomfortable wasn't making it any less difficult.

They were stressed from a lack of sleep, the conditions that Amanda was dealing with, and having to decide what they would do with the twins and their survival. The decision on the twins weighed extremely heavy on them. All I can remember during all this was how the pregnancy had turned from being such a joyful occasion to one wrought with such despair. I couldn't imagine being Mario and Amanda's age and making such a difficult decision.

It was a horrific weekend that they were going through, and Daryl and I were with them at the hospital. I could see they were exhausted, and the stress of what to do was crushing them. They asked Daryl and me what they should do. I was hesitant to answer. What kind of advice or wisdom could I provide them whenever I never had to make such a decision? But they needed something. They were struggling and looking for insight, so I told them what was in my heart.

I told them that Vinny's umbilical cord was not going to resolve itself and that taking the babies out might be his best chance of survival, but those chances were not great odds, and having to take Mila out along with him would reduce her chance of survival. Mila was doing well and deserved an opportunity to live. Mario and Amanda were given the option to be discharged and have Amanda go to her OB/Gyn to be monitored daily. I told them that if it were me, I would go home and get a good night's sleep and a good meal.

Amanda and Mario decided that to give Mila a fighting chance at surviving, they would monitor the babies daily and hope and pray that Vinny would survive a few more weeks when the possibility of both of them surviving an early delivery was more in their favor. There was always the possibility that Vinny would pass away in the womb; if that occurred, then Amanda would have to carry him to term.

The Loss

Amanda went to her daily monitoring sessions the following week. Vinny seemed to be holding his own, and Mila was doing well, also. This was a good sign.

We would talk with Amanda daily, and she would let us know how the monitoring went and if she felt Vinny move. When she felt him move, she thought he would make it. Then there would be days where she wouldn't feel Vinny move for an extended time, and she would start to worry. Daryl and I tried to keep her calm so her blood pressure wouldn't rise, but I don't know how that was possible. How could she not be worried 24/7? I know I was.

Amanda's monitoring sessions were every other day the following week. During one of these sessions, Amanda discovered that Vinny's heart was no longer beating. He had passed away. The date was June 10, 2019.

When Daryl and I found out, my heart sank to my feet. I can't even remember the conversation we had with Amanda and Mario. All I remember is later that night going into my garage at my home, sitting on the floor, and just crying. I was crying for the grandson that I would never meet. The grandson that I couldn't spoil or take to a baseball game someday or teach how to skip a stone on a pond. I know these were dumb things to be grieving over, but it was what I felt.

I composed myself, prayed for Vinny, and thanked him for giving Mila a better chance to survive. I told him I would meet him at some point, but for now, I knew he was an angel who would take care of his sister.

The next day I had a conversation with Amanda and talked to her about Vinny. She was understandably upset. I told her that I had thought of a way to honor Vinny. I told her that since Vinny and Mila shared space inside of her, maybe the thing to do was to share a part of Vinny's name with Mila. I said the feminine version of Vincenzo was Vincenza. I told her to give

Mila two middle names. Her new name could be Mila Rose Vincenza Romanelli. It would always be a way for Mila to know that a part of Vinny was with her throughout her life.

Amanda said she would think about it. It sounded nice, but she was having difficulty knowing that Vinny was inside of her, that he was stillborn, and that she would have to carry him until Mila was born. How do you try and help your daughter navigate through something like that?

Amanda couldn't bring herself to go into the nursery at home. Everything was set up for two babies, and each baby's name was hung on the wall above their crib. There were two of everything, and now only one baby would occupy the nursery. Mario had the unenviable task of disassembling the nursery. Something amazing happened, however. A friend of Amanda's and Mario's cousin showed up to help. It was a display of kindness that I know will not be forgotten by either Mario or Amanda.

Six Weeks

For the next six weeks, Amanda and Mario did not have an easy time with the pregnancy.

There were still monitoring sessions that had to occur to ensure that Mila was progressing as she should. Daryl and I met Amanda at one of her ultrasound sessions. Mario was working and needed to complete a job, and Amanda never wanted to go alone to the sessions. She was apprehensive as to what bad news could come next.

The tech was performing the ultrasound, and she stepped out of the room when she was done. This was a little unusual. When the test is complete, the tech will help you clean up, and you are clear to leave. She returned to the room and said she wanted one of the OB/GYNs to look at the ultrasound. I could see the anxiety in Amanda starting to rise. The OB/GYN came into the room almost immediately and started to do the ultrasound again, looking at a particular area of the baby.

Amanda was doing the best she could to keep her composure. I remember thinking this poor child did not need another issue to deal with. I started praying that whatever the tech saw would not be significant.

After five minutes or so of looking at the ultrasound screen, the OB/GYN told us that the tech thought she saw something in the head region which could be a potential risk for learning disabilities. The OB/GYN said that Mila's head was positioned in a way that was making it hard for her to see what the tech thought she had seen. The doctor told us it was her obligation to tell us this, but she said not to be alarmed because she didn't see anything, and the tech may have been mistaken because of the positioning of Mila's head. She said that, hopefully, by the next appointment, Mila's head would be at a better angle so they could tell if there was anything to be concerned about.

As we walked out with Amanda, we told her not to stress

over this because the doctor sounded very optimistic about nothing being there. I know our intentions were meant for the best for Amanda when we told her that her being stressed would only drive up her blood pressure and possibly endanger Mila, but that was like pouring gasoline on a match. She was already carrying a stillborn baby, was swollen to the point where it hurt for her to walk, and now she is told her other baby may be developing a learning disability. Her anxiety was climbing as we tried to reassure her.

How many negative things could you put on one person with a history of anxiety? What can you say to someone that will put them at ease in that situation? We talked to Amanda about what she would do if Mila had a learning disability like Down's Syndrome. Would she love her any less? Would she not want her? Amanda said, "Of course not." Amanda said she would love her even more if that were possible.

We reminded her that the doctor did not seem overly concerned and that the next appointment was in a few days, so let's focus on being positive.

I remember talking to Amanda via the phone the next day, and I could tell she was still upset about Mila. Whenever possible, I always wanted to remind Amanda of the strong woman she was and how it would be her job to raise Mila to have that same strength. I would remind her about some of the lowest points in her life and how she overcame them by just living one day at a time. I would remind her that while we can try to plan for the future, we can't predict the future. All we can do is deal with the circumstances and events as they present themselves to us, and that strength comes from knowing that and knowing that we can overcome almost any obstacle. These were all things I used to remind her of during her addiction and attempts at sobriety. I felt I had to give her something she could hold onto until her next ultrasound.

At Amanda's next ultrasound appointment, Mila's head was better positioned for the tech and OB/GYN to see. They both were happy to report that they saw nothing indicating that Mila might have a learning disability!

Finally, here was some good news!

Daryl and I couldn't be at that appointment, we were moving to our new home, but we were on cloud nine when Amanda called us with that news. It felt great to be on the right side of a situation, and Amanda desperately needed that to happen.

A few days later, it was the campground's Fourth of July celebration, where we had fireworks shot over the camp's lake. Amanda never missed that fireworks display, even during her addiction years. Amanda and Mario usually stayed at our campsite the weekend after the Fourth of July. They came up late Friday afternoon. Mario, I, and a couple of other guys were going to golf Saturday morning. When we returned, we would spend the afternoon at the campground's pool before joining our friends for a cookout and then watching the fireworks.

It was late Friday night when Amanda started complaining that she was feeling contractions. Amanda was concerned. Mila was only 30 weeks, so she had Mario pack up their car, and they headed back to Pittsburgh to go to the hospital.

They called us the following day to tell us that she was having Braxton Hicks contractions and that they were home and going to spend the rest of the weekend there. I felt terrible that they wouldn't be able to spend the day with us, but I was happy that nothing serious came out of the whole situation.

July 20, 2019

The date July 20, 2019, will forever be etched onto my brain. It will be a day I will never forget. It began as a celebration with the expectation of a new family member entering this world. What it turned into was something from a horror movie.

It started in the early hours of the day with Amanda and Mario going to the hospital because she was experiencing contraction pains and her cervix was starting to dilate. Daryl and I arrived at the hospital around 8 am at Amanda's birthing suite. Mario's parents, Debbie and Joe, were already there.

Amanda was in bed, and she and the baby were being monitored as is standard practice. Amanda was complaining about being hungry and her back being sore, but she was not permitted to eat, and we were sure her scoliosis was causing her back pain.

We were all talking about going on vacation to the beach, possibly in September. Deb and I were on our cellphones looking at rentals and talking about how many bedrooms we would need and did we want a place with a pool.

Daryl and I had gone straight to the hospital when we woke, so I was hungry. I said I was going to the café to get something to eat. This prompted Amanda to say, "I wish I could go get something to eat." I remember teasing her by ensuring her that I would eat enough for both of us.

Mario, Joe, and I went to the cafeteria to get some food. Mario told us Amanda was 5cm dilated, and they were reasonably sure she would deliver today. I was only glad that this episode of their lives was going to be behind them and that they could concentrate on having a happy little family.

We finished eating and headed back to Amanda's birthing suite. The nurse was in the room with Amanda. She was checking the monitor and indicated that everything looked ok.

Amanda was still complaining about her back, so the nurse asked her if she would feel better on her side. Amanda agreed, so the nurse helped her to get on her side. When this was done, Amanda said, "I just felt something pop." The nurse asked her about it, but it didn't seem like a big deal.

After a few more minutes, Amanda asked the nurse if she could be examined again to see if she had dilated any further. Since Amanda hadn't been examined in the last couple of hours, the nurse said she would ask the doctor to come in and examine her. The nurse left the room, returned a couple of minutes later, and said the doctor would be in momentarily.

There was a family waiting room across the hall from Amanda's room. I said that when the doctor came in, I would be in the waiting room until they were finished. A couple of minutes later, the doctor came in. Debbie, Daryl, Joe, and I got up and proceeded to the waiting room.

We weren't in there more than a few minutes when a nurse came rushing out of Amanda's room and said something to the effect that the baby was coming. That was a surprise, but we had been told that sometimes the exam could lead to the baby's birth.

It got a little confusing because of the flurry of people who went in and out of Amanda's room. I couldn't tell you if they were doctors, nurses, or just support personnel, so correctly identifying any of them from this point on was impossible.

A couple of staff members entered Amanda's room, and then we heard a code calling on the overhead speaker. At this point, more staff was rushing into Amanda's room. Daryl, Joe, Debbie, and I were starting to get concerned. I tried to stay calm and reassure the others that Amanda and the baby were in the best hospital possible. I began to think something terrible was happening to Mila. I kept thinking that Amanda and Mario had been through so many trials and tests throughout the pregnancy that to come out of it without a child would crush them.

More and more people were going into Amanda's room. I

couldn't figure out where they were all going. It was like a clown car; but in reverse. The door would occasionally open, and I could see a crowd of people in there, but I could not see what was happening. I knew I couldn't hear Amanda's voice, and I would have thought she would be more vocal if anything terrible happened to Mila.

Time stood still as chaos swirled around us until a nurse came out of Amanda's room to us and said the baby was fine. During the examination of Amanda's cervix, her water had broken, and Amanda began giving birth to Mila. While pushing Mila out, Amanda stopped breathing and went into cardiac arrest. There was an audible gasp but I'm not sure by whom. The nurse continued her narrative by telling us the doctor did a forceps delivery of Mila and then kept their attention on Mila while the rest of the team was working on Amanda. The nurse told us that Amanda's heart had restarted. We were so relieved to hear that. They were going to bring Mila out in an incubator since she was two months premature, and she said we could see her for a few minutes on her way to the Neonatal Intensive Care Unit (NICU).

Mila was brought out of the room in an incubator, and she was so tiny and thin, but she was ours, and I immediately fell in love with her. We saw her for a few minutes, and then they whisked her off to the NICU. When the nurses were bringing out Mila, the door was open for a moment, and I could have sworn I saw someone doing the chest compression portion of CPR. My attention was diverted to Mila, and after she left, we were directed back to the waiting room.

People were still coming from and going into Amanda's room, and there still seemed to be a flurry of activity. Daryl was visibly upset and said she was going into the room to find out what was happening. I remember telling her not to do that. I knew they would call security and remove us from the area if we became an obstacle. She opened the door to Amanda's room and attempted to work her way in, but they stopped her and directed her back out. A minute later, hospital security was on the scene. The same nurse who had spoken to us earlier came out of Amanda's room with Mario and said something to the security guard and then came over to us and said that the security guard was going to take us to another waiting area on the floor. We followed the nurse and the security guard to this waiting room, and then the nurse told us that Amanda had gone into cardiac arrest again, but they restarted her heart.

I'm guesstimating at the time right now because every minute seemed like an hour. All I knew was that my daughter's heart had stopped twice, and I didn't know for how long that had happened. I kept hoping she wouldn't end up brain-damaged because she lacked oxygen. The nurse told us she would be back with another update, but they were trying to stabilize Amanda right now to get her to an ICU.

Amanda and Mario had chosen the most extensive health system in Pittsburgh to have their baby. This health system was compromised of numerous hospitals. They wanted to get Amanda to an ICU in another one of their hospitals which was only a few blocks away.

We sat in the waiting room for what seemed like an eternity. Another nurse came in and said they had removed Vinny from Amanda and that if we would like, we could see him. I looked at Daryl, and we said we wanted to see him. I felt that this little boy had been through so much in his short life that we couldn't let him go without seeing him and telling him he was loved. The nurse told us it would be a few minutes before we could see him, but she would be back to get us.

We just sat in that waiting room, lost in our thoughts. I kept asking myself, "How could this happen?" A few minutes ago, we were all talking about going on vacation, and now my daughter was fighting for her life. Mario was sitting with his head in his hands and just sobbing. He told us that when Amanda was pushing to deliver Mila that Amanda made a gurgling sound and then passed out. He said the whole room became organized chaos. They pulled Mila out of Amanda and then started doing CPR on Amanda. He just kept watching in horror as they got her heart started, but soon after, it stopped again, and at that point, they removed him from the room.

We all sat in the room, praying that Amanda would pull through and survive this episode. Not a word was spoken amongst us. We were all just stunned. The nurse came to get Daryl and me to see Vinny. I don't remember how far I walked or what the room looked like. I was in a haze. All I remember is the nurse saying something to the effect that we needed to understand that Vinny passed a month ago and that what we would see wouldn't be easy.

I can't recall what they had Vinny in. It could have been a bassinet or in some box. That wasn't important. What was important was seeing my grandson for the first time and feeling my heart break for him knowing he could never see me, Daryl, his mom or dad, or his great big loving family. He had the start of fingers and toes, and the nurses put a little cap on his head. They did their best to make him presentable to us.

I prayed for Vinny and asked God to take care of him for me until I could be with him. I cried for him as I was crying while I wrote this. I told him that he made the greatest sacrifice by giving his life so his sister could live. I told him I knew he'll always be her guardian angel and protect her for the rest of her life. I told him I would never forget him. As we were leaving the room, I turned to thank the nurse. She was gazing at Vinny, and a tear ran down her cheek. I remember thinking about how something like this must affect these nurses.

Daryl and I have Vinny's ashes in his urn, sitting on our dresser, waiting for him to go home with his mom, dad, and sister. My grandson will never be far from me. He will live with me in my heart forever.

As we walked back to the waiting room, I vowed not to tell anyone what Vinny looked like at his death. To this day, I haven't.

When we were back in the waiting room, the nurse informed us what was going on with Amanda and told us that they had called on the ECMO team from the main hospital a few blocks away. She explained that ECMO was a heart-lung machine that would keep Amanda alive while they transported her to their main hospital. I discovered many months later that using ECMO on a patient is the equivalent of a 'Hail Mary' pass at the end of a football game; it's your last hope for victory. The nurse told us that Amanda's heart had stopped a third time, and they were able to restart it. They had done a total of 37 minutes of CPR on Amanda. You didn't have to be a neurologist to know that 37 minutes of CPR and the heart-stopping three times were not good things for Amanda's brain.

She also told us that they believe Amanda suffered an Amniotic Fluid Embolism, or AFE for short. I had never heard of such a thing, but she told us it is rare. She told us an AFE is when amniotic fluid gets in the mother's bloodstream and travels to the lungs causing immediate cardiopulmonary arrest.

The nurse said that Amanda was to be placed on the ECMO machine before they transported her to the other hospital. Before they transported her, they would let us come in and see her. While waiting for that, the nurse asked if we wanted to go to the NICU and see Mila. We all did, except for Mario. He said he didn't want to see the baby until Amanda could. I wasn't sure when that would happen, but I know you can't judge how someone processes something of this magnitude. We all process events like this differently, and there is no right or wrong way.

The staff took us to the NICU via a backway so that we could bypass other families. When we got to the NICU, they directed us to a screened-off area where they had Mila in an incubator. She was so tiny. Her eyes were covered, and she had a nasal cannula delivering oxygen. We were told by the staff not to be alarmed. Mila was fine and they took this precaution with all preemie babies.

We all looked at Mila with nothing but love in our hearts. She was my grand princess the minute I laid eyes on her. We had to get Amanda back so she could see and love her daughter.

After about 15 minutes, we were told they were getting ready to transport Amanda. Before we entered the room, one of the staff told us that Amanda's abdomen was distended, which was a cause for concern. They thought she had internal bleeding, and they would take her to the operating room to perform surgery on her and see what was causing her abdomen to be distended.

As we were all brought into the room, the staff was standing around the bed, just waiting for us to finish so they could rush her off to the OR. They all looked emotionally and physically exhausted.

What had happened to my daughter?! Someone who resembled my daughter Amanda was on the bed, but this girl's face was bloated, and her stomach looked like she had never delivered a baby. She was Amanda, but she was beginning to look unrecognizable. Joe and Debbie approached her bed. They were both crying and said they loved her. Mario was next, and he whispered something in her ear and kissed her. Daryl also walked up to her crying and told her she loved her and to stay strong. Then it was my turn. I tried to hold back my tears, which was becoming extremely difficult. I had a message for her, and I wanted her to hear it. I know my daughter. She is a fighter. She fought back from addiction to regain her sobriety and have the life she always wanted; a life filled with love, laughter, and family joy.

I put my mouth close to her ear and said to her, "Amanda… it's Dad. I love you, and I don't want you to give up. Don't. Ever. Give. Up." I kissed her cheek, backed away, and watched the staff prepare her to leave.

We were taken from the room and told that she would be going to the OR on the third floor of the main hospital and that there was a family waiting room for us to use. The maternity hospital had their security provide transport for us to the main hospital.

I can't even tell you what day it was, but it was sunny and warm. It was a beautiful day but not from my perspective. We arrived at the main entrance and were led to the surgical waiting area on the third floor. All we could do was wait. As we sat there, other family members started to arrive. Brothers, sisters, aunts, uncles, cousins, and even some friends of Amanda all came to the hospital to be with us. None could believe it as the story was retold to them.

We waited for what seemed like an eternity. Finally, a surgeon entered the waiting room and told us that Amanda was out of surgery but still very critical. Their main concern was her liver. Her ribs had severely lacerated her liver during the chest compression phase of CPR. They were trying to stop the bleeding. They said we would be given more details once she was in the Cardio Thoracic Intensive Care Unit (CTICU). We were told where the waiting room was located for that unit. The whole family proceeded there. It was a small waiting room with other families waiting for information about their loved ones. We took up every seat that was available and waited.

I had a million thoughts and scenarios running through my head, and none had a happy ending. My mind was in shock. I was numb from fear but knew that I had to stay focused so I could listen to the physicians when they came to talk with us. I knew that if I broke down that it would only make matters worse. I had to hold on for Amanda's sake.

Amanda was transported to the CTICU from the OR, and the nurses had to do several things with her before we could see her. Because of the situation's circumstances and severity, we had a nurse liaison assigned to us. She informed us that only three people were permitted into the unit at one time. She gave us other unit rules we had to follow and let in Mario, Daryl, and me.

Amanda was in the first bay to the right as soon as we walked in. There were machines, hoses, lines, and IVs everywhere, and all there to keep her alive. When we saw Amanda, she was swollen from head to toe. I knew her body was retaining fluids, which was not a good sign. I kept all my thoughts to myself, but I knew my daughter was at death's doorstep. I kissed her head and told her that I loved her. What

I wouldn't have given for her to open her eyes and tell me she loved me too.

Amanda wanted to look her best for her after-delivery pictures, so she had her hair, eyelashes, eyebrows, and fingernails all done. I thought that she was never expecting this to be her after-delivery look. I silently prayed to God, asking him to hold Amanda closely but to please let her come back to us unscathed. I couldn't stand seeing my beautiful daughter looking like she did, so I walked out and let someone else in to see her.

We were told the CTICU physician would be in to see us and brief us on what had happened to Amanda and what they were currently doing. I sat in the waiting room and talked to people who asked questions, greeted family members as they came, and for the most part, tried to stop the screaming in my head.

At one point, a woman walked into the room. She wore a hoodie, stylishly torn jeans, multicolored sneakers, and a ball cap. At first, I thought she was another patient's family member, but then she started talking. She introduced herself as the CTICU lead physician and the one who went to the maternity hospital to put Amanda on ECMO. She was soft-spoken, so I had to listen to catch every word. She told us that it was believed that Amanda had suffered an AFE and that during CPR, her liver had been lacerated by her ribs. She said that a byproduct of an AFE is Disseminated Intravascular Coagulopathy (DIC). DIC prevents the blood from clotting, so with her liver being lacerated, it would not be able to clot and begin healing. Amanda had been fed numerous units of blood and would continue this course until the DIC resolved itself, which could possibly take days. The surgeons had packed her liver in gauze to help stem the bleeding. They had left her abdomen open to bring her back to the OR as necessary to repack the liver with clean gauze. She said, "Right now, it was a waiting game to see when and if the DIC would resolve itself." I had a distinct impression that Amanda's odds were not good. The physician, we'll call her Dr. Nickle, said they would continue to monitor Amanda and for us to bring any needs we had to the nurse liaison.

At some point, I asked the nurse liaison if I could get a ride back to the maternity hospital to get my car and move it to where we were. She said she would arrange for transportation for us when we were ready. It was getting late, and I knew Daryl and I couldn't stay at the hospital overnight, so I told Daryl that I was exhausted and wanted to go home and get some sleep so we could return early the next day. I knew Daryl was ready to leave. I could see that she was also emotionally and mentally drained.

I asked the nurse liaison if she could arrange for us to see Mila when we were brought back to the maternity hospital, and she said she would check and see. After a few minutes, she came for us and told us that, under the circumstances, the NICU would let us in to see Mila.

Security drove us back to the maternity hospital, and we were directed to the NICU, where we were taken back to Mila's room. Mila's nurse greeted us and said she was doing fine. They had taken away the oxygen cannula because she was doing so well. She was still hooked up to an IV and was being monitored, and her eyes were covered. She looked beautiful. She was long and skinny but had tuffs of red hair. I smiled because Amanda had said several times when she was pregnant that she hoped the baby would have red hair like Mario. The nurse let us touch her, and as I gazed at such perfection, I only kept thinking that I hoped Amanda would soon see her.

I started calling Mila "Sunshine" because she sent me home with a smile at the end of a very dark day. She was my sunshine.

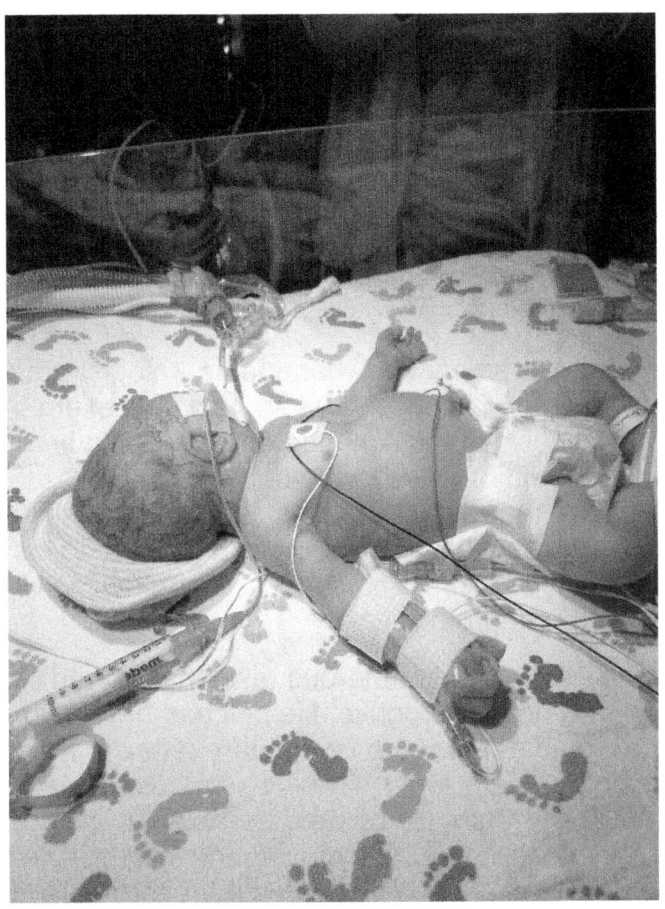

Mila in the NICU. This photo was taken after Amanda's heart stopped for a third time.

The Rabbit Hole

On July 21, 2019, Mario called us to tell us that Dr. Nickle wanted to have a family meeting to discuss Amanda's status. We were already on our way because we were told that a neurologist was coming to examine Amanda, and we wanted to be present.

We were at Amanda's bedside when the neurologist arrived not more than 15 minutes later and began doing his exam. A bunch of machines surrounded Amanda, and the sand bed she was on added a ton of noise to the bed bay, so it was hard to hear what the neurologist was saying. I tried getting as close as possible to see what he was doing and listen to his comments. Dr. Nickle was present, so most of the talking was directed to her by the neurologist.

The neurologist performed numerous tests that looked like he was looking for a nerve response. He pinched her cheeks, hoping that she would perform the involuntary reflex to try and swat the source of the pain away. There was no response. Her finger didn't even twitch. He opened her eyelids and shined a penlight into them, quickly moving the light from left to right on each eye. I could see there was no response. With every test he did, my heart sank lower and lower in my chest. I'm not a doctor, but I could see that none of this was going well.

The neurologist finished his exam, and he and Dr. Nickle stepped away and had a discussion. Earlier in the day, Amanda had an electroencephalogram (EEG) done on her brain. We did not know the results of this test and assumed that Dr. Nickle would discuss it with us at the family meeting.

The CTICU nurse liaison arranged for our family to have a waiting room all to ourselves. Daryl and I went back to this waiting room after the neurologist exam concluded, and the room was filled with all our families. There must have been at least 30 people there. There was probably more, but I was shaken by what I had seen during the neuro exam, and while I was greeting people with hugs and kisses, I was doing this on autopilot.

After a short period, Dr. Nickle and the nurse liaison entered the room. I remembered Dr. Nickle's soft-spoken voice, so I walked up to the front of the crowd to hear what she had to say. Dr. Nickle went through the litany of problems Amanda was currently facing.

She stated that along with the severe damage to Amanda's liver during CPR, all her other organs had failed her. She was getting blood transfusion after blood transfusion. She was on dialysis. She was still on the heart/lung machine. She was on a respirator to help her breathe. She was being kept alive mechanically. She was swollen so much that she looked like a balloon in a Thanksgiving Day parade. There was concern that the circulation in her limbs was being compromised because of the swelling.

Then Dr. Nickle gave us the worst news. The EEG had shown very little brain activity. Based on her extensive expertise, her opinion was that Amanda would not survive.

When I heard those words, my world stopped spinning. Had I heard her correctly? Did Dr. Nickle say that my daughter was going to die? I asked her if there was any possibility that she was wrong. She said the only thing that could save my daughter now was a miracle. She said the next 24-72 hours would be a critical period for Amanda.

My head slumped to my chest. I turned away and walked to the back of the waiting room, looking out the windows. Cars were passing on the street below. People were walking on the sidewalks. It was a beautiful sunny day in Pittsburgh, and everyone was unaware that inside this room, I was falling down a rabbit hole like Alice in Wonderland. I turned, sat in the nearest chair, put my head in my hands, and began sobbing. I kept thinking about how this could be happening. My daughter had survived what I thought was the most challenging thing anyone could survive, and that was a heroin addiction. She had turned her life around in storybook style and had the happy ending she wanted; getting married and starting a family. This couldn't be happening now!

My sister Mary Jo came over to me, put her arm around me, and tried to console me. I could hear others sobbing in the room, but I didn't look up to see who they were. This wasn't natural! A parent should never have to bury a child, but here I was, faced with that grim reality.

I finally looked up and saw Daryl sitting in a chair, crying. My son was next to her. I kicked myself in the ass for forgetting about her. One of her babies was dying, and I wasn't there to console her. I have always been her rock when we faced tough times; now, I was not where I needed to be at our most challenging time together. I wasn't next to her.

I walked over to her, knelt, and put my arms around her. We both cried for a few minutes, and then I told her we would get through this. I told Daryl that Amanda was a fighter and that I knew she wouldn't give up or throw in the towel. I said these things to her, but I think I was saying them to convince myself.

I told myself that I had to stop crying. My daughter wasn't dead yet; if anyone could survive this, it would be her. I got up and said to the others, "It isn't over yet." I said, "We need a miracle so let's start all praying for one." I said to Daryl that I was going to go and see Amanda. I had something to tell her.

I walked into the CTICU, and it felt like all the staff's eyes were on me. I walked up to Amanda on the right side of her bed and looked at her. I just stood there and looked at her, trying to will her to open her eyes and show some life. I looked at all the machines, wires, and IVs keeping her alive. I put my head down by her ear and said, "I know you can hear me. The doctors think you will not survive this, but I know you are. You will leave this hospital someday and surprise a whole bunch of people. You're going to do this because you have a beautiful baby girl waiting for her mom, who needs to see and know the bravest, strongest woman I know. I love you and haven't given up on you, so you can't give up on yourself."

Other people started to come into Amanda's bay, and since we could only have so many people in her bay, I stepped out. I was done crying. For the rest of the day, I stood behind a solid wall I had built and helped other family members believe she would survive.

When I saw Daryl after she visited with Amanda, I told her I wanted to go to the maternity hospital and visit Mila. I needed to see our granddaughter. She was the lone bright spot of these last two dismal days.

The nurse liaison arranged to have security drive us to the maternity hospital. We went straight to the NICU and visited with Mila. She was still in the incubator, but the nurse said we might be able to start taking her out the next day and begin holding her. She was doing well, and the NICU staff were so good to her.

I kept thinking that if only we could get Mila to be with Amanda, that somehow would make a big difference in Amanda's recovery.

Who did this?!!

July 22, 2019, started as Daryl and I made our way to the hospital early. We had heard that Amanda was going into the OR so the surgeons could look at her liver and check her uterus and other organs.

Her blood was still not clotting, so we knew that the packing around the liver would need to be changed along with all the wound vacs that were removing blood from her abdomen.

When we arrived at the CTICU, we pressed the button on the ICU door. As it opened, I saw several nurses and physicians standing just outside Amanda's bay. There appeared to be paramedics with a stretcher in front of them. Mario and his parents were there when I looked into Amanda's bay. Mario was holding Mila and beginning to put her down by Amanda's side.

I couldn't believe my eyes! The one thing I thought might give Amanda the extra drive to continue her fight for her life was happening. I was overcome with emotion. Mila must have just arrived because she was a little fidgety with Mario, but as soon as she was placed by her mom, she seemed to settle right in and relax. It was amazing to see. It is an image burned in my mind that I will never forget.

I stood there for many minutes, just looking and not saying anything. I was afraid that if I opened my mouth, I might start crying again, and I was tired of losing my composure in front of people. With all the machines' noise surrounding her, Mila was comfortable and sleeping. I hoped that Amanda could feel and know she had a daughter waiting for her.

I turned and looked at the staff and could see there wasn't a dry eye among them. I saw our nurse liaison and walked over to her. I didn't want to start crying, so I took a deep breath and asked her, "Who is responsible for this? Who did this? Whose idea was this?" She looked taken aback, and I realized I had said this too harshly. She said, "It was the NICU's idea." I told her, "Is anyone from the NICU here?" She pointed to two nurses dressed in blue scrubs standing by the paramedics.

They looked nervous as I walked over to them. I stopped before the first one I came to and hugged her. All I could say to her was, "Thank you so much!" I turned to the other nurse, hugged her, and told her the same thing. I then stepped back and said how much having the baby here meant to us and how much it meant to my daughter, Mila, and Mario. I walked back to the nurse liaison and hugged her, too, because I realized I must have appeared to be angry. I told her I was sorry for doing that to her and that I knew she had something to do with arranging this also.

I looked back in Amanda's bay and saw the smiles and tears on my family's faces and then turned to the nursing staff and physicians and said, "Thank you." It was all I could say. No other words would come out. I was choking up. It took all I could to look them all in the eyes and smile.

The baby stayed with Amanda for close to an hour, and then we were told the ambulance crew was needed for another pediatric case, so Mila had to return to the NICU. It was hard to watch them get her ready to leave. Amanda did not move or indicate that she knew the baby was there, but I could feel she knew her baby was next to her. I knew the mother-baby bond was more substantial than any other force known to man. I prayed that bond would give her the strength she needed to survive.

As we walked out of Amanda's bay and to the waiting room, I couldn't wait to find a chair and sit down. The day had just started, and I was already feeling emotionally drained.

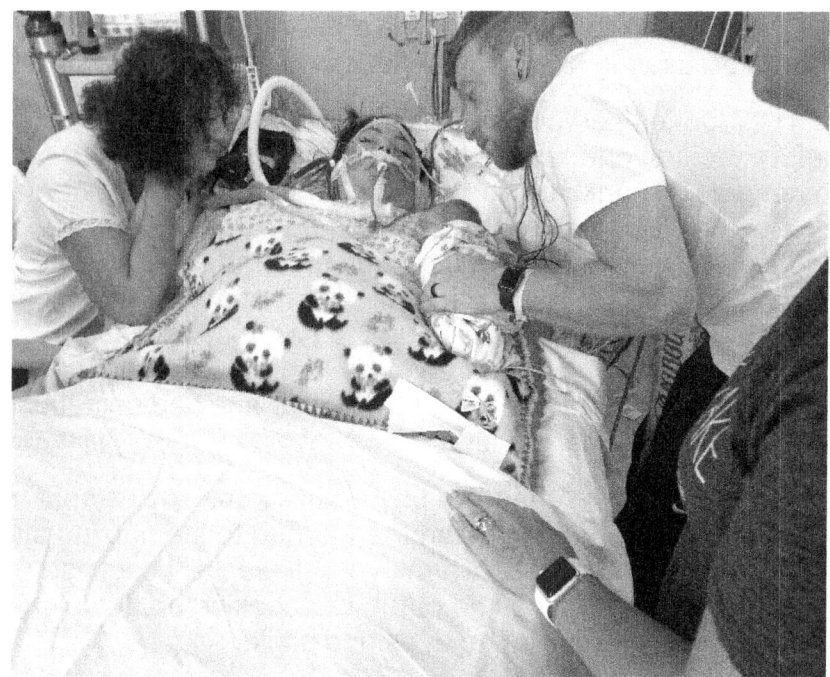

Mila meets her mom for the first time. Our hope was this would not be her only time with her mom. I am forever grateful to the NICU and CTICU staff for arranging this.

A Little Bit

Forty-eight hours and then seventy-two hours passed, and Amanda was still holding on. On day 4 of the AFE event, Amanda's blood showed signs of clotting. The DIC symptom of the AFE was resolving itself. Amanda was going into the OR for the 5th time to check her liver.

The surgeons were going to repack the liver and look at her uterus with the OB/GYNs. Her uterus suffered some damage, and it was in question as to whether the uterus was damaged enough to be removed, and if it was, when would it be a good time to do that?

The surgeons were also becoming concerned with her right leg. One of the insertion points of the ECMO machine is the right femoral artery, and unfortunately, this can cause blood clots to form below the insertion point and cut off circulation to the leg. The surgeons hoped the clots would break up and circulation would return to normal. They couldn't put Amanda on blood-thinning medication that would break up the clots because her liver wouldn't heal. It was a real catch-22. Her liver was more vital to her recovery, so it wasn't much of a choice.

After her fifth visit to the OR, when we were in her bay with her in the CTICU, she opened her eyes! It wasn't long, and she certainly didn't respond to us when we called her name, but it was the first time she had done anything other than lay in bed.

We told her nurse, who came over and examined Amanda. She said that sometimes, the opening of the eyes is an involuntary reflex. She said something to the effect of let's hope it leads to something more.

As far as we were concerned, this was a sign of hope. She had already lived longer than the CTICU physicians thought she would live. They still told us she was very critical, and there was still a good chance her liver would die. They were unwilling to say she was any less critical than when she arrived in the CTICU.

Amanda was still fighting for her life, and every chance I could get with her, I would tell her that she was one of the bravest, strongest women I knew and that she had the most beautiful little girl she needed to come back to so she could teach Mila how to be a strong woman. I told her how proud I was of her for becoming the person she was. I told her I loved her every chance I could. I just kept hoping and praying that the last time I said, "I love you," wouldn't be the last time she heard it.

Week One Plus One

It was July 28, 2019, and Amanda was still hanging on. I can't say we were optimistic. It was hard to be optimistic when we saw nothing that showed any outward signs of improvement every day.

Amanda was still hooked up to all the same machines, including the ECMO, and the physicians were concerned about her being on the ECMO for so long. Being on the ECMO machine for an extended period can lead to severe complications. Her right leg was looking like it was becoming necrotic. Her left leg was also starting to show signs of the same.

The physicians were talking about weaning Amanda off the ECMO machine. Still, they then discovered Amanda had developed a blood infection that required it to be treated before they did anything else.

She had been through seven visits to the OR primarily to repack her liver, check on her other organs, and change the wound vacs. Each visit to the OR came with heightened tension. I kept thinking, "How much can my tiny daughter's body withstand?" I was hoping that she was unaware of how dire her situation was.

It's crazy how you think in a situation like this. For one instance, I hoped she could hear me as I kept encouraging her to fight through this. In another instance, I was hoping she was oblivious to her surroundings and how critical she was. I was all over the place with my thoughts.

Her husband, Mario, never left the hospital. The CTICU staff arranged for him to access a small conference room next to the waiting room. They put a recliner in it for him to sleep on. He was not leaving her side. He would be up and with the physicians as they made their rounds in the CTICU. He studied her daily report, including her labs, and began understanding the values and how they correlated. He asked the nurses and staff about all the machines and all the tests so he could realize firsthand how each functioned and worked together. It reached the point that if I had any questions about how Amanda was doing, I asked Mario first.

I tried to imagine what he was going through, but it was impossible for me. He was a 26-year-old man with a successful business, a beautiful, loving wife, and who was looking forward to raising his new family. Now, everything was turned upside down on him. How would he survive this? I wasn't sure about the answer to that question. I kept a close eye on him in case any cracks in his character appeared. He only saw his daughter when she was brought to Amanda from the NICU. He was so fearful of not being close to Amanda if she turned for the worse. Amanda was everything to him, and I knew he was struggling not to fall apart. I often thought that his way of coping with the situation was to get involved in her care.

Every afternoon before Daryl and I would go home; we would go to the NICU to see Mila. We could hold and cuddle her, and it was so good for our hearts to do that. She was helping Daryl and me stay sane through this insane situation.

On this day, before we left Amanda, we got a call from the NICU that they were transferring Mila to our local Children's Hospital. They were concerned that Mila's stomach was a little distended and wanted her examined by the specialists at the Children's Hospital.

Mila was examined at the Children's Hospital. The doctors determined that she had a hole in her intestine that would require surgery to cut out the affected intestine and then wait for her intestines to heal and grow so the surgeons could reattach them. Mila would require a stoma on her intestine and a colostomy bag. She would be in the hospital for about 3 to 4 months.

Upon hearing this news, I was at the point of thinking, "What else could go wrong." Our little ray of sunshine now had her health problems that had to be dealt with. Mario's mother took charge of being with Mila. The NICU at the Children's

Hospital were private rooms for each child, and each had a couch bed built into the room so parents could stay with their sick babies. Debbie was cleared to remain with Mila and did so right from the first night.

We now had a new destination in our daily route. Daryl and I would drive to Pittsburgh to be with Amanda, and then right around dinner time, we would go to the Children's Hospital to visit Mila and give Debbie and Joe a chance to get dinner. We would then leave and get home at around 8 or 9 pm to get some rest and start the next day with the same itinerary.

This wasn't how I envisioned my retirement, but I was thankful that my daughter and granddaughter were still with us.

The Beat Goes On

The physicians were getting increasingly concerned about Amanda remaining on the ECMO machine. Her blood infection cleared, and they didn't want to wait another day. The ECMO machine is comprised of two cannulas (tubes) attached to blood vessels in the heart. The one cannula transfers blood from the heart to the machine via a pump, where the machine then oxygenates, removes carbon dioxide, and warms the blood before returning it through the other cannula to the body.

The big concern was if Amanda would go into cardiac arrest or heart failure when they removed her from the heart portion of ECMO. Her surgery was scheduled very early on August 3, 2019. This was going to be her ninth visit to the OR in 13 days. We had no idea how long she would be in the OR. I believe the ECMO removal was going to be done first. If she survived that, they would examine and possibly remove her uterus due to its damage during the AFE. The last thing they wanted to do was to close her abdomen.

Since Amanda's abdomen had been open for almost two weeks, and with the swelling, it would not be possible to pull the stomach muscles and skin back into place as before her initial surgery. The surgeons would have to put a mesh over the open portion of her abdomen. That mesh would probably stay in place for at least a year or two.

Amanda was in surgery for over 11 hours. It was concerning but also reassuring. The longer she was in there meant that she had survived removal from the ECMO. Every few hours, we would get an update. The first update confirmed that the ECMO had been removed successfully. The next update informed us that her uterus had been damaged beyond recovery and had to be removed. That was a hard one to hear. It meant that Amanda would never be able to have another child. I knew how upset Amanda would be when she discovered that having more children would not be possible.

Here I was not even sure she was going to survive any of this, and I was worried about her not being able to have more babies. Boy, did I have to refocus my priorities!

When the surgery was finally over, the surgeons told us they had accomplished everything they had set out to do. They expressed concern about her right leg again. They said it looked like the muscles below her knee were beginning to die. They were preparing us for the possibility that Amanda would lose her right leg below the knee.

All of this was too much to process. I couldn't wrap my head around the idea that my daughter giving birth had led to all this hardship for her and her husband. How were they going to manage all of this if she did survive? We left Mario at the hospital with our daughter to see Mila, who had just survived her surgery to repair the hole in her intestine. Looking back, I don't know how any of us managed all this hardship. I kept telling myself that someday we would all look back on this period and marvel at our resilience.

Dad

As we moved into the second week of August, we no longer saw as many people visiting Amanda. My 91-year-old dad was there daily. He would visit my mother's gravesite, who had passed away three years prior, and then come straight over to sit with Amanda. Daryl and I usually showed up around noon. It was good to have my dad there. He and I would go to lunch or find ourselves in the waiting room alone and talk about life and how precious it was. My dad was still grieving from the loss of my mother, and I was grieving over the loss of my daughter's future.

Eight years before my mom's death, she had a major stroke that left her mostly bedridden. I remember when that happened that I couldn't imagine how my dad would survive without her. My mom had a dominant personality, and from what I could see, she ran the household. I imagined that my dad would be lost without her.

When it became apparent that my mom would survive the stroke but have limited mobility, I couldn't see her surviving for long unless she was in a nursing home. My mom did go to a nursing home when she was discharged from the hospital, but she was only there for 100 days when my dad checked her out and decided to take care of her at their apartment. I remember arguing with my dad over how he would care for her. He was in his eighties, and I couldn't fathom how he would do it. I remember thinking that this was a disaster waiting to happen.

My dad cared for her for eight years until she died from natural causes. There were bumps in that road, but they both survived for better or worse. My mom never had a bed sore while my dad cared for her. He was attentive to her every need. To say he surprised me would be an understatement. He had his moments with my mom, just like any married couple. He was depressed at times. But I think the one thing that drove him on was imagining how scared my mother must be. My dad became a nurturer, a role I had never seen before with him.

My dad taught me a lot during those eight years. He taught me how strong the bond of marriage truly is. He taught me that, for better or worse, were not just words in a vow but were a genuine promise between two people.

My dad taught me more life lessons in those eight years than in the years preceding.

Now my dad and I had the chance to talk about something we both had in common—the fear of losing someone you love. We would talk about my mom and Amanda. I let him know how afraid I was of Amanda dying. I told him that when Amanda was using heroin, I expected her to die every night; but for some unfathomable reason, I was prepared for that. But now I wasn't prepared. I had allowed myself to see a future for Amanda that had nothing but love and happiness, and not knowing if she would survive was crushing for me.

My dad reminded me that Amanda was very much alive and that I should not let her current situation mean she would not have love and happiness in her future. He told me he thought the same thing when my mom first had her stroke. As time passed, he realized how much more he and her connected as they navigated their way through what they thought was an impossible journey. He said that he and she discovered just how much love and happiness they found together during that time.

These talks with my dad helped me get back on track and keep myself centered. I've always believed that sharing your hopes and fears with others permits them to share theirs with you and that, together, both parties' benefit. Sharing allows comfort, support, and empathy to come to the forefront. Sharing brings out possibilities, and possibilities bring out hope. I learned from Amanda's addiction years that I could never give up hope.

Thanks, Dad, for reminding me of that.

New Outlook

I had been living on the edge of my seat for over three weeks, and it was taking a toll. I was tired, losing weight, feeling overly sad, and I felt like I had been through a 15-round fight. I didn't know if Amanda was going to live or die. If she did live, I didn't know if she had any brain injury. We kept asking the CTICU doctors if there was a test we could do to see if Amanda had cognitive abilities. The doctors told us they weren't interested in any of those tests. They were more concerned with keeping her alive. They said they would perform those tests when the time was right.

I was going through all the chaos of Amanda's medical condition and letting it get the best of me. Decisions needed to be made almost daily, and the ramifications of those decisions could be life-altering for the entire family. It was dizzying and, at times, frightening. At times I couldn't think straight and was apprehensive that if I didn't understand all the medical jargon and made a choice, it could be the wrong one. I needed to stop this tornado of chaos and stop it quickly before it consumed me and made me a detriment to everyone who needed me. I couldn't see where this whole event was going to go. I knew I had felt this way before. It was when Amanda was using drugs heavily.

Through my talks with my dad, I knew one thing: I couldn't lose sight of hope. I lost hope when Amanda was using heroin heavily, but then I rediscovered hope and learned how to find my center. I learned how to alter my perspective.

I had to alter my perspective to survive the trauma that Amanda's addiction caused, and I needed to change my perspective now. I decided to take all the tools I had learned during Amanda's addiction while attending the Bridge to Hope and put them back into play.

I had to stop and recognize that I was going through the grieving process again. I had to take an inventory of all the stages of grief and where I was in those stages. I knew it was important not to skip any grief stages and not rush through them to get to the last stage of Acceptance.

As I took this inventory, I realized that I had processed Denial, Anger, Bargaining, and Depression. Now I was faced with Acceptance. I couldn't accept that my daughter might die. I couldn't accept that she may never regain consciousness again. I couldn't accept that she may permanently have a brain injury. I hoped that she was going to pull through all of this. I hoped we would have Amanda back totally intact and ready to be the mom to Mila she so wanted to be. I hoped that this nightmare I was in would come to a dramatic and happy ending.

I understood that my acceptance was that I had no control over what was occurring. Once I accepted that I had no control over what was happening to Amanda, I could find peace. I knew I had to take this whole ordeal one day at a time.

At this point, I understood that Amanda had prepared me years ago for what was happening. My daughter's addiction years and all the emotions and trauma then were similar to her current condition. As strange as it was, she taught me years ago how to cope today. My daughter had laid the groundwork for navigating this journey with her. All I had to do was follow it. I found comfort in recognizing this.

Support From Those We Know the Least

Right after I retired in January 2019, Daryl and I went to Florida and stayed at a condominium resort where we rented a first-floor condo that was wheelchair accessible. It was a two-bedroom, two-bath condo, and this would be a test for us to see how going from 2500 square feet of living space to 1500 square feet would affect us. We stayed at this resort for two months and determined that we could easily live in a reduced-size home with some furniture downsizing.

When we returned from Florida in April, I contacted our real estate agent and Daryl, and I actively began looking for a new single-level home. We found a single-level condo in an active senior community not far from our current home. By the end of May, we closed on this condo and moved into our new neighborhood by the end of June.

The community we moved into was active and had numerous monthly social events. Daryl and I were looking forward to attending these events and getting to know our neighbors.

The community had a website with a community directory, posted rules and regulations, and a message board for the community members to communicate with one another.

Daryl and I have two small dogs that had a complete run of our fenced-in backyard in our old home but would need to be walked three times a day in our new location. The dogs enjoyed their walks; it was an excellent opportunity to meet and talk to people in our neighborhood. One of our dogs was diabetic and required two insulin shots per day.

The day Amanda had her AFE, Daryl and I didn't get back to our home until very late at night, and I was late getting an insulin shot into my dog. I knew this was going to be a problem for us moving forward.

The day after Amanda's AFE, I went onto the community website and posted on the message board my need for someone to help walk our dogs and to give my diabetic dog its insulin shot. I explained what had happened to my daughter in the post. I posted this message around 9 am. By 9:15 am, I received a phone call from one of my neighbors. They said they would gladly walk our dogs and inject the insulin. This neighbor, whom I don't believe I had previously met, told me she was sure others would also volunteer and would be happy to coordinate a dog walking schedule with all who wanted to help. I returned to the message board and posted this new info to my previous post. Faster than you can imagine, 25 people volunteered to walk my dogs. I was shocked. I would never have imagined that so many people would be willing to step up and help us in our time of need. It was then that I knew I was living in a remarkable community.

Over the next few weeks, we would come home to cards in the mail, food, and gifts from our neighbors who felt such deep compassion and empathy for us because of the nightmare of events we were going through. Daryl and I will never forget their kindness and warmth toward us.

Liberty Hills will always hold a special place in my heart, and I am so thankful that Daryl and I decided to move here.

The Pressure

Even though Amanda was no longer on the ECMO machine, she was still on a ventilator. The doctors were talking about performing a tracheotomy on her so the intubation would not damage her vocal cords. It was August 7, 2019, and Amanda was still fighting an uphill battle.

Her liver was still considered critical and was not functioning well. This was verified by her yellow-tinged skin color and her daily lab report. Her kidneys were still not working, but the doctors told us the kidneys are always the first organ to fail and the last organ to recover.

The biggest hurdle that Amanda was now facing was weaning her from her vasopressor medications. These medications kept her blood pressure at reasonable levels; without it, she would have no blood pressure. Her blood pressure with the meds was low in my eyes, but according to the doctors and nurses, it was not dangerous.

They started the weaning process, and it was evident that Amanda's body was not ready to resume that workload without continuing their use. This was not the outcome the medical staff was prepared for. The doctors decided they would all have to confer and devise another game plan.

I was certain Amanda would be ok when they began weaning her from the vasopressors. She had been fighting against all odds, and while she was still critical, she seemed to be improving in my eyes. Maybe it was wishful thinking on my behalf. I know I had to keep telling myself not to get too high with the highs or too low with the lows. I kept repeating to myself, "One day at a time."

Our granddaughter Mila was improving daily. She was fed through a tube in her nose, but she was gaining weight. The NICU nurses were trying to train her on how to feed from a bottle. They said she had to learn to suck, swallow, and breathe simultaneously. I had always thought that babies just instinctively knew how to do that, but I was surprised when the nurse told us that with preemies, it's a learning process.

It was always so good for us to see her at the end of our day. She loved being swaddled and held; I certainly didn't mind providing her with that. She would make a purring sound when she was sleeping. I initially thought it was snoring, but Daryl told me, "Mila does not snore. She purrs." I didn't care what noise this little girl made. All I knew was that she already had me wrapped around her little finger, and I didn't mind.

No Words

The surgeons and CTICU doctors were not painting a good picture concerning Amanda's right leg. The leg was dying at the foot and calf, and her thigh muscle was showing continuing signs that it, too, was dying. The surgeons were doing everything they could to save her leg. They had made lacerations in the leg muscles to help relieve the swelling. It wasn't working. With Amanda's liver in distress, her kidneys not functioning, and the blood clots in her leg, it was a losing battle for them with her leg.

The surgeon called a family meeting and told us that, in her opinion, for Amanda to survive, they would have to amputate her right leg. I didn't feel anything when she told us this. I had been living this horrible dream for so long that another piece of traumatic news wasn't even fazing me.

I remember the conversation being about how much of the leg they would need to amputate. The surgeon told us that the whole leg didn't look good but that they would attempt to take her leg from right above the knee.

The mental images I had of Amanda with the lower portion of her leg missing were frightening. If she survived, and there were still no guarantees that would happen, how would she feel about the decision we were making? Amanda was a girl through and through. She loved having her hair colored and done perfectly on a routine basis. She would get her eyebrows and eyelashes done religiously. She was always dressed fashionably and loved wearing heels. How would she see herself with the lower portion of her leg gone?

To this point, the surgeons had done everything they could to keep Amanda alive, and they had our complete faith. If it was their opinion that this gave Amanda her best shot to move forward, then I was on board. I remember looking into the surgeon's eyes and saying, "You do whatever you have to do to save her life." My only hope was that someday I would be able to explain to Amanda why her lower leg had been amputated.

On August 8, 2019, Amanda's leg was amputated from just above the right knee. The surgery had gone well, and now it was a waiting game to see if the rest of her leg would begin recovering and how the amputation affected the rest of her condition.

It was a draining day for Daryl and me. Even when we visited with Mila later that day, I couldn't bring myself to find any joy. Her snuggles and cuddles couldn't bring a smile to my face. It was a sobering somber day.

I assume I did what I did every night when we came home from the hospital. I walked the dogs, fed them dinner, gave them their meds, and then sat in front of the TV. I assumed I did these things because I don't remember doing them that night. It was as if I was sleepwalking. I remember going into my bathroom to shower, waiting for the water to warm up, getting in the shower, and then sitting on the floor and crying. I sat there for a long time as the water poured over me, and tears came down my face. Why was this happening to my baby girl?!! After all she had done to turn her life around, why was God letting this happen!!?? Was this penance that God was extracting from her because of her past!!?? I had forgiven her for all the trauma and turmoil she caused Daryl and me. Why wasn't God forgiving her? I remember telling God, "You got your leg. Now you better not take her life."

I guess God doesn't take kindly to threats because on August 17, 2019; the surgeons had to take the rest of her right leg up to the hip because it was septic and causing her additional liver distress. It was her 13th surgery… how appropriate.

What's Left?

The CTICU attendings rotate every week, but the one who spent the first week caring for Amanda hadn't seen Amanda in over a month. On the first day he was back, he called a family meeting. The family meetings had become the CTICU attending, our nurse advocate, the CTICU nurse currently caring for Amanda, Mario, Daryl, my son Dan, my dad, and myself.

He started by telling us how well Amanda was progressing. One month ago, he firmly believed that she would not survive the first 48 hours, but now her liver was healing and her other organs, except the kidneys, were functioning quite well, her lab values were also trending in the right direction, and she was being weaned from the vasopressor medications. He was enthused about her progress.

Removing her right leg had been the difference maker. Within 48 hours of the removal of the leg, Amanda's swelling had decreased by 90%, and she appeared to be much more alert. While we agonized over the removal of the leg, it was the best move we could have made.

After meeting with the attending, I felt somewhat better about Amanda's prognosis, but inside, I was still very concerned about her mind. Amanda probably had a brain injury during the AFE. She had to have CPR for 37 minutes. There had to be a time when blood was not getting to her brain. The big mystery to me was how much time it was and how much of an injury she had. While we were all praying for her to have all her organs functioning and supporting her, I was worried that she might have a significant brain injury where she might spend the rest of her life institutionalized.

I shared my thoughts with Daryl, who said she also had the same concerns. We agreed to keep our thoughts to ourselves for the time being.

Amanda was going into the O.R. the next day so the

surgeons could work on her right hip to get it ready for a prosthetic. While Amanda was far from being fitted for a prosthetic leg, the work had to be done now.

The surgeons were also looking at Amanda's left leg. There was some necrotic tissue on her left leg and foot, and there was still a chance it may also have to be amputated. We kept praying that they could save the leg.

Mila had a second surgery because she was getting air in her stomach and would not take a bottle. She had also become quite adept at pulling her feeding tube from her nose. The nurses were trying everything to keep the tube in, but no matter what they did, she somehow found a way to take it out. We found it humorous that this little peanut of a girl could be so feisty! The doctors wanted her to start being bottle-fed, so they examined the stoma and decided it needed to be widened. Somehow doing that would stop the air from getting in her stomach.

Mila was not much of a complainer. Whether she was having a diaper change or getting poked by a needle, she would yell out once and then stop. She was a real soldier, just like her mom. I couldn't wait for the day when they could both consciously meet each other.

The Village

When tragedy strikes, there are several ways that we respond as human beings. The event's size and scope will determine if our coping skills are overwhelmed and what that response will be.

I can say that Amanda's AFE was a tragedy I was unprepared for. I was probably in shock for days, if not weeks, afterward. I knew if I felt this way, everyone else probably felt the same.

I was very concerned for Daryl. Her muscular dystrophy had lowered her stamina, but here we were doing 14-hour days, and some days, we were living off pure adrenaline. I kept a close eye on her and didn't like what I saw. While my wife wanted to always be with either Amanda or Mila, I knew she couldn't keep up with the routine we had been on for the past six weeks. The last thing any of us needed was for her health to become a problem, so I had to make a decision that I knew might upset her. I told Daryl I needed us to take a couple of days off each week. I told her I couldn't keep up with our current pace and felt we needed to reign ourselves in. She agreed, so I let Mario know our plans for going forward.

Mario had been at the hospital around the clock for Amanda's entire hospitalization. The CTICU staff were becoming concerned for him. They were afraid that he would "burn out" and not be ready to help Amanda if she ever regained consciousness. I tried talking with Mario to get him to go home at night and sleep in his bed, but he refused. He was not going to leave the hospital while Amanda's condition was still critical. He didn't want to miss any tests, physician rounds, or procedures. He would get Amanda's daily report and pour over her lab values. He asked every question possible on what each value meant. He wanted to look at the information and know exactly how she was doing without waiting for someone's interpretation. Mario learned everything he could about the various machines keeping Amanda alive. Watching him interact with the CTICU nurses, attendings, fellows, and residents was amazing. He knew them by their first name, and they spoke to him as if he were a peer, not a family member.

Mario's mother, Debbie, was staying with Mila every day. She would only leave when other family members would come in to visit and then go out for lunch or dinner with her husband, Joe, or other family members or friends. I knew this wasn't easy for Debbie or Joe, but they never complained or bemoaned their situation.

My son Dan rarely missed a day when he didn't come in to visit Amanda. He was working full-time, but he had arranged with his job that he could work remotely and still be at the hospital.

My dad would visit on most days. He would come in at 11 am and go home around 2 pm. I insisted he leave at 2 pm so he wouldn't have to drive in rush hour traffic. I couldn't help but be in awe of him. He was a 91-year-old man driving 50 miles daily to see his granddaughter.

My sister, Mary Jo, was at the hospital consistently. She would help Debbie with Mila when Debbie needed a break, and she was always well within reach whenever I needed her.

All the siblings, aunts, uncles, cousins, and friends who came in to visit or drop off food or provide moral support were vital to us.

This was our village. I knew we had to be a village because it would take one to help us all survive this tragedy. I was very proud of this village. This village was going to be the glue that was going to hold everything and everyone together.

Treadmill Results

Amanda had been in a coma for a little over 5 weeks. Daryl and I had been on autopilot for over a month now. At this point going to the hospital was becoming our routine. It was almost like being on a treadmill where you walk for a very long time without actually going anywhere.

It was so routine that we knew the best location in the hospital parking garage to park our car. We knew what route would get us to the correct bank of elevators the quickest. We knew which elevator to wait for to save steps walking to the CTICU. We would always stop in the visitor lounge first to see who from our family may be visiting that day. At times we would find my father there, my son Dan, my sister Mary Jo, or some other family member or friend. We would next check the staff conference room that Mario was housed in to see if he was there. Mario was always my preferred first contact because he would update us on Amanda's latest condition. This is what we did daily.

Not much was changing with Amanda's condition. Her lab values and other test results were slowly changing but they were still not great. I just kept telling myself that as long as the results kept improving, I had to continue to believe that she was going to survive.

Daryl and I would make our way into the CTICU and to Amanda's bedside. Daryl would always sit by the head of Amanda's bed and talk to Amanda. Daryl would speak to Amanda as if Amanda could hear and comprehend what Daryl was saying to her. While Daryl was doing this I would usually go to the cafeteria and grab us some lunch that we could eat outside Amanda's bay.

As I stood in line at the cafeteria, I recognized that I was starting to get mentally exhausted by this daily routine. I was beginning to wonder if this could possibly be the only way we would interact with our daughter going forward.

I came back with our lunch which we ate outside of Amanda's bay. Afterward, we were back at Amanda's bedside. Daryl was talking to Amanda on one side of her bed, and I was on the other side. Dan arrived and was standing at the foot of the bed and watched Daryl talk to Amanda.

Dan said to Daryl that he couldn't understand why she was continually talking to Amanda. He said to her, "You know she can't hear you." Daryl disagreed with this and let Dan know that.

Her belief was that Amanda had to be talked to and told that she was loved, she was a mom, and that she was going to survive. Daryl told Dan she truly believed that Amanda could hear her and that it was all of our responsibility to talk to her.

Thankfully, there was no staff around as this discussion was beginning to escalate. Dan was as firm in his belief as Daryl was in her belief. I intervened and asked them to tone it down and to just agree to disagree. I remember telling Dan if it was bothering him seeing his mom talk to Amanda then he didn't have to stand there and watch it.

Dan left. I knew he wasn't happy, but I sure couldn't understand why he chose this moment to voice his opinion in such a negative way.

I began to realize just how deeply Amanda's current condition was adversely affecting all of us. While we were experiencing the same chain of events, each of us was processing them differently. It's hard to see that when you are in the moment and frankly my family's moment was almost six weeks old.

Dan was living in his reality, and I can't tell you exactly what that was in its entirety, but it certainly included the belief that Amanda was unaware of her surroundings. I think he was coming to the acceptance that this may be the way she would remain for the rest of her life.

If that was his outlook, then I could understand why he reacted the way he did. Watching someone you love suffering and dying before your eyes day after day is emotionally draining.

I could relate to that feeling. When Amanda was using heroin, I was facing the possibility of her death daily. I had to come to an acceptance that her death was imminent and how little I could do to prevent it. Helplessness is such a depressing and heavy feeling and I think Dan was experiencing this. I knew that he loved his sister and would do whatever he could to help her survive. Not knowing what to do though is very frustrating.

Daryl's reality of Amanda was one of hope and promise. I believe that is the only reality a parent can have in a situation such as ours. That was also my reality but as time was marching on, my reality was becoming distorted.

At the beginning of Amanda's coma, I was faced with the likelihood of Amanda's impending death. As she survived into the second week, I began to have hope that she would somehow survive this episode. As the weeks progressed and she was not showing any sign of coming out of her coma, I questioned my hope for her.

By the fifth week of her coma, I would stand by her bedside looking at her and ask myself, "Is this it? Is this what she'll be like until she passes?" These were very dark moments for me. I was having a very difficult time with the possibility of Amanda never being herself again.

Her spirit of joy, happiness, and promise was all fading before my eyes. It was on days like these that I would have to mentally kick myself in the ass and readjust my perspective back to having hope. I must admit, I was kicking myself quite a bit during that fifth week.

I left Daryl with Amanda and found Dan in the waiting room. There was no one else in the room and I asked him what was going on with him. I wanted to know why he felt the need to question his mom talking to Amanda.

Dan didn't answer. I was expecting that. When Dan gets upset with something he'll let you know his thoughts but after that, he doesn't feel the need to explain himself. Because of this, I knew I was going to have a one-way conversation. It was going to be brief.

I simply reminded Dan that his mother was watching her baby girl wither away in a hospital bed. I let him know his mother's way of coping with this impossible situation was to continue to have hope. It was her duty as a mother to always have hope for her children and if expressing her hope came out by talking to Amanda then he needed to respect that.

I left him with that and went back to Amanda's bedside and continued to watch Daryl talk to her baby and attempt to will her out of her coma. She had my total support and I prayed she was going to be right.

This treadmill we were all on seemed to be never-ending and it was slowly increasing in speed. We were all becoming weary. I wasn't sure how much longer we could stay on it and survive as a family.

A Miraculous Day

August 28, 2019, started like every day for the past six weeks. Daryl and I got in our car at around noon to go to the hospital. We again discussed our concern that Amanda had a brain injury and may never regain consciousness. We couldn't even comprehend what life would be like if this was going to be Amanda's future. All I could think was that her life would not be long if she were in a never-ending coma. The chance of her getting pneumonia, bed sores that would get infected, or any number of items that could go wrong was a genuine possibility.

It was a somber ride to the hospital, and I just kept reflecting on the past six weeks and all the myriad medical problems that Amanda had faced. She had beaten almost all of the odds to get this far, and her lab values continued to improve slowly. There was still reason for hope, but with the passing of each day, I could feel it slipping away.

When we arrived at the hospital, we went to the CTICU. My dad was leaving, and I asked him if there was any change with Amanda, and he half-smiled and shook his head no. He said her eyes would open now and then, and he would speak to her but that she wasn't responding.

We walked into her room, and she was sleeping, so I asked Daryl if she wanted anything for lunch. She told me what she wanted, and I told her I would return with her food in a few minutes.

I took the express elevator to the cafeteria, bought our food, and sat down for a few minutes to catch my breath. I was tired. I hadn't been sleeping well for a few weeks, and the stress was beginning to catch up with me. I knew that if I was being affected this way, Daryl must also feel the same; and for her, that wasn't healthy.

I snapped myself out of my stupor and headed back to Amanda's room. When I got to her room, Daryl was standing by Amanda and talking to her. Daryl looked at me and said that Amanda had nodded when Daryl asked her questions. I looked at her skeptically. I knew how badly Daryl wanted Amanda to respond because I wanted it to happen as much as she did. I asked Daryl if she was sure that Amanda nodded to questions, and she was emphatic that she did.

I stood beside Amanda and said to her, "Amanda, it's Dad. Can you hear me?" She ever so slowly nodded her head, "Yes"! I was stunned. Could this have just happened? Did I see things? Did I see something that wasn't there? I asked her, "Do you know what happened to you?" She ever so slightly shook her head, "No"!

I looked at Daryl and said, "Go get Mario!" Daryl left, and in minutes, Mario was in the room. I said, "Mario, she's answering questions!" He said, "Are you sure?" So, I looked at Amanda and asked her if she could hear me. Amanda, again, ever so slightly, nodded her head, "Yes."

With that, Mario quickly left the room. During this episode, Amanda's nurse, who was in another patient's room, walked into Amanda's room. I told her that Amanda was answering questions. She looked at me with surprise and then went to her bedside and asked Amanda questions. She answered them all with nods or shakes of her head.

While the nurse was with Amanda, Mario returned with the CTICU attending and several fellows and residents. The CTICU attending that week was Dr. Nickle. She was the attending who saw Amanda the first day and then delivered the news that she wouldn't survive 48 hours.

There was now a crowd around Amanda's bed, and Mario was standing in front of me with Daryl to his right at the foot of Amanda's bed. Dr. Nickle approached Amanda and said, "Amanda, this is Dr. Nickle. Can you hear me?" When Amanda nodded, she said, "Oh my God." Everyone was looking at each other in disbelief. My daughter was hearing questions, comprehending their meaning, and then answering them correctly! Her brain was working! She was able to process words, form thoughts, and produce reasonable

251

answers!

What happened next was something I wasn't prepared for. I was already on cloud nine and shocked at what I saw when Dr. Nickle took it one step further.

When Amanda had her first neurological exam the day after her AFE, the neurologist kept asking Amanda to move her finger or wiggle a toe. She did neither. We later found out how important that little request is. When the brain hears a command, a chain of neurological responses takes place. The brain must understand the question and send a neurological stimulus via nerves to the muscular part of the body it wants to respond. The muscle then performs the desired action, which sends a signal back to the brain, and the entire cycle is complete. I never realized all that was involved in wiggling a finger or toe.

Dr. Nickle picked up Amanda's left hand and asked Amanda to move her finger. I realized right then the importance and possible severity of this request. I watched with bated breath. If that finger moved, then the possibility of Amanda having any impactful brain damage was greatly reduced. I didn't want to face the possibility of Amanda's finger not moving.

Amanda's left index finger moved just a tiny bit! That was all Dr. Nickle needed to see! She turned to the nurse behind her and said, "Praise God!" as she wrapped her in a hug.

Mario fell to his knees in front of me and started to sob loudly. People were hugging and crying and just dumbfounded. I just stood there with tears coming down my face. I couldn't believe the scene in front of me. Daryl was bent over, hugging Mario. I bent down, put my arms around both, and kept repeating, "I can't believe it! I can't believe it!"

I hugged every nurse, doctor, and staff member I could see and repeatedly told them, "Thank you!". The medical staff of the CTICU had been with us through all the ups and downs over the past six weeks. They were the ones who kept telling us never to give up hope, even though they knew that

Amanda's survival was a long shot at best. They were the ones who helped arrange for Amanda to get visits from Mila. They were the ones who would clean her up and wash her hair and put it in a ponytail and always tried to make sure she was comfortable. They treated us like family and talked to us with kindness and love. They had become invested professionally and emotionally with Amanda. Amanda's age and circumstances drove home that something like this could have happened to them or their wives. They all got to share our joy now. Since the staff rotated around to different patients every few days, most of them had already taken care of Amanda, and as word spread about Amanda, they all came up, when they could, to see her and hug us and tell us how happy they were for us.

I was on the phone calling my family to spread the good news, and as I sat outside Amanda's room, other CTICU staff would stop by to peer into her room. I would say to them, "Can you believe this?" They would just smile the biggest of smiles I had ever seen.

Later that afternoon, the CTICU physician staff made rounds of all the patients. When they got to Amanda's room, the nurse gave them the report on Amanda, which they all already knew but still listened to. When she finished the report, some doctors made their way into Amanda's room and asked her questions, which she answered correctly. Standing next to one of the more tenured residents, I asked him, "So what can you attribute to what Amanda did today? How did this happen? What caused this to happen?" I had so many questions that I didn't know how to put them into words. He looked at Amanda for a few seconds, turned to look at me, and said, "Pure and simple. This is a miracle. A true medical miracle."

Then, I began to understand the importance of what I had seen. While most people go through life and hear about miraculous events that either occurred in the past or are currently happening, they have never had the opportunity to see one first-hand. I had not only seen one, but I was also a part of the miracle. I was a witness to a miracle. I couldn't believe that my daughter's name and the word "miracle" would forever be linked in the same sentence.

I was cynical about miracles before this day, but I can tell you now that I firmly believe in them. Just see my daughter, and you'll also become a believer.

Wet Bed

Over the next few days, while Amanda was alert, she couldn't speak. She was fragile, her vocal cords had been damaged due to the intubation, and her tracheotomy was also a factor. She was trying to communicate using a picture board that Speech Therapy provided, but it wasn't easy to figure out what she wanted or needed. We knew she was in extreme pain. Her back was killing her. She had been lying on her back for an extended period, and her scoliosis was probably an additional item. The doctors and nurses worked with Amanda to make her comfortable.

The news about Amanda's recovery had spread throughout the hospital. I would see nurses, doctors, therapists, and other clinicians I did not recognize stop by to see a real live and breathing miracle.

I talked with our nurse about Amanda's kidneys and when they might start working again. The nurse was telling me the same thing as the physicians. The kidneys were the last organ to recover, and there was no timetable for their recovery. She told me about how other patients with kidney failure would suddenly pee the bed, and the staff would throw a "Pee the Bed Party" because it usually meant the kidneys were starting to function again. Others did not recover and had to remain on dialysis therapy for the rest of their lives. While I hoped for the best, I wouldn't complain if Amanda had to stay on dialysis. She was alive and awake, and I wasn't going to complain or question anything about her recovery process.

Amanda was still considered critical. Her lab values were improving, but she was still deep in the woods regarding her overall condition.

Daryl and I were getting ready to leave to go and visit Mila when the nurse came in to check Amanda's wound sites. We had to step out of the room while she was doing this. A couple of minutes passed when the nurse pulled the curtain back and said, "Somebody wet the bed!" I couldn't believe it. We were talking about this a couple of hours earlier, and now she wet the bed. It was as if Amanda had willed herself to pee. While this was significant in that it meant her kidneys had started to function, it didn't mean that her dialysis was over. Some other nurses came down to Amanda's room primarily to change her bed linens, but they also celebrated with Amanda because of her "accident."

When the nurses were done with Amanda, we went back into her room and told her the good news that she had peed the bed. Amanda didn't seem to comprehend what we were telling her or its significance. We stayed for a few more minutes but then went to see Mila.

When we came into Mila's room, Deb told us how Mila was no longer on an IV for nutrition. She was getting all her food from her feeding tube and her bottle. This was also good news for us. Mila was getting close to having to go into surgery to reattach her intestines. The doctors told us that Mila would go home the week after her surgery if all went well.

While this was undoubtedly good news, it raised another set of issues for us. Where would Mila go once she was released? Mario was still at the hospital all day and night and hadn't established a connection with Mila. He was Mila's father, but Mario had built a wall that he had difficulty tearing down.

On the day Mila was born, Mario did not go and see her. The first time he saw her was when the NICU nurses brought Mila to visit Amanda a couple of days after her AFE. Mario told us he did not want to see Mila unless it was with Amanda. To him, that was the way it was supposed to be. I didn't know if he was blaming Mila for what happened to Amanda or if this was what he needed to do to cope with the situation. In any case, Mario taking Mila home was out of the question. We couldn't take Mila with us. We went to the hospital daily to be with Amanda. Debbie knew she was the most logical person to take care of Mila and did it without hesitation.

The Bond

Amanda was becoming more alert as each day passed. She was somewhat sedated so she wouldn't be in immense pain, but she wasn't without pain because the doctors were worried that if they sedated her too much, she wouldn't be alert enough for them to get a handle on how well her cognitive capabilities were.

With Mila being off her IVs, the nurses of the NICU at the Children's hospital coordinated with the nurses of the CTICU and arranged for Mila to come and visit her mommy so she could lay eyes on her for the very first time.

The CTICU nurses washed Amanda's hair, put it in a ponytail, and tied it with a yellow ribbon made from the drawstring of one of the disposable gowns everyone wore when they entered Amanda's room. We had prepped Amanda for the visit, telling her how beautiful her daughter was. Amanda's room was decorated with pictures of her family, friends, and baby. I don't know how much Amanda could comprehend that the photos of the baby were her baby. I wasn't sure what to expect when Mila arrived and was presented to her mom, but I knew I had to record it.

We didn't know precisely when Mila would arrive, so Daryl and I got to the hospital much earlier than usual. The dicey thing with Mila was the transportation. Mila had to be transported in a pediatric ambulance; there weren't many in the city. If the ambulance designated for Mila had to be used for an emergency or something more critical, the whole event could have been canceled.

We had asked Debbie to keep us posted via text when the ambulance crew arrived at Mila's room in the NICU and again when they were in the ambulance on their way. It was a bit nerve-racking waiting for the first text from Debbie. When the text came, we all started breathing again. Now all they had to do was get in the ambulance and make their way to Amanda's room. It seemed like an eternity before a text arrived stating they were on the way. Now the anticipation began for everyone as to what Amanda's reaction would be when she saw Mila for the first time.

The air was electric when the ambulance crew arrived outside Amanda's room. There were many nurses and technicians who had been working with Amanda who were milling about. Mila arrived on a gurney inside what looked like some medieval rack that held her head strictly in place and had her buckled in every way imaginable. She was the most protected little treasure I had ever seen. She was swaddled in a blanket and had a red bow with black polka dots on her head.

Debbie told us she had just been fed and was fast asleep. I was hoping she would open her eyes when Amanda saw her so they could see each other for the first time. I don't know what I was expecting to happen. Amanda wasn't communicating very well, but she looked radiant. The nurses had covered Amanda from head to toe with sterile blue sheets in order to lay the baby next to her. Once the ambulance crew had Mila ready, they carried her into Amanda's room and gave her to Mario, who placed Mila on Amanda's left side, right below her head.

Amanda was able to look down and see Mila, who was soundly sleeping. Amanda just stared at her as Mario talked to her and told her that this was their daughter. Amanda didn't have any overt reaction. She couldn't take her eyes off Mila. I don't know what she was thinking at the time. I showed Amanda the video of her and Mila's first meeting, and she told me she doesn't even remember it happening. ICU memory is terrible but can also be a blessing because she doesn't remember any of the trauma she suffered.

At one point, Mila squirmed a little as if she were trying to stretch and opened her eyes just a little and looked directly at Amanda, and Amanda returned the look. It was a beautiful moment. It was a moment that was branded in my brain. They both just held that look for seconds, and then Mila closed her eyes and went back to sleep. She never made a peep while lying next to Amanda. Amanda even closed her eyes. I could only imagine how draining this was for her.

The visit lasted 45 minutes, and then it was time to take Mila back to the NICU at the children's hospital. Mario reached down, picked Mila up, and brought her to Amanda's lips, where Amanda gave Mila her first kiss from her mommy. Which is another moment I will never forget.

While Mila and Amanda were together, I was aware of the commotion outside the room as the clinical staff strained to see inside the room. It was an event that no one thought they would see just a couple of months ago.

I left my daughter that day feeling like everything was going to be all right. I knew that Amanda had a long road to recovery and that there would probably be many ups and downs along the way, but when Amanda kissed Mila, that meant more to me than anything else. That kiss was magical. It was the beginning of a new phase of our journey.

Amanda meets Mila for the first time. The mother-child bond is undeniable.

Another Life Gone

Amanda was still going to the OR on a twice-a-week schedule. She had wound vacs and dressings that needed to be cleaned and drained consistently. The wound vacs were in place to help her open wounds heal quicker by applying negative pressure to the injury.

Amanda had four wound vacs. She had two on her abdomen, one on her right hip near her amputation, and one on her left leg, where the physicians lacerated her calf to relieve pressure and to remove necrotic tissue.

Amanda usually went on Tuesday and Friday to get the wound vacs and dressings changed. She was on approximately her 20th visit to the OR. Amanda was still not retaining her short-term memory, so we had to keep telling her why she was going to the OR. I'm sure she was frightened by all of this, and constantly reminding her was a little trying on us.

The surgeons usually tried to take Amanda to the OR early in the morning, but since her visits to the OR weren't critical, she would get bumped to later times. On one difficult visit, Amanda was bumped numerous times until she was taken later in the afternoon. Her visits to the OR were usually 90 minutes long. On this visit, when she went to the OR, Daryl and I decided to leave and visit Mila.

Mila was having a few setbacks of her own. She had developed an infection, so she was being treated with IV antibiotics. She was still on a feeding tube because the staff was still trying to figure out what formula worked best for Mila. Mila was vomiting up most formulas or wouldn't want to drink some of them. Until the staff could figure out what formula would work with Mila, she stayed at the children's hospital.

It was towards the end of our day. Daryl and I were relaxing at home when we got a call from Mario telling us that Amanda had been emergently taken to the OR. We asked what had happened. He told us that she had returned from her latest OR visit and was resting soundly. A little later, he noticed that she was in some distress. Her blood pressure was dropping. He went to get her nurse when alarms started sounding in the room. The nurse assigned to Amanda was already coming into Amanda's room, followed by other staff and physicians. They examined Amanda very quickly and noticed that the wound vac on her amputation site was drawing out large amounts of blood. They immediately called the OR and rushed Amanda to the OR. Amanda was awake and alert the entire time and was frightened beyond belief. Amanda later told me she thought she was going to die.

When Amanda came out of the OR, the surgeons told Mario that the wound vac at her amputation site had somehow shifted and latched onto her femoral artery, drawing blood out of her body. The CTICU staff had caught it fast enough that they could limit the amount of blood being drawn and therefore limit any additional damage to Amanda.

Daryl and I were relieved that this was caught and resolved so quickly but were very upset that Amanda had to witness all the chaos it caused. This was one of those scenarios where minutes mattered. We were thankful that Mario was there to alert the nurse that something was wrong with Amanda. Mario told us that Amanda was resting comfortably and would probably be out until the morning.

Like a cat with nine lives, Amanda had just lost another life. That analogy stuck with me. As I thought back about her past, I realized how true it was. Her life was spared when she crashed head-on into a concrete median. I have no idea how many times her life was spared while she was mainlining heroin. Every time she used heroin was like playing with a loaded gun. Miraculously, she survived an AFE that by all rights she had no reason to survive. The odds of a woman having an AFE during or after childbirth is 1 in 50,000. The odds of surviving the first hour of an AFE is 1 in 5 and those who do survive usually have some type of neurological damage due to the lack of oxygen to the brain during the AFE. Amanda didn't appear to have any brain damage, but it was still too early to tell. The doctors told us that in all probability she suffered at least one stroke if not more during her AFE. If I counted every time her heart stopped during her AFE then she lost three more lives. I, still to this day, cannot wrap my mind around all of this. How does a person try to comprehend what Amanda had been through without thinking that some divine intervention had occurred? Nothing else really explains it.

I went to bed that night thanking God, again, for sparing my daughter. I was certainly tired of having to do that.

Fear and Trauma

The day after Amanda's emergency OR visit, I had the opportunity to be at her bedside alone with her. Amanda was talking with the assistance of a speaking valve placed over her tracheotomy. Her talking sounded like very strained whispering. She couldn't wear the valve for long because it made it harder for her to breathe, and she would get tired and was still very weak physically.

I was sitting by her bed and talking to her about something insignificant. I can't recall what it was. At one point, Amanda looked at me and began moving her lips, trying to say something. Her speaking valve wasn't in place, so I asked the nurse if she could insert it.

Once the valve was inserted, Amanda looked at me and said, "Am I going to die?" Those five words hit me hard. All this time, I was sitting at her bedside, yammering about nonsense when all that was going through her head was if she was going to survive. I couldn't, and still can't, imagine what she was experiencing. All the trauma her body had been through was one thing, but her mind was also traumatized, and this was my first glimpse of how mentally traumatized she may be.

I got my face in front of her and said, "Amanda, I want you to look at me while I say this to you." She resisted at first, but I kept insisting. Finally, I said, "You need to look at me while I say this to you, so you understand how important this is."

She looked up at me with fear and anticipation. I said, "You are NOT going to die. You have survived so many bad things in your life and have conquered them all. When you were using heroin daily, God could have decided to take you at any moment, but he didn't. When you ran your car head-on into a median, and it was the only day you ever put on a seatbelt, you could have died then, but you didn't. When you were homeless and facing a life of misery and early death, you decided to live life the way it was intended for you and did it. You have faced so many obstacles and overcome them all, and you will overcome this one as well. You will do this because that is just who you are. You are a fighter and a survivor. You don't give up."

"You have a baby girl who needs her Momma to show her how to be a strong, independent woman, and you will do that. You are destined to do something great in this world and have yet to do it. I don't know what it is, and I can't tell you what it may be or when it will occur, but you will do something that will help others in a meaningful way. Mila is also a survivor, and she is also destined to do something good for this world."

"So, you need to know this. You are NOT going to die. I guarantee it. Do you believe me?"

While I was saying all this, it was very emotional. I had tears running down my face. Amanda looked at me with tears and said, "I believe you." Then she closed her eyes and relaxed.

This wasn't the first time I had to reassure Amanda that she wouldn't die. She still had many miles to walk on her journey, and her journey would have many obstacles in its path. My only wish was that she would be able to mentally handle these obstacles and if she waivered then I needed to be ready to help her with words, with actions, but mostly… with love.

The Left is Left

A few days later, the surgeons told us that the next time Amanda went into the OR for wound vac changes and wound care, they would assess if her left leg would also need to be amputated.

As we left our house for the drive into the hospital, my mind was spinning about what todays OR outcome could mean for the rest of Amanda's life. Missing one leg was going to be challenging for her, but two legs were a game changer. I couldn't see how she could adjust to life, probably being restricted to a wheelchair for the rest of her days.

I prayed the whole way into the hospital that day, hoping the surgeons would come out of the OR with nothing but good news. When we arrived at the hospital, Mario was sleeping in the conference room the CTICU staff let him use. Amanda was already in the OR and had been there for a couple of hours. We sat in the family visiting room with my dad and my son Dan. We didn't talk much about Amanda's possible amputation. None of us wanted to talk about the possible outcomes or what life for her might be like missing both her legs.

From previous experience, I knew that OR visits that just dealt with wound care took anywhere from 2-3 hours. As the end of the third hour approached, I was starting to get concerned and nervous. I was playing over scenarios in my mind about what the outcome of this could be. Amanda didn't even know she had lost one leg and may now lose the other. How would she process this when she was finally told? How accepting would she be of not having her legs? What would her life be like going forward?

Every minute felt like an hour, and every hour seemed like a day. We were coming close to the end of the fourth hour, and we still hadn't heard anything. Inside I was churning. Outside I tried to remain calm to keep everyone else's spirits in check.

Finally, the surgeon came out and told us that Amanda's left leg did not need to be amputated. They found that the leg had good blood circulation and was not dying. I don't know if I did it outwardly, but inside, I breathed a sigh of relief. I was dancing on the inside. The surgeon said the wound changes took a little longer because they wanted the plastic surgeons to come in and look at Amanda's various wounds. Some of the wounds would need skin grafts in the future, and they needed to determine how that would be done.

After the surgeon left us, I felt like Amanda had dodged a huge bullet. With all the bad things that had happened to her, she finally was getting a significant break. Hopefully, this was going to be a new trend for her. I know I was praying that it would be.

Intestinal Fortitude

Mila, for the most part, was doing ok at the NICU. She had some minor setbacks while she was there. She still wasn't bottle feeding with formula and still had the feeding tube in her nose. She was taking in donated breast milk, but that would not be an option when she was discharged. Mila also had an infection that the doctors were treating with IV antibiotics. These things were delaying her surgery which would reattach her intestines and remove her stoma.

The stoma was a source of pain for Mila because the bag they had attached to her was not making a good seal around the stoma, causing the bag to leak. When the bag leaked, it would need to be changed out. Removing the bag was painful because it was attached to Mila's skin with adhesive, and the more they changed it, the more irritated her skin became. The bag was intended to stay on for at least 3-4 days but was being changed almost daily. The surgeons had increased the stoma's size to alleviate this, but it was unsuccessful.

Getting Mila's intestines reattached was the only thing that would solve this. All the NICU nurses were attentive to Mila and quick to comfort her when she was crying. Mario's mom, Debbie, was still staying with Mila almost daily and at night. She would go home occasionally to sleep in her bed and get rejuvenated, but for the most part, she lived at the children's hospital. She would tell us stories of when she would be sleeping in Mila's room, waking up and finding a nurse holding Mila, and soothing her when she was having a rough night. The nursing staff was just amazing!

Finally, Mila was cleared for surgery to reattach her intestines in late September. The intestinal tract had grown enough to make the surgery possible, along with her infection clearing up.

Mila was in surgery for a few hours but came out of it in good shape. The surgery was a success, the stoma was gone, and Mila had a long horizontal incision just above her belly button. She was asleep most of the day of her surgery, but when we saw her the next day, she was back to being her lovable self.

The next step in her recovery was to get back to the bottle feeds. Mila still wasn't taking her bottle feeds, and the staff believed that the formula they were trying to use with her was upsetting her stomach. It became a process of elimination for the nursing staff from the various formulas at their disposal.

The nursing staff wasn't pushing the limits with Mila. She had a rough start to life and was still a preemie, so they were handling her with kid gloves. We all appreciated the staff and physicians at the children's hospital. They treated us very well and treated Mila like the princess she deserved to be.

Parched

After Amanda was no longer intubated and was aware of her surroundings, she constantly asked for something to drink. Because she was in a coma for so long, she wasn't permitted to drink anything. The only thing she could have were sponge swabs moistened with water. These would be rubbed inside her mouth to try and relieve the dryness she was feeling but right from the beginning, Amanda made us aware that she was not satisfied with the swabs.

When Amanda first came out of her coma, it was challenging to figure out what she wanted because she wasn't speaking and had minimal finger movements. We had a list of items the CTICU staff provided us with that were the most requested. We would go down the list with Amanda until we got to the item she wanted. Most of the time, it was for water and food—neither thing she could have.

We would offer her the swabs, and she would take them at first, but as the days wore on, she was getting frustrated and wanted something she could drink. Since Amanda's short-term memory was not functioning yet, we had to explain daily that she could not have water or food until she passed a swallow test.

The speech therapists were the ones who performed the swallow test, and they scheduled Amanda to have the test, but they weren't very optimistic that she would pass it. They explained that it's not unusual for someone who had been intubated for an extended time and then had a tracheotomy for an even longer period not to pass the test on their first attempt.

They administered the swallow test to Amanda, who passed on the first attempt! The speech therapist was amazed. After the test, Amanda was approved to have thin liquids.

It was a joy to watch her drink water. She swallowed it

slowly and under the watchful eye of her nurse. After it was determined that she was handling the water, she was approved for flavored waters and pureed foods.

Amanda wasn't a fan of the pureed foods the hospital gave her. She's always been a very particular eater. Pasta was always her favorite dish, and she didn't like the pureed pasta and meatballs they brought her.

Not long after she began ingesting food, she would be overcome with nausea and vomiting. This wasn't too concerning to the physicians. They believed that being nauseous was bound to happen since she had not eaten anything for months. The feeding tube was still providing Amanda with nourishment, so she would not starve.

Unfortunately, this was the beginning of months of nausea for Amanda that perplexed one physician after another who encountered her.

Hard Day Away

It was the middle of September, and I was away on a golf trip I had signed up for before Amanda's AFE. It had been a tough two months, and I was looking forward to being about 60 miles away for two days playing golf with my neighbors and friends.

Dr. Nickle had approached us the Friday before I left and said that she wanted to tell Amanda about her right leg being amputated. I asked her to please hold off until I returned from my trip, but she was afraid that Amanda might discover that her right leg was missing and felt it was best to tell her before that happened. I wasn't asking her to hold off for long. We could tell her in five days rather than three. I was hoping Dr. Nickle would wait until I returned.

I drove out to the golf destination on Monday morning. I had an early afternoon tee time and was looking forward to taking my mind off my daughter's situation. I finished my round about four hours later and had an enjoyable time. I was sitting in the hotel lounge waiting for the other groups to complete their rounds when my cell phone rang. It was Amanda.

I answered the call saying, "Hey, Sweetie! How are you feeling today?" She said, "Dad, did you know they took my right leg off?" My stomach sank. Dr. Nickle didn't wait for me to get back. She had told Amanda that afternoon. I was sick that I wasn't there, but I couldn't let that deter me from telling Amanda what I knew I had to say to her. First, I told her I was extremely sorry I wasn't there when she was told about her leg being amputated.

I told Amanda, "Your right leg was in terrible shape and dying. It was in such bad shape that it wasn't permitting your liver to heal. The fear was that if your leg wasn't removed, your liver would fail, and you would die. It was one of the most difficult, yet easiest decision we ever had to make, and we made it with love. If I had to do it all over again, I wouldn't change anything."

I also told Amanda, "I never loved you because of your right leg. I loved you because of who you are. I couldn't imagine life without you in it, and I wasn't willing to take a chance with your life to keep a leg that would probably be useless to you even if there was some way they could have saved it."

Amanda had me on speakerphone, and Daryl and Mario were with her, echoing my sentiments. We then all told her about the medical community's significant prosthetic advances. We tried painting a rosy picture of life for her with a prosthetic leg. She'll still be able to drive a car, take her baby for walks, and do anything she wanted. I was saying all these things to her, but in the back of my mind, I knew that if it were me on the other end of this conversation, I would be extremely depressed over the loss of a limb.

My next fear was if Amanda was suffering from "ICU memory", we would have to explain the amputation of her right leg to her again and again until she could retain that information. I prayed that would not happen.

I didn't sleep well that night. My mind kept spinning around the conversation I had with Amanda earlier. I kept hoping I had said the right things and that she would remain positive and want to live her life to the fullest.

The next day I didn't do well at all. I woke up after a few hours of sleep with a pounding headache. It was a pounding behind my eyeballs that I couldn't shake. My tee time was early Tuesday morning, and I didn't play well. I couldn't wait to get off the golf course and return home. My heart just wasn't in it. Thinking that distracting myself would give me a mental break had been a bad mistake. I did nothing but think about Amanda the whole time.

Driving home, I could only think about seeing Amanda the next day and letting her know I loved her.

Progress

It was the beginning of October. Amanda and Mila were both making some progress. Mila's improvement was more pronounced. After her intestines had been reattached, the big quest was to find a formula that didn't upset her stomach. That took many tries with various formulas, but it appeared that the NICU staff had found one that worked for her.

Mila was getting close to being discharged. She had been putting on weight, but, in the beginning, it was at a slow pace. The physicians were taking it slow with her because of her feeding issues and wanted to ensure that when Mila was discharged, there would be no return visits.

Amanda's physicians had told us in early September that she would probably be in the CTICU until December. Now there was talk that she might be moved from the CTICU soon. She was communicating better and taking in fluids and some pureed food, but she was still extremely nauseous. The physicians felt that maybe the feeding tube she had was in a location in her stomach that was causing nausea. They decided to move the feeding tube beyond her stomach and into her intestine in the hope that it would help her.

This procedure was done at her bedside and didn't take more than 30 minutes to be completed. A few days later, Amanda was still experiencing nausea which would cause her to vomit after she ate or had too much to drink. This wasn't causing the physicians too much concern because she was getting nourishment from the feeding tube.

The physicians began trying different nausea medications on Amanda, hoping one would help her. Amanda was already on a boatload of meds, and the thought was that a combination of the meds was causing her nausea. Unfortunately, figuring out the correct combination would be a trial-and-error process that could take weeks or months.

Amanda's daily lab report kept improving gradually, which

was why there were discussions about moving her out of the CTICU. For us, this was great news! We took it to mean that Amanda was becoming less "critical." But we weren't becoming delusional by this thought. The doctors kept reminding us that Amanda's recovery would probably be measured not in weeks or months but in all probability, it would take years.

While I heard those words and my mind understood them, I didn't realize what that timeframe would be like. I didn't understand the scope of the journey we would be on or all the highs and lows that would come our way.

State of Minds

When something of the magnitude that happened to Amanda starts to settle somewhat, it allows those involved to begin processing the events that brought them to where they are and the ramifications surrounding them.

Let me explain what I mean. Until Amanda came out of her coma, I would not permit myself to speculate on what the future might be like for her. I'm not saying those thoughts didn't enter my mind, but when I didn't know if she was going to survive her coma or from all the damage done to her body, I would stop myself from trying to gaze into the crystal ball so I could predict what her future may be like.

It was the middle of October, and Amanda had slowly gained some traction in her remarkable recovery. She had been to the OR on 30 occasions since July 20th, and the doctors were now discussing performing skin grafts that needed to be done on her right hip and abdomen.

I knew Mario was struggling. He was doing a great job of being invested and in control of Amanda's well-being, but he wasn't addressing his trauma. His family and the staff suggested that he reach out to get some help with processing all that he had been through and talk about it with a neutral party that could hopefully either begin to make some sense of a senseless situation for him or help him to recognize the importance of vocalizing his fears and uncertainties.

How does a young man grasp the enormity of the situation without fear or trepidation? The answer, of course, is that you can't. I knew he probably wasn't fully comprehending how life-changing this would be for him, Amanda, and Mila. I don't know how I would have dealt with my wife coming so close to death at such a young age. I don't know how I would face the future knowing that the woman who meant the world to me would be disabled for the rest of her life and that I would probably be the primary caregiver for my child. I remember when Daryl and I had our son Danny how comforting it was knowing that I had her by my side to take care of him. That Daryl would give him that motherly love he would need. I would have been in a panic if Daryl hadn't been there. I don't know how I would have functioned. I hate to project my feelings on others, but I couldn't help but think Mario was facing the future with an overabundance of fear.

Because of my knowledge of the causes of opioid addiction, I was very much in fear of Mario returning to using heroin to suppress his feelings. One of the bad things I learned when attending Narcotics Anonymous meetings was of how people who had years of "clean" time returned to using because of some trauma they had experienced.

I knew Mario and Amanda were not attending NA meetings as they used to because life was getting in the way. They had a business they were building, which kept them busy, they were pregnant, and getting their home ready for a newborn. They surrounded themselves with friends who were all in recovery, so they all kept tabs on each other and supported each other when life became difficult. Right after the AFE, Amanda and Mario's friends were all at the hospital and helped by either spending time with Mario, being at Amanda's bedside, or helping to decorate her room with pictures of family, friends, and Mila. They supported Amanda and Mario, but as time wore on and days turned to weeks, life took over, and slowly her friends returned to work and their lives. Their visits became shorter and less frequent.

I am not judging anyone! This is what happens in situations like this. You must go back to your life and try to get back to visit as soon as you can or as soon as your schedule allows. I only tell you this because as Mario was spending all his time at the hospital taking care of Amanda, he was neglecting taking care of himself. I asked him numerous times if he thought that calling his NA sponsor was something he needed to do. But he always said he was fine. I couldn't force him to make that call, but I wished he would.

I also offered to take him to an NA meeting. I had no

evidence that he was using narcotics, but that wasn't why I thought it would be good for him to go. If you've ever been to an NA meeting, you've seen and felt the love in those meetings. You've seen how they embrace someone who is struggling and stay with them and provide support for them. I thought Mario needed that right now. But I've also learned that you have no control over this; all you can do is plant a seed and hope it takes root and grows.

I was also concerned for Daryl's state of mind and her physical state. With her having Muscular Dystrophy, I was always watching her to determine if she was handling the pace of our days. I would let her sleep until late morning, then we would be off to the hospital to spend the afternoon with Amanda and then the evening with Mila. We usually got home by 8 pm for a late dinner before doing it again the next day. When I saw indications that she was in pain, I would tell her we were taking a day off to decompress.

As far as Daryl's state of mind was concerned, I knew she was one tough girl. We had both lived through Amanda's addiction years and survived those because we believed in each other and what we were doing. We communicated our thoughts and planned everything accordingly. We're a great team together. We always have been. I knew if we lost Amanda, we would be damaged, but we would be damaged together and fix each other. Our bond, which started more than 40 years ago when we were just a couple of kids in high school, is stronger than anything I've ever experienced and has never weakened.

Graduation Day

It was the middle of October, and Mila was doing so much better. She recovered very well from her surgery, and the staff had finally figured out what formula Mila could hold down.

The doctors told Debbie that Mila would be discharged in a couple of days, which made us a little anxious about raising a baby and the care a baby needs. Of course, we all had children, but we were in our later years of life, and caring for a baby full-time was daunting.

Mila's graduation day came up, and the children's hospital staff had Mila dressed in a cap and gown in her car seat. Debbie carried her down the hallway with staff lined up on both sides down to the elevators waving pink pom poms and playing graduation music through the overhead sound system.

We couldn't witness it because Amanda was going into the O.R. again, and we wanted to spend some time with her before her procedure. Thankfully Mario recorded it on his phone, and Debbie posted it to Facebook for all of us.

Mila was going to live at Debbie and Joe's home. They had set up a nursery for Mila in a spare bedroom. I didn't envy Debbie and Joe having to get up at night and take care of a newborn, plus all the daily responsibilities that came with that.

Thankfully my sister, Mary Jo, and her husband, Alan, were able to take Mila for a few days every couple of weeks to give them a break. Plus, my sister loved every minute she had with Mila.

Daryl and I would take her for a night when we could, and having Mila around brightened our spirit. She was getting little tuffs of bright red hair and had the bluest eyes I had ever seen. I would tell everyone she had my blue eyes, but truth be told, her eyes were much bluer than mine.

Mila settled into a routine of care with her family, and we all began raising a child until her parents could take those reins.

Moving Day

The hospital Amanda was in had to do some repairs to the AC units on the roof of the building she was in. The windows to the ICU looked out onto a road that was going to be closed so a crane could lift the units onto the roof. The hospital determined that for all patients and staff to stay safe, they would be moved out of the units that faced the crane and road. This was done in case the crane malfunctioned and the AC units hit the side of the hospital while it was being lifted. All the CTICU patients in Amanda's section of the CTICU were temporarily transferred for the weekend to a PACU until the work was completed.

The PACU was not intended for ICU patients like Amanda, who had many IVs and medical equipment that had to move with her. Once Amanda was in the PACU, the CTICU physician in charge realized that the cramped quarters were not a good fit for her. Within hours he had Amanda transferred to the Trauma ICU. At the time, we didn't know that Amanda was finished with the CTICU for good. The Trauma ICU was her new home now.

One of the problems with moving to the Trauma ICU was that they had some stringent visitation rules. Until then, Mario was spending every day and night at the hospital. While Amanda was in the CTICU, Mario spent all his waking hours in her room and slept in a small conference room at night. He also was able to go into her room at any time. The trauma ICU did not allow the family to walk in without first calling into the unit and getting let in by the staff. They also had visiting hours that ended at 9 pm. This prevented Mario from staying until Amanda was sound asleep. While this was difficult for Amanda to accept, it was good for Mario because it gave him a chance to decompress without feeling guilty that he was neglecting her.

Amanda didn't last long in the Trauma ICU as they deemed her to no longer have a "Critical" status. They had her moved to the Trauma Step Down Unit within a week. She was placed in a private room where her next care phase began. We always hoped that physical and occupational rehab would intensify, but Amanda was constantly nauseous and in extreme pain. She was throwing up almost everything she ate. The doctors were always trying new anti-nausea meds, but this was a situation where a new med was introduced, and then time would have to pass to determine if it would work.

Amanda slept quite a bit because of how weak she was and the pain medication they had her on. She was getting dialysis every other day, which also took its toll on her. My poor girl was surviving, but it wasn't the most pleasant way to survive.

Sharing My Thanks

When Mila was in the NICU right after she was born, my nephew brought it to my attention that the Nurse Director of the NICU was his best friend's mother. She told my nephew that if we needed anything while Mila was there, we should have the staff contact her.

A few days after Amanda's AFE episode, we discovered that the AFE Foundation, which is located in southern California, was coming to the maternity hospital, where Amanda suffered her AFE, to conduct a presentation. We asked my nephew if he could contact the NICU Director and let her know we would be interested in attending it.

We found out a few days later that we could attend, but since it was meant only for the clinical staff, we would need to sit in the back of the auditorium and keep a low profile.

On the day of the presentation, as we were told, Daryl and I entered the auditorium quietly and searched for seats in the back. Unfortunately for us, all the seats towards the back were occupied. The only seats available were closer to the middle front of the auditorium. Since most of the people were clinicians, they were in nursing attire, had scrubs, or wore white lab coats. I felt like Daryl and I stuck out like sore thumbs. I was hoping no one would approach us and ask us to leave. I felt like it was so apparent that we didn't belong there.

Shortly after Amanda's AFE, we heard the maternity hospital had another patient who had suffered an AFE a few months before Amanda's. Despite the efforts of the clinical staff, this mom did not survive. I had heard that a documented AFE had never occurred within its walls before this episode, so the hospital administration arranged for the AFE Foundation to be present and conduct the presentation we were attending. The odds were astronomical that a second AFE would occur at the same hospital, separated by a few months.

Two AFE staff members were conducting the presentation. Miranda Klassen, the Executive Director, and Stephanie Arnold, Director, were introduced, and the presentation began. Both women were AFE survivors and related their experiences as they discussed the topic of AFE. As they were speaking on the subject, I was transported back to the day of my daughter's AFE. I found myself feeling very emotional. I knew I was suffering from PTSD. At one point in the presentation, they spoke about the two recent AFEs at the hospital and took a moment to point out that Daryl and I were in the audience. So much for keeping a low profile. I felt like all eyes were on us then. I was still having difficulty and was thinking about getting up and leaving the room so that I could breathe.

Somehow, I made it through that presentation, and at the end, both Miranda and Stephanie approached Daryl and me. There was a hope that these women could visit with Amanda so Amanda could see that not only was survival from an AFE possible but that having a meaningful, purpose-filled life was also possible. Mario's mom, Debbie, had found the AFE foundation online and had been interacting with Miranda for a few weeks. Debbie had asked Miranda previously if she could visit Amanda when she was in Pittsburgh.

They did visit my daughter, but when I asked Amanda about the visit a couple of months later, she could not remember them being there.

While speaking to these ladies, another woman and man approached us. They introduced themselves as the CEO and Director of Nursing of the hospital. They passed along their best wishes for a complete and speedy recovery for Amanda and said if we needed anything from them, please ask.

Without hesitation, I asked if it was possible to meet with the clinical staff that was a part of the team who provided for my daughter's immediate care after the AFE. I told them how I worked at a sister hospital for almost 30 years and many of those years were spent interacting with the clinical staff. I told them that from those interactions and friendships I had made with the staff, I knew there were many occasions where they had seen their patients in the worst medical condition imaginable. Some of these patients did not survive, and I had seen the reaction of the staff when that occurred.

I told them that on the day of Amanda's AFE, when Daryl and I were escorted to the room to see Vinny, we had passed the doorway to the nursing station on that floor. I saw in the nursing station that the staff was having a meeting and did not appear to be in the best shape. Their mood was somber, and I knew that this was the staff that had attended to my daughter. I told the CEO and Director of Nursing that meeting with the staff was essential for me so I could let them know how much their efforts meant to my family and me.

I think they were taken aback by this request, but the CEO said he didn't consider it unreasonable. The Director of Nursing asked me to give her a couple of weeks so she could find out what staff was in the room on that day. She gave me her contact info, and we left and went back to Amanda's room.

A few weeks later, I contacted the Director of Nursing, and we selected a mutual date, time, and location for the meeting. On the day of the meeting, I kept telling myself to keep it together when I met these wonderful people.

I was greeted by the Nursing Director and taken to a conference room where the staff had already assembled and had a lunch buffet in place. I wasn't expecting the food, and my stomach was so nervous that I passed on eating. After I was sure everyone had food and drink, I moved to the front of the room and introduced myself as Amanda's father.

I told them about my exposure and interactions with the clinical staff where I used to work. I talked about how I had seen the staff at the nurse's station on the day of my daughter's AFE and had seen its effects on the staff.

I told them of my daughter's status when she went into surgery to repair her liver, how we were told she was not going to survive, how many surgeries she had been through, how we feared she may have suffered permanent brain damage, and how we celebrated her miracle recovery from her coma.

I told them all this so they could understand that my daughter would not be alive without them and their efforts, no matter the rib lacerations to her liver. They had done the unthinkable and performed CPR on her for 37 minutes. I had never heard of such a thing. I told them that the only thing I could think of that drove them to work so hard to keep Amanda alive was the death of their previous AFE patient.

I told them I was traumatized by all I had experienced over the last couple of months. I told them that if they felt traumatized also, they needed to share that so they could begin to heal. I thanked them for saving my daughter's life, and I promised them that she was going to make a difference somehow, someway, and that they should take comfort in knowing that what they did on that day, no matter how small, was going to be remembered and celebrated by my family and me forever.

That staff, on that day, had saved Amanda's life, and they should have nothing but pride in knowing they did what they were trained to do and did it very well.

When I was done speaking, I had almost every staff member come up to me and express gratitude for requesting this meeting and how much it meant to them.

In the six months prior to Amanda's AFE, there were twelve AFEs nationwide. Amanda was the sole survivor. As did the previous twelve, my daughter could have died in that first hour. These heroic people were bound and determined not to let that happen to Amanda. I will be forever grateful for their determination and commitment to patient care.

Thanks & Giving

Thanksgiving was approaching quickly, and Amanda was still battling severe nausea. She was having difficulty holding any food or liquid. She still had a feeding tube, but even with that in place, she was vomiting so much that we were concerned that she might not get enough nutrition even from the feeding tube.

The doctors were trying everything, but the rub was that when they would start a new antinausea medication, they had to wait a couple of weeks to see if it worked. Amanda was also very combative with the clinical staff. She was in so much pain that she didn't want anyone touching or poking her. She didn't like the rehab staff touching her body because everything hurt her.

We, as a family, knew that Amanda couldn't continue this behavior. We told the staff to ignore her complaints and do whatever they had to do. We talked to Amanda about being less combative, but she was still not mentally with us. I tried to imagine what it must be like to begin delivering the baby you couldn't wait to hold, only to wake up weeks later unable to move or communicate, in severe pain, and not knowing anything about what caused you to be where and how you were.

No matter how often we would tell her how close to death she came, she didn't experience it. She didn't see it. She didn't understand it. All she knew was that she didn't want anyone to touch her because it hurt; she couldn't eat regular food without getting sick and couldn't do anything for herself.

Amanda was still on dialysis, but because she was frequently urinating, the kidney doctor was leaning towards taking her off daily dialysis and having it done every few days. Amanda was making progress, but it was prolonged. She still could not move her arms or use her hands. She had regained enough strength to start moving her head, but it was not with any significant range of motion.

During the time Amanda was in the CTICU, she had an O2 saturation clip on her left earlobe to measure the oxygen in her blood. Because of her deteriorating condition, she developed a sore under the clip. The staff moved the clip to the other ear and then tried a clip on her fingers and different locations. One problem for Amanda, though, was when she fell asleep, her head would always tilt to the left, and she would wake up a short time later because the wound on her ear would begin hurting.

The nursing staff of the unit she was in wanted to help heal that sore on her earlobe. The nursing staff was trying everything to help her keep her head from turning left. We finally rolled up some foam the nurses gave us, enclosed it in a pillow cover, and used that to prop up the left side of her head and not permit her head to roll to the left. This was just one of the little things that Amanda had to battle. There were so many more.

Thanksgiving came to Amanda's room with some help from a chain food restaurant selling Thanksgiving meals. Daryl and I grabbed all the traditional food and headed to the hospital to spend the day with Amanda, Mario, and my son Dan. The day before, Mario's aunt and his cousin helped put up Christmas decorations in her room to give it a festive mood and hopefully brighten Amanda's outlook. The room was decorated as much as the hospital permitted, but I thought it looked very festive, and it did seem to put Amanda in a holiday mood. Of course, we had a football game on the TV, ate our meal, and thanked all the nurses, techs, doctors, and support staff who gave my daughter the care she needed. We bought a tray of cookies and brought them to the nursing station. The nurses were grateful for the cookies and shared them with the other support staff.

Thanksgiving had more purpose for us in 2019. Instead of mourning the loss of our daughter, we gave thanks for our current blessings and whatever future blessings we knew were coming Amanda's way.

Specialty

We had heard rumblings from the nurses and doctors that Amanda was at a point where they felt she could be transferred to a specialty hospital. This specialty hospital was located on a specific floor in another building within the same hospital complex.

Before the move, Mario and I arranged to meet the Director of this specialty hospital and see what Amanda's accommodations would be. We were happy to know that she would have a large private room and that they would bring her current bed with her. Having the bed was extremely important. Amanda was in a sand bed whose sole purpose was to ensure she did not develop any bed sores. Even with this bed, Amanda would become uncomfortable and need to be turned to take pressure off her back. We also discussed the need for a different call button for Amanda because her fingers were not strong enough to push the regular controller. Their solution was to put Amanda in a room across the hall from the nursing station so it would be easier for the nurses and support staff to check on her periodically during the day and to be able to see into her room so they could provide timely assistance.

When Mario was in the room, he would turn Amanda himself and place pillows under her so she could not roll back. She could only lie on her back or sides. When the surgeons no longer needed to get to Amanda's liver to wrap it in gauze, they couldn't close her abdomen because the core stomach muscles had relaxed, as did the skin. They couldn't perform the surgery to reattach Amanda's stomach muscles because her condition was so critical that they were concerned she might be unable to survive the surgery. The surgeons placed a mesh over her open stomach and skin grafts over the mesh to protect the wound from infection. The plan was to revisit the core muscle reattachment surgery when she was physically stronger. This was just one of the many surgeries Amanda had done and was one of the reasons she would make numerous trips to the O.R.

I had not seen Amanda's stomach or the stump that used to be her right leg. I couldn't bring myself to look at them. Anytime the nurses had to do anything with her stomach or leg stump, I would leave the room. I couldn't do it. I was ashamed of myself for being like that, but I couldn't do it. I always made an excuse about respecting Amanda's privacy, but that wasn't the real reason.

On December 3, 2019, Amanda was moved to the specialty hospital. Their charge was to continue Amanda's current care and rehab her muscles. At this point, Amanda had regained some movement in her fingers and a little strength in her hands. She still could not feed herself or give herself a drink. She didn't have that mobility or strength yet. Her lungs were also still fragile. She struggled to cough, and her diaphragm was also very weak. Because of this, Amanda would have to have her lungs suctioned out almost daily. She hated it. The respiratory therapist would have to slip a small tube down her throat to her lungs, and it would pull out phlegm that was accumulating in her lungs. I've never had this done, so I couldn't even imagine what that must feel like. There was no way it could be pleasant.

After a few days of Amanda being in the Specialty hospital, it became apparent that the hospital was understaffed. In the ICU, because the nurse-to-patient ratio is so low, they are usually in the room in seconds or minutes when you call for a nurse or support member. At the specialty hospital, this was not the case.

Mario started going back to work during the day, so when Daryl and I would show up at noon, we were the ones who would help with Amanda's needs until Mario would show up after work. The first full day that Amanda was in her new location, she complained to us that she would try to press the call button for the nurse, but she couldn't do it. She said she would try to call out, but her voice was weak, and she was sure they couldn't hear her. We took this with a grain of salt, thinking that this wasn't an ICU, so a slower response time was something that Amanda would have to get used to. We thought she might be exaggerating about the 30 minutes.

When we were there, Daryl and I would take care of most of her needs, and if we needed anything special from the nurse or support staff, we would go to the nurse's station to get what we needed.

As I wrote earlier, Mario would turn her as she needed when he was with Amanda. When it was just Daryl and me, I would try to turn her, but if I couldn't get her in the right spot or if she was still complaining about a part of her body being in pain, I would have to call for help.

When we first arrived, the staff was attentive to helping us move Amanda, but as time passed, we noticed that they would take longer to respond to our requests for assistance. Sometimes we waited at least 30 minutes for someone to help us. When someone would show up, they would apologize for the wait but tell us they were assisting other patients. We just figured this was not an ICU, so we would have to get used to extended wait times.

Here Comes Santa Claus!

One of the things that saddened Amanda was that she couldn't spend the holidays with Mila the way she had envisioned before July 20th. She wanted to be there when Mila had her first pictures taken with Santa. She wanted to be with Mila when she saw her first decorated tree. She couldn't do many things that she wanted, which bothered her.

Mario, Daryl, and I would tell her that Mila was too young to experience these things and that her next holiday season would be one that she would remember and would be more meaningful to her. Amanda wasn't buying it, and it showed.

Mario's mom, Debbie, somehow found a couple that would dress up like Santa and Mrs. Claus and visit people who needed holiday cheer. Debbie reached out to this couple and arranged for them to come to Amanda's room.

Amanda's room had been decorated with holiday decorations. We put up battery-operated lights, a small decorated tree, and other banners and signs. Not only did this brighten up Amanda's room it also brightened up her mood.

Debbie brought Mila into the hospital so she could meet Santa for the first time and also get her first picture with Santa with Amanda being present. Daryl and I arrived at the hospital a little earlier than usual, just in time to see Santa and Mrs. Claus. They looked very authentic! They were dressed in red outfits trimmed with white fur, and this Santa did not need a fake beard! It was the real thing!

They spent about an hour and came with small gifts for Amanda and Mila. They did this on their own. Debbie wanted them to bring Amanda a festive mood and get pictures with Santa, Mrs. Claus, and my daughter's family. It was lovely of them to take time out of their lives to be with us. We got some great photos and videos. We all felt very blessed for this special day.

After they left, I thought, "This is what the holiday season is about… giving to others without expecting anything in return."

The holiday season had kicked off on the right foot, and we hoped this would inspire Amanda to work hard to regain mobility! We were all looking forward to a better 2020.

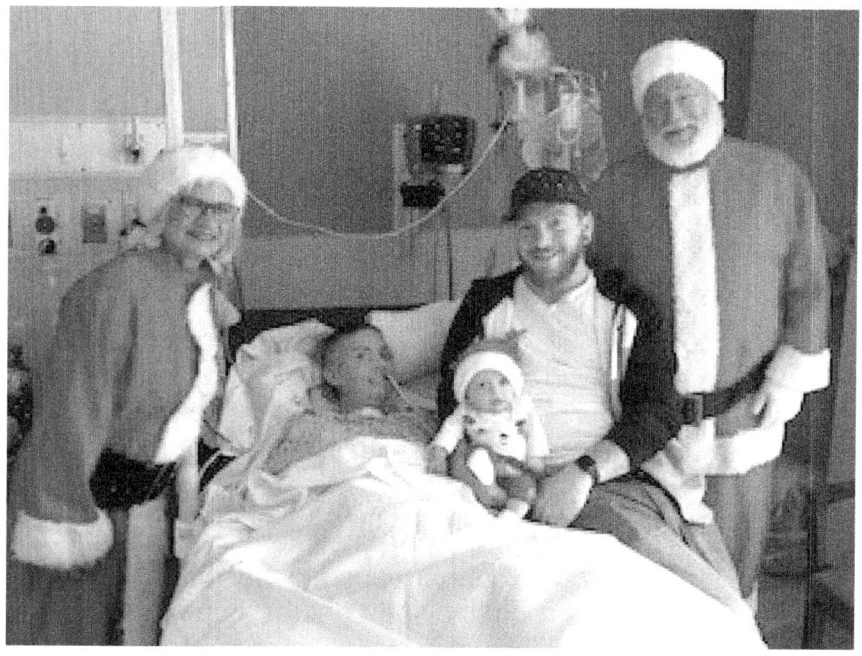

Amanda, Mario, and Mila get a very special visit From Santa and Mrs. Claus. Special thanks to Mr. and Mrs. Claus for making a family smile during the holiday season.

A Message from Amanda

On December 11, 2020, Amanda posted her first message on Facebook since her AFE. (I edited out the names of the hospitals but below is that message.)

Sorry I've been so MIA. I've been kinda tied up lately fighting for my life! 😊 I just want to give everyone an update since so many people have asked for one. First of all I'm not the one typing this because I haven't regained the full use of my hands or fingers. I've been in the hospital for 145 days and while I had a very difficult beginning I am now well on my way to a miraculous recovery. In the next few weeks I will begin an intensive rehab at ***** and after that I will be able to be at home with my baby girl Mila. I want to thank everyone who called, texted (even though I haven't been able to respond), wrote, sent cards, visited, contributed to my GoFundMe, and everything in between. I may not have been able to acknowledge each you but I felt you all in my heart. I swear because of you I was able to survive this. I do have one request though... I would love to have visitors. Disclaimer: I may not look my best but I'm still me. I'm in ***** Hospital in the ****** Hospital located on the 8th floor. This is where I'm beginning my rehab. I want to give a special thanks to my mom and dad for being there every step of the way, to my mother and father in law, Debbie and Joe, for taking such good care of my baby, and especially my husband Mario, who has lived at the hospital with me and only leaves my side to keep our business running. You are my rock! I'm so grateful to be alive and see another day. Keep praying for me and hopefully I'll be home soon.

Cue Balls

When Amanda came out of her coma, it had been roughly six weeks since her AFE. While she was in the coma, the CTICU nurses did what they could to wash her hair and body and keep her clean, but if you knew my daughter, you would understand how meticulous she is about her appearance.

Amanda would have her hair, nails, eyebrows, and eyelashes done consistently. She always wanted to look her best for Mario and enjoyed the pampering. She had all those items taken care of before she went into the hospital to give birth so that she would look great for photos with Mila right after her birth. Over time her eyelashes had to be removed along with her hair extensions.

I had started to notice that when I would visit Amanda, I would see stray strands of her hair on her pillow. I would remove them and throw them out. I saw Daryl remove a few strands of hair and throw them in the trash. As the weeks rolled on, it became apparent that Amanda's hair was coming out more and more.

Amanda was on many different medications while in her coma and immediately after regaining consciousness. We were told that the combination of drugs and the trauma to her body were factors in her hair loss, and this was not unusual in patients who suffered the amount of trauma that Amanda did.

When Amanda was in the Step-Down Trauma Unit, Mario arranged to have Amanda's hair stylist come in and style Amanda's hair. With the help of the nurses and support staff, she was able to wash Amanda's hair, dry it and style it to a degree. This was great for Amanda's psyche. It made her feel a little more like herself.

By the time Amanda made it to the specialty hospital in December 2019, it was very apparent that her hair was getting very thin. There was no stopping the hair loss. It was significantly damaged and coming out very quickly. We started discussing with Amanda the thought of having her head shaved so that new hair could grow.

Amanda was resistant to this. It upset her to lose her hair, and the thought of shaving her head was just too much. Daryl would remind Amanda how Daryl's sister Terry, who had cancer and underwent chemotherapy, had lost all her hair and had her head shaved. She reminded Amanda how quickly Terry's hair grew back and thicker than ever.

Amanda was struggling with this. Deep down, she knew she needed to shave her head, but being able to admit it was more complex. Finally, I told Amanda that if she shaved her head that I would do the same thing right next to her after she was done.

That seemed to be the kicker. Amanda agreed to have her head shaved if I would do it. I volunteered Mario to shave his head, but Amanda said, "No!!" She loved Mario's red hair and didn't want him to shave it off.

On December 19, 2019, with Daryl, Debbie, Joe, Mila, Mario, me, and Amanda's hairstylist in attendance, Amanda had her head shaved, and then I followed suit. It didn't take long to take the hair off. Once it was gone, my head felt a little lighter, but my heart felt full because I saw how well Amanda handled having her head shaved.

I had Daryl take a picture of Amanda and me while holding Mila. We posted the photo on the Facebook page called Amanda's Journey. In the post, we told followers how Amanda was losing her hair and had to shave her hair and how in the spirit of the moment, I shaved mine also. We asked followers to judge who had the best toe-head, Amanda, Mila, or me.

I didn't win, but I didn't care, because I felt like a winner already.

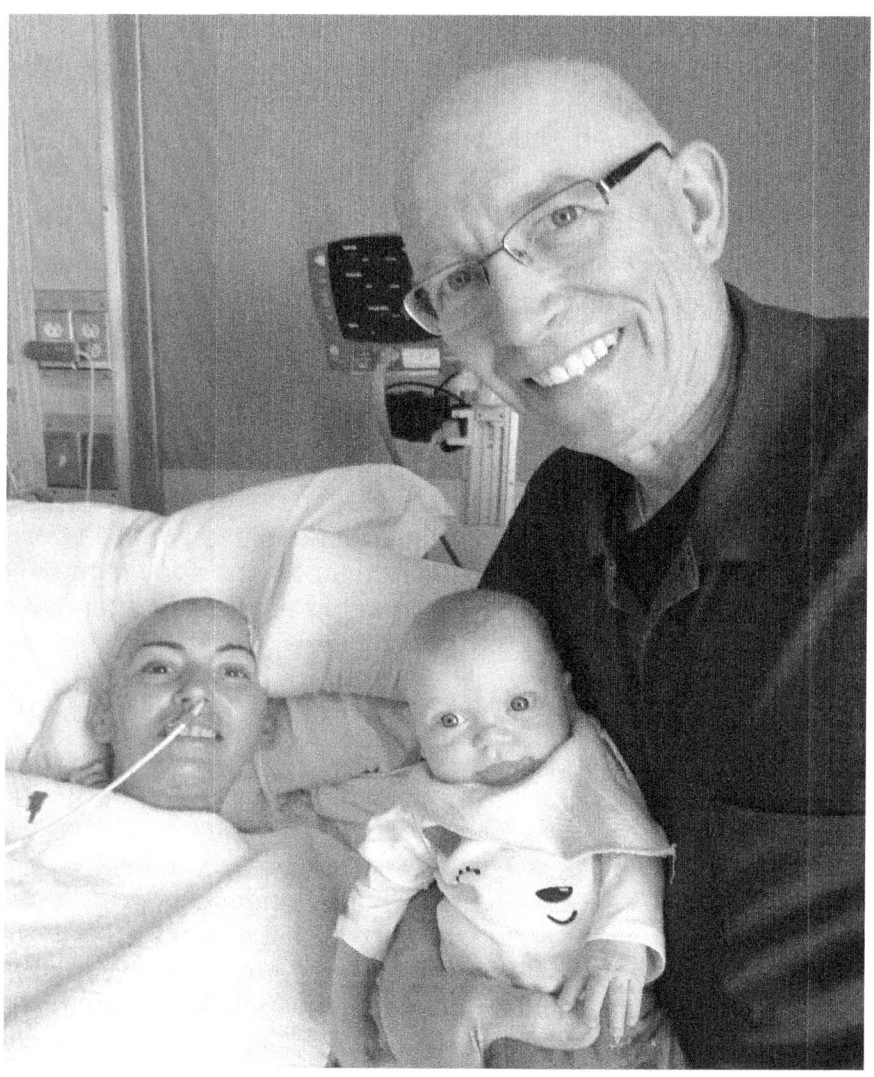

Which one of the Cue Balls looks the best?! Note two things… Amanda still had her feeding tube which kept her nutrition levels at an appropriate level and the foam pillow which stopped her head from rolling to her left so that her left ear could heal.

All I Want for Christmas Is...

I wasn't feeling much holiday spirit on December 25th. I was grateful for having my daughter with us today, but it wasn't the way I knew she would have wanted to celebrate her first Christmas with her new daughter. I hoped she could see through all her pain and uncertainty about what life had in store for her, but that was a big ask.

Amanda was still in constant pain. She was constantly nauseous. The doctors were concerned with her nutrition and her weight loss. She still had the feeding tube, but she and Mario wanted it removed. They were told by the doctors if she ate well and held down her food, they would remove it. The problem was that she had a hard time holding down her food. The doctors were still trying to figure out what was causing her nausea without success.

On the morning of December 25th, I made a lasagna to bring to the hospital for a family meal. Mario's family was coming in with Mila, as were Daryl, my son Dan, and me. Lasagna was one of Amanda's favorite foods, and I was hoping she could enjoy it with the rest of us.

Everyone showed up at Amanda's room around mid-afternoon, and the staff set up a table in the hallway which we could use to place all the food on. All the decorations were up, and the lights were lit. There were wrapped gifts waiting to be unwrapped, but something was missing.

I don't know. Maybe it was just me. For some reason, I felt that Amanda wasn't feeling festive. I know it was hard for her. This wasn't what she was expecting for her first Christmas with Mila. Of course, it was just another day as an infant for Mila, but Amanda was stuck in bed with a body that wasn't responding as she wanted it to. She couldn't hold Mila, and when she tried to feed Mila a bottle, someone had to put the bottle in Amanda's hand and guide it to Mila's mouth.

Sometimes this worked; other times, Mila and Amanda

would get so frustrated that Mila wasn't getting her bottle properly that someone else would have to take Mila and feed her. You could see the anguish on Amanda's face when this occurred and the tears in her eyes. She was a mom but not a mom. She couldn't do the "mom" things she wanted to do with Mila.

At one point, I approached Amanda's bed when no one was in earshot, and I asked Amanda if she was ok. She said she was but then wanted to know why I asked. I told her that she didn't appear to be okay from what I saw. I told her she seemed to be withdrawn. She told me that she was just a little tired from all the activity of the day but that when she saw everyone in her room there to help her, Mario and Mila celebrate, she was just so thankful that she was around to see it.

I realized on that day that Amanda was going to be not just a "survivor" but that she was going to be a "thriver." She wouldn't let her circumstances stop her from being the mother she wanted to be for Mila. Of course, there were setbacks in this process, but she wasn't going to let those setbacks stop her from moving forward.

Once again, my daughter made me very proud. After all the years that her addiction wanted me to do nothing but cringe, she was now making me see how that time and her sobriety had shaped her character. She was one hell of a courageous woman.

Next Steps

Amanda and Mario had been lobbying for the removal of the feeding tube from Amanda. They had concluded that her nausea was being caused by the feeding tube. Please don't ask me how they came to that conclusion, but it didn't seem unreasonable. The doctors finally agreed to remove the feeding tube, but if Amanda's nutrition did not improve, she would have the tube reinserted. Everybody agreed.

The day the tube was removed, Amanda's case manager came into her room to tell us about the next steps in Amanda's recovery process. Within a few days, Amanda would be transitioned to a specialty rehab hospital within the maternity hospital where Amanda had her AFE. This specialty hospital was going to work on improving Amanda's strength. They were going to work on her sitting on the side of the bed for an extended period and work on her arm strength. They were going to start moving and exercising her arms.

Amanda needed to go through this process because the recovery phase after that was for her to be sent to a Rehab hospital specializing in brain trauma. The rehab process at this hospital was intensive and was done for extended periods during the day. Amanda had to be physically prepared to attend this program.

This day was nothing but good news. First, the feeding tube was removed, and now a game plan to help Amanda regain her physical capabilities was developed. The future was looking bright.

With New Year's coming up in a couple of days, we were sure looking forward to closing the book on 2019 and opening the door to a bright, promising 2020.

Happy New Year… NOT!

December 30, 2019, started as a day like any other. Daryl and I went to visit Amanda and spend the day with her. She was coughing quite a bit but not more than she had been. Amanda's lungs were still compromised and not nearly inflating the way they should. She would do breathing exercises using a breathing apparatus daily to build up her lung strength, but it was going to be a long, arduous process.

When Mario arrived, Daryl and I left to go home and start our dinner. We had settled in for the evening, watched a little TV, and then decided to get some sleep so we could visit Amanda a little earlier. Daryl and I wanted to end our visit with Amanda early in the evening to avoid any New Year's Eve traffic.

On December 31, 2019, my cell phone was on the night table charging so it would be ready for me when I awoke. I'm not sure what time of the morning my phone rang, but it was still dark, and I saw by the caller ID that it was Mario.

Mario has a deep tone to his voice and is always calm when delivering news, but I knew this had to be a big deal. Mario told me that Amanda was in the ICU back at the main hospital. He said that a couple of hours prior, she was having difficulty breathing. She was trying to cough up mucus from her lungs, but she wasn't strong enough to get it up. He said Respiratory Therapy came in to suction her, and they pulled out some mucus plugs, but she was running a fever and still having difficulty breathing. They rushed her to the ICU, where a chest x-ray showed she had pneumonia! I couldn't believe it. What could happen next?! I was so frustrated with this latest development. She had been moving along so well, even with her restrictions, and now she had pneumonia. Mario said that the ICU doctor put her on a BiPap machine to help her breathe, and they started IV antibiotics and that she was now resting comfortably. He told us we didn't need to rush into the hospital and that we could see her as we usually did.

When we got to the hospital the next day, we had to rotate into Amanda's room since the staff said we could only have two visitors in her room simultaneously. Daryl and I went in, and Amanda looked very tired. Her voice was weak, and she still had trouble breathing. She still had a fever, but the antibiotics seemed to be working. The ICU doctor said that Amanda was responding well to the treatment and that pneumonia was one of the hazards for someone on their back for such a long time.

We hoped this was just a bump in the road and that Amanda could beat this and get back on track again. I mean, seriously, what else could go wrong here??!!

Quick Turn Around

Late in the day on January 1, 2020, it was decided by the ICU doctor to transfer Amanda to a Pulmonary Step-Down Unit (PSDU). It was determined that while she still had pneumonia, it wasn't severe enough to warrant an ICU bed. The PSDU could treat pneumonia along with helping Amanda get back on track with her mobility rehab.

The PSDU manager, I'll call her Maggy, said that goals needed to be set for Amanda and that we all needed to be on board with Amanda attaining those goals. Maggy noted that the physical and occupational therapists would begin working with Amanda as soon as she had regained her strength from her latest medical event.

The goal was to increase Amanda's range of motion and to help increase her lung and diaphragm strength. Maggy also wanted Amanda to get out of bed for an hour each day to begin learning how to sit in a chair. I know that doesn't sound like much, but for someone who had as much physical trauma and was bedridden for a little over five months, one hour in a chair was physically and mentally demanding.

One of the new experiences that Amanda was starting to have was Phantom Limb Pain. Phantom Limb Pain is pain a patient feels after amputation of a limb. At one time, physicians thought that this pain was a psychological problem. Later, it was discovered that these pains are initiated in the brain and spinal cord. When I asked Amanda what those pains felt like, it would vary from hour to hour, day to day. She said that she sometimes felt tingling or pins and needles. Other times it was a cramping or stabbing pain.

I had a hard time with Amanda's pain. I knew she didn't imagine her pain, but it concerned me whenever she would not want the support staff to do whatever they were there for because of her pain. I know it frustrated the staff, but they were obligated not to perform their duties if Amanda declined them. At times it would frustrate us to come in and visit Amanda and find out something to help Amanda wasn't done because she was in pain.

When we discussed the goals with Maggy, we mentioned how staff would not perform their duties because Amanda complained about her pain. We told Maggy Amanda was always in pain and that when asked at what level her pain was, Amanda would always say it was somewhere from 8 to 10 on the pain scale. I didn't doubt this was true, but if her pain was constant, how would she ever improve if pain stopped her ability to improve? Maggy agreed that Amanda had to fight through the pain to begin moving forward. Maggy suggested that Amanda be given her pain medication 30-60 minutes before her PT/OT sessions. These discussions were done with Amanda, and while she wasn't thrilled about the additional pain she was going to experience, she agreed to the goals if she was given her pain meds in the agreed-upon timeframe.

Thus began Amanda's road to regaining her mobility. Within a matter of days, Amanda had worked through all her PT/OT sessions; she was sitting up on the side of the bed, with support, for about 30 minutes a day, and not only was she sitting in a chair, but when her pneumonia cleared, she was able to be placed in a specially designed wheelchair and taken for walks around the hospital and was able to go outside on warm days.

These items made us all feel very optimistic about Amanda moving forward in her recovery. We were thrilled with the progress of the PSDU PT/OT staff and how they were helping Amanda work towards her goals.

What The…???!!!

Here we go again! During the night, Amanda was having difficulty breathing. But this time, she started to "desat." "Desat" is short for the medical term desaturation. Desaturation is when saturation (oxygen) levels drop, or oxygen gets lower.

This was an emergent situation, and the PSDU staff had to intubate Amanda so they could perform a bronchoscopy procedure on Amanda. A bronchoscopy is a procedure where a doctor inserts a thin, bendable tube through the mouth or nose into the lungs. A light and a tiny camera on the bronchoscope permit the doctor to look inside the lungs' airways.

The doctor discovered that Amanda had numerous mucus plugs in her lungs that had to be suctioned out. After they removed all the mucus, it was decided that they would keep Amanda intubated for a couple of days just in case they had to remove more mucus plugs.

Amanda was transferred back to the ICU. The doctors wanted to take some cultures to see if Amanda had an infection that was causing all this mucus buildup over the last couple of days.

When Daryl and I visited her in the ICU, Amanda was sedated due to the intubation, so we decided to go home early so we could have some time to recharge.

A couple of days after this episode, Amanda was extubated and kept in the ICU while the doctors waited to see what the cultures showed. They didn't want a repeat performance of what had occurred initially.

A couple of Amanda's friends came to visit her to cheer her up, and while they were there, they did her nails, eyes, skin, and hair. Amanda was feeling better after that. Having her friends come in and visit and spend time taking care of her was good for her. Amanda and her friends were very close before the AFE, and knowing they were still there for her lifted her spirits.

The day Amanda was extubated, I was by her bedside, and I said something to the effect that she had experienced an exciting couple of days. She then told me how scared she was when that happened. She said that she was coughing a lot and that suddenly she couldn't breathe and felt like she would die any minute. She said that the people at the PSDU were very concerned about her, and everything was happening quickly. She said she thought to herself that she survived the AFE, she survived almost bleeding out because of the wound vac slipping onto her femoral artery, and now she was going to die because she was suffocating on her own fluid. She said she believed that she was going to die this time.

There are times when you want to scream. When you want to hold somebody or something accountable for everything going wrong. I was so angry at this whole situation. I had just about had enough of all the shit that my daughter was going through. I was beginning to think that God was torturing her. For what reason God was doing this was beyond me, but I had just about had enough of it. How much more was my daughter expected to tolerate? Why couldn't she get home and be with her daughter Mila?

I had to internalize this anger because I didn't want to upset Amanda. I told Amanda that she was not going to die. No way was that going to happen. She had to believe that; I reminded her she had a purpose in this life. She had something to accomplish. I told her she had a husband that loved her more than I had ever seen a man love a woman. He spent every free hour with her, and his attentiveness to her was something she could count on. He was her real-life guardian angel. I don't know if I was trying to convince her or myself. I was running out of reassurance that she would get past this AFE alive.

Daryl and I spent the day with Amanda. She seemed a little tired, but she was breathing normally. She was exhausted from all the excitement, fear, and medications. I was happy to see her resting peacefully before we left, and I prayed that she would remain at peace for the remainder of her hospitalization.

This was a tough couple of days.

Car Talk

From where Daryl and I lived, it was about an hour's commute into the city to visit Amanda at the hospital. These car rides were mainly highway driving; thankfully, we were rarely stuck in traffic. There were many rides where Daryl and I would talk about anything we could think of to try and take our minds off the madness we were dealing with. Sometimes we would not say anything as we were both lost in our thoughts. There were times when we would ride home happy about the events of the day, and there were times when we would ride home in despair.

We didn't have a crystal ball. We couldn't see what the immediate future held for us, Amanda, or her family. We had questions about what the next five years may be like. We didn't know how Mila would respond to not being able to spend her infant days with her mother. Would there still be a bond… a connection?

We would talk about how Mario and Amanda would survive this. They would travel a journey like none of us had ever experienced. We knew this would be a real test of their marriage, and we prayed they would pass it.

We were all working on autopilot. We had all settled into our routine for approaching each day and making each day work. The real test for us was when Amanda had a setback. It was how we responded to these setbacks that mattered most. These setbacks could either question what we were doing or set our resolve on conquering them and gaining the strength we needed to move forward.

The day Amanda contracted pneumonia was one of those days when I was questioning everything. I remember riding home with Daryl and talking about how much more Amanda could endure. I was at a low point. I felt like we had been in this fight for so long, and every time we gained a little ground, we would lose more ground. We were told by the doctors early on that what we were dealing with doesn't happen very often, so understanding a course of recovery was difficult. This course of recovery had no clear path. So, in essence, Amanda was a trailblazer, and we had to be prepared to blaze that trail with her wherever it would lead us.

Daryl and I talked about all this quite a bit on our drives into the city and then back home again. I wouldn't know at the time if we thought these conversations were therapeutic or if we benefitted from them. I know now that they were, and we did.

Isolation

So now this… Daryl and I were on our way to visit Amanda in the ICU when we received a call from Mario telling us that Amanda had been transferred to an isolation room in the ICU. The doctors said they simultaneously had a patient in the ICU, while Amanda was there a few days before, who later contracted Shingles.

Because their paths may have crossed, and Amanda's immune system was compromised, they had to isolate her so other ICU patients would be protected from Shingles if she contracted them.

When Daryl and I arrived at the ICU, we asked to speak to the ICU doctor. He came over and began explaining Amanda's current situation. The explanation was pretty much what Mario told us. Our request to speak to the doctor was to let him know that Amanda had chickenpox as a child and asked him if they could test to see if that part of her immune system was good.

The doctor told us there were precise criteria for placing someone in isolation, and Amanda met that criterion, and they had to isolate her to protect other patients. He also told us that she would be in isolation for a minimum of 21 days!

We asked if it was still possible for Amanda to get the same PT/OT treatment that she was receiving in the PSDU. We explained that she was starting to move forward with the game plan the PSDU staff had put in place, and we were hoping they could continue.

The doctor explained that PT/OT would still be seeing Amanda daily, but they would be constrained with what they could do because of the room size and the isolation restrictions they would have to adhere to.

This was highly disappointing. Amanda was starting to thrive in the PSDU. They were very vested in Amanda and would push her to do things she didn't think she could do. They were working with her on extending her range of motion for her arms and fingers. They were getting her to sit at her bedside for an hour daily. We saw progress. Amanda saw improvement, and now it would, for the most part, stop.

To get into Amanda's room, we had to put on disposable gowns, booties, gloves, head covering, and N-95 masks. Yes… we knew what an N-95 mask was before the Covid pandemic.

Amanda's room was a negative air pressure room that would stop airborne diseases from escaping. To see Amanda, you would have to go into a changing room that was attached to Amanda's room and put on all the protective gear. You could then open the door to her room and go inside.

It was a pain in the butt because every time you had to leave the room, you had to discard all the protective gear and then put on new equipment when you wanted to re-enter.

Amanda was very disappointed. She didn't like being isolated. She was already feeling "isolated" because of her circumstances and now being in isolation cemented that feeling with her. It also meant that she could not see Mila until her isolation was over. This really upset her.

This was one of those days when I felt down. Again… what more could go wrong here? But I knew that Daryl and I would need to go in and make it appear that this was just a speed bump. So that is what we did. We told her we all knew this would be a long road and there would be delays along the way, but we also knew that when she was cleared to leave isolation, we would get her back to the PSDU so her progress forward could continue.

I was sure this would be a long 21 days, and if her muscles deconditioned again, we would be back at square one on restoring her mobility. I prayed this wouldn't be the case.

7 Days

Amanda had been in ICU Isolation for almost seven days when her case manager approached us and said that Amanda was going to be transferred back to the specialty hospital where she contracted pneumonia. We told the case manager we weren't happy with that transfer and wanted her sent back to the PSDU. We felt the PSDU was more attentive to Amanda and were invested in her recovering her mobility.

The case manager told us that Amanda still needed to be in a negative pressure room because of her isolation needs and that PSDU did not have that type of room, whereas the specialty hospital did have a couple of them. She said they could also provide Amanda with her rehabbing needs while in isolation at the specialty hospital.

Daryl, Mario, and I were not confident she would get the attention she needed due to staffing inadequacies at the specialty hospital. We asked if there was another specialty hospital she could be transferred to, but again, because of the need for a negative pressure room, there were not many options.

While we were not happy with this move, at least Amanda would be out of the cramped ICU isolation room and in one where she could begin her rehab again. We also knew that we would have to be ready to help support Amanda when she was in the specialty hospital.

Amanda wasn't thrilled about this move, but she also realized there wasn't much we could do and that, hopefully, after her isolation time was over, she would be transferred to the main rehab hospital, which was a part of the health system.

No More Sand

When Amanda was transferred back to the specialty hospital, we were told they would like to have Amanda removed from her sand bed and placed on a regular mattress. The specialty hospital rehab staff said it would make it easier to have her sit on the side of the bed as a part of her rehab. They said the sand bed made it very difficult for her to sit up without assistance and slowed her recovery.

Amanda and Mario were upset because the sand bed had kept Amanda somewhat comfortable and from getting any bed sores which were very likely if she wasn't moved consistently. Amanda still couldn't move or reposition herself on her own. She was still frail. She couldn't even bring a cup up to her lips to take a drink.

The specialty staff assured us that they would turn Amanda as requested or, at the least, every 2 hours. Amanda couldn't push a nurse call button yet. Her fingers didn't have the strength or flexibility. The staff told us they had a pressure-call control they could install for Amanda, so all she would have to do was put minimal pressure on it to call the nurse.

A couple of days later, Amanda was moved to a regular bed, and the sand bed was removed. As soon as Amanda was moved into the new hospital bed, she immediately complained that it was uncomfortable. This was not unexpected because the sand bed was like laying on a cloud. We told Amanda that she needed to be patient in order for her body to adjust to this new surface.

It became apparent very early that Amanda was uncomfortable in this new bed. She constantly complained that it hurt her back, her shoulders, her neck, and the back of her head.

It wasn't long after they had Amanda in her new bed that she needed to be turned. This was an excellent test to see how quickly the staff responded. Amanda was able to exert enough pressure to trigger the call button, and someone from the nurse's station called in over the speaker and asked Amanda what she needed. Amanda's voice was not very strong because of the intubation she had done the prior week. We wanted her to do the talking so we could make sure they could hear her. It was evident that the staff member couldn't hear what she was saying. She ended up saying that someone would be in momentarily.

Close to 15 minutes later, a support staff member came in and helped turn Amanda onto her side. I'll admit it wasn't easy to turn Amanda because even after being turned, she would still be uncomfortable and need extra attention. A staff member could be there for up to 15 minutes to get her in the right spot.

Mario had been helping to turn Amanda for quite some time since he was with her all night and into the morning until he went to work. If she were uncomfortable in the middle of the night, he would help turn her.

Mario would help the specialty staff turn Amanda and show them how to get her in the most comfortable position using pillows and foam pads. It was meticulous work and not that easy. I know that when I was alone with Amanda and would help, it was not easy to get her to feel comfortable. It could be downright frustrating at times.

For the next few days, Amanda did nothing but complain about how uncomfortable and unhappy she was because the new bed was making everything hurt. I know she was driving the staff crazy because she called them almost every hour to move her. They would try to get her comfortable, but it would just get to the point where Amanda would say that she was ok for the moment. I could see the frustration she had, and the staff also had.

We all started complaining about the bed Amanda was on to the nurses and the nurse manager. I believe that Mario even complained to the director of the specialty hospital. It was finally approved for Amanda to get a sand bed. We were thrilled. I believe the mattress showed up the next day, and

Amanda was transferred to that bed.

We all hoped this would help bring Amanda more comfort. She still had upper and lower back pain, however. Her left ear lobe was also still healing from earlier when she was in CTICU. It was concerning how long it took for the ear lobe to heal, but her skin was fragile from all the trauma she had suffered. The ear would heal and start to look good, but then Amanda would sleep on the left side of her head, and the ear would look bad again. It took quite a long time for her left ear lobe to heal.

Staffing Needs

Amanda was constantly in pain. It was difficult to watch her in such agony, knowing that there wasn't much we could do to help her. She was always uncomfortable. She would call the nurse station to have someone move her, but it would take up to 30 minutes to get someone to come into the room to move her.

We felt terrible for the support staff. We knew they were doing their best, but they were woefully understaffed. The support staff-to-patient ratio was very reasonable in every unit Amanda had been in. In this specialty hospital, that ratio seemed very inadequate. The specialty hospital was a transitional step in a patient's recovery process. The specialty hospital would prepare patients for the next steps they would have to take. In Amanda's case, they needed to get her ready for the brain injury rehab hospital. From my perspective, the specialty hospital was dealing with a patient whose care they weren't prepared for. Amanda's needs were too great for this hospital.

I cannot tell you how many times we had to go out to the nurse's station to ask for someone to assist Amanda, and then when someone would show up if they needed another support person to help them, there was usually an additional delay. I told them I didn't believe the delay was their fault. They appreciated the understanding. It wasn't the case that they would not respond. They were always with another patient, and the hospital needed additional support staff. Unfortunately, Amanda was suffering because of this.

The one thing that was moving along as planned was Amanda's rehab. She was doing a range of motion exercises and spending more time sitting in a chair. She was beginning to gain strength back in her hands and fingers. She reached the point where she could pick up the suction hose and place it in her mouth when removing any mucus she coughed up. It wasn't a smooth maneuver for her, but it was a beginning.

Amanda had been at the specialty hospital for a couple of weeks when a nurse noticed a red spot forming on Amanda's tailbone area. The wound specialist was called in, and she examined it. When these exams occurred, I would leave the room to give Amanda privacy.

When the wound specialist came out of Amanda's room, I asked her what was happening. I wasn't aware of the red spot. She informed me about discovering a red area on Amanda's tailbone. She told me it was the beginnings of a bed sore but that they caught it very early. She said it would most likely heal without issue. They ordered Amanda a unique jell pillow that would be placed under her back to take the pressure off the area.

This bed sore, and another which developed on Amanda's hip, did not get better. They both got exceedingly worse, and it took almost a year for them to heal. If you had or know someone who had a bed sore, then you know how painful these are.

Amanda had so much pain because of these bed sores and had to stay on painkillers longer than she should have.

I hated those bed sores. They couldn't heal fast enough for me.

Plugs

On February 11th, 2020, Amanda had to have a bronchoscopy again. Amanda's O2 levels started to dip a couple of days before this procedure, so a CT scan was scheduled. Amanda was having difficulty bringing up mucus. She was bringing some mucus up but just not all of it.

Her right lung collapsed early on when Amanda's organs were failing. It had been regaining its functionality, but it wasn't nearly where it should be. The CT scan was ordered, which showed that her right lung was still partially collapsed, and she would need a bronchoscopy to get out the mucus plugs she couldn't cough up on her own.

The bronchoscopy went without a hitch, and Amanda's O2 levels returned to an acceptable level.

There was a discussion about transferring Amanda to a different specialty hospital housed in the maternity hospital where Amanda had her AFE.

The case manager at the current specialty hospital told us that the rehab facilities were better suited for Amanda's next rehab phase. They had a rehab room that the patients were moved into daily, and the staffing was more abundant.

I thought the current specialty hospital staff couldn't wait to get Amanda transferred out from under their care. From my perspective, Amanda's needs were so much more than the staff could handle. Amanda had developed two bed sores under their supervision; they were ready to move her along and have her be someone else's problem.

We weren't unhappy about the move. I was frustrated with the staff/patient ratio and the response time to her needs. Plus, I was always concerned about how Amanda was treated when no other family member was with her. Amanda had complained to us about how she would call for a nurse and that it would take a long time for someone to show up.

Arrangements were being made for the transfer, and as soon as a bed opened at the other specialty hospital, Amanda was headed there.

V-Day

Amanda was moved to her second specialty hospital, and the next phase of her rehab began. We expected that Amanda was going to start rehab to gain back her arm strength and to begin rehabbing her left leg. Her left leg had not moved since her AFE, and we all knew that her left leg had to recover for her to gain mobility.

Before Amanda was moved to her new room, Mario and I met with the manager to see what room she would be placed in and discuss her various issues. One of the first items we wanted to discuss was the type of bed Amanda needed. The manager wasn't aware that Amanda would need a sand bed, and once we relayed her past experiences with a regular bed and the bed sores she developed, a sand bed was ordered to be in place. This was such a good sign for us. This specialty hospital appeared attentive to our concerns and didn't want to push its agenda on us as the last specialty hospital did.

This hospital also had an equipped rehab room and a better staff-to-patient ratio. The rehab staff indicated that Amanda would be taken to the rehab room twice daily and given an hour of rehab time per visit. I was excited about this because it was what I was hoping for. I wanted to see Amanda walk again, and knowing that her left leg had atrophied to unacceptable levels, I knew she would need some intense rehab. I was encouraged that it sounded like this was also the desire of the rehab personnel.

On Valentine's Day, Mila was brought in to visit with her mommy and daddy. Mila's pediatrician had given her the green light to begin solid foods, and Amanda was insistent that she be the first to feed her daughter solid food. Amanda had already missed so many firsts with Mila, and I can't tell you how many tears she wept because of all she missed.

I believe that by this time, Amanda had come to grips with the seriousness of her injuries and what it would take to regain some normalcy. What she couldn't come to grips with was all the little things she was missing with Mila. Debbie would do all she could to try and include Amanda in all of Mila's infant accomplishments, but Debbie didn't have a crystal ball that she could use to know when Mila would do something for the first time.

Amanda's ability to grip had not fully recovered. She could not close her fingers enough to hold a spoon. The rehab staff jury-rigged a baby spoon with foam around the handle so Amanda could grip it while she fed Mila.

With assistance, the baby cereal was mixed in a bowl, and Amanda got a small amount on the spoon. She brought the spoon up to Mila's lips and got a tiny amount in her mouth. Mila tasted it and immediately began crying.

Mila wanted nothing to do with solid foods. Amanda was very disappointed. She wanted Mila to love being fed by her, but Mila wasn't enjoying this feeding. I could see Amanda's eyes begin to tear up, but she held it together.

Amanda looked so forward to being a mom. I'm sure she had all these thoughts before Mila's birth about motherhood, all the firsts she would experience with Mila, and the pure joy of watching her baby grow and fall in love with her momma.

Several times Amanda told us she believed Mila thought Debbie was her mother. I know that wasn't fair to Debbie. Debbie was doing what she had to do in a very unusual situation. Daryl and I would always tell Amanda that Mila knew Amanda was her momma. We just hoped we were convincing enough.

We would always tell her about the day Mila visited Amanda for the first time after the AFE. We told her about how Mila was acting fussy until Mario brought her to Amanda's bed and laid Mila next to her and how Mila immediately stopped fussing. We told her that Mila intuitively knew that she was next to her momma and that she was safe.

Amanda loved that story, but it was still hard for her not to be participating in Mila's first year the way she had envisioned.

Reducing Expectations

Amanda was doing very well in her new location. The rehab team was getting her out of bed twice a day and either sitting her in a chair in her room or taking her down to the rehab room.

Most of Amanda's workouts centered on regaining strength in her hands and arms. Her progress was slow, but it was progress.

All the rehab personnel were female and right around Amanda's age. I felt they were vested in Amanda's recovery because Amanda's back story moved them. I'm sure that while they couldn't put themselves in Amanda's shoes, they could certainly relate to what they would want to accomplish in rehab if it was them in Amanda's place.

Daryl and I would sit in the rehab room and watch how hard they would work Amanda. Sometimes, they would work through Amanda's objections and press her to do more. With their coaching, Amanda would always give it her best. I was hoping that Amanda would not get discouraged because of her slow progress.

The one thing that I was getting impatient with was the rehab on Amanda's left leg. It didn't seem like anything was being done to her leg. I would ask the rehab staff when they would begin rehabbing her leg, and the usual answer was that they had to get her arm strength up so the arms could help support her leg rehab.

I think these questions to the staff prompted a visit from a rehab physician who worked at the rehab hospital, which was going to be Amanda's last step in her recovery process.

He came into Amanda's room and did a brief examination of Amanda's hands, arms, and leg. When he was finished, he told us that he had reviewed Amanda's case, particularly her rehab progress throughout the AFE recovery process.

He said that before he provided us with his analysis of Amanda, he wanted to know what our expectations were for Amanda during her upcoming stay at the rehab hospital.

We agreed that the goal was for Amanda to regain her mobility and independence. We wanted her to be fitted for a prosthetic leg and see her recover the ability to stand and walk.

The doctor listened intently to each of us and then paused. I remember that pause because I interpreted it as a bad sign. I'm unsure if he was looking for the right words or manner to deliver his findings.

He told us that in Amanda's current condition, she was not ready for the rehab hospital. He said the sessions at the rehab hospital were very intense and would require Amanda to be able to do multiple hours of rehab throughout the day. Patients there began their sessions at 9 am, would receive a break for lunch and rest, and then have an extended afternoon session. Depending on the schedule, she might even have an early evening session.

Amanda's stay at the rehab hospital would depend on her progress. If Amanda progressed forward, she would remain at the hospital until it was determined that she had reached her potential.

So far, this didn't sound too bad to me. Before I retired, my job as a systems analyst was at the rehab hospital. I primarily worked with the Cardiology Department, but since I had been employed at this hospital for almost 30 years, I had the opportunity to interact with personnel from various departments. While I didn't know any of the rehab staff personally, I had heard about how the rehab department operated and how committed they were to their patients. I had seen the interactions between the staff and their patients on occasion and was impressed.

My mother was one of those patients when she suffered a significant stroke several years prior. There were days when I would attempt to visit my mom only to find her in a rehab session. I would watch from the hallway and note how well the rehab staff treated her.

I wasn't prepared for what the rehab doctor told us next. He said that Amanda would not regain any movement in her left leg! He did not see any muscle movement in response to stimulation. I know in my mind that I disagreed with him, but I don't recall if I or anyone else said that to him. I always expected Amanda to regain her leg strength once the rehab staff started working on her. This was a tough pill to swallow.

The doctor told us not to lose hope for the leg, but it was his job to ensure that expectations were kept in line with reality. He also told us his opinion was not 100% accurate but based on what he was currently seeing and what damage had been done to the leg, he was confident in it.

The doctor asked us if we had any questions, and I don't believe we did. I think we were all stunned. We always talked about how Amanda would walk again, and to hear now that was probably not going to happen, was a real blow.

I don't know what Amanda was thinking, but after the doctor left, I remember Daryl and me telling her about all that she had overcome so far and that the doctor's opinion was just that. It was an opinion.

We reminded Amanda that the doctors said she wouldn't live past 24 hours, but she did. We reminded her that the doctors said she would probably be on dialysis for the rest of her life, but she wasn't. This doctor told her that her left leg would no longer move, and she had to prove him wrong.

It was hard to keep Amanda's spirits in a good place, especially when you have doubts of your own.

Left Progression

It was the beginning of March 2020, about one week after the doctor from the rehab hospital had visited us.

Amanda had been working very hard in her PT/OT sessions. The PT/OT staff had heard about the rehab hospital doctor's opinion. They saw how it affected us, and I think they took it as a challenge.

The rehab staff were doing exercises that improved her grip and arm strength. Her progress, in my eyes, was minimal, but the rehab staff set me straight with what a significant improvement Amanda was going through. They would even help Amanda stand with their assistance.

When they helped Amanda stand, the smile on her face was priceless. She felt good about her rehab and looked forward to attending her sessions. The sessions got Amanda out of bed and her room, which helped her mentally.

Daryl and I had just arrived for our daily visit. We walked into the room, and one of the PT/OT staff was with Amanda. Amanda seemed in great spirits and said we needed to see what she could do now. She told us she could move her left leg!

Daryl and I moved to the foot of her bed, and the rehab clinician told us to watch the muscle above her knee. She then turned to Amanda and said, "Show them." I was staring intently at her leg and saw the tiniest twitch of her leg muscle above her knee.

I looked at Amanda and said, "Do that again!" The muscle twitched again. I was ecstatic! I couldn't believe what I was seeing. After what the rehab doctor had told us, this was another miracle happening. Reflecting on this moment, I don't know why I was so incredulous over my daughter's leg muscle movement. I mean, she thumbed her nose at all the naysayers that continued to tell her what she couldn't or wouldn't be able to do. I'm probably portraying that wrong. These doctors weren't naysayers; they delivered what they believed to be a truthful assessment of Amanda's medical condition. They weren't being hostile or dishonest. They were doing what they were trained to do. They were keeping us grounded. I can now appreciate what they were doing.

They didn't know my "miracle" girl. They didn't know that, somehow, she was a survivor who just wouldn't let any human's words get in her way of being the person she wanted to be.

She was supposed to die within 24 hours, and she didn't. She may never have the function of her kidneys again, and she did. She may never move her left leg again, and she did.

That's my daughter. She's a fighter, a survivor, and she will be a thriver.

I don't know why I had my doubts about her leg movement. I shouldn't have. I decided then that my daughter was on a quest to become whole again in whatever image that was for her. I was a part of this quest and had a front-row seat to watch it happen.

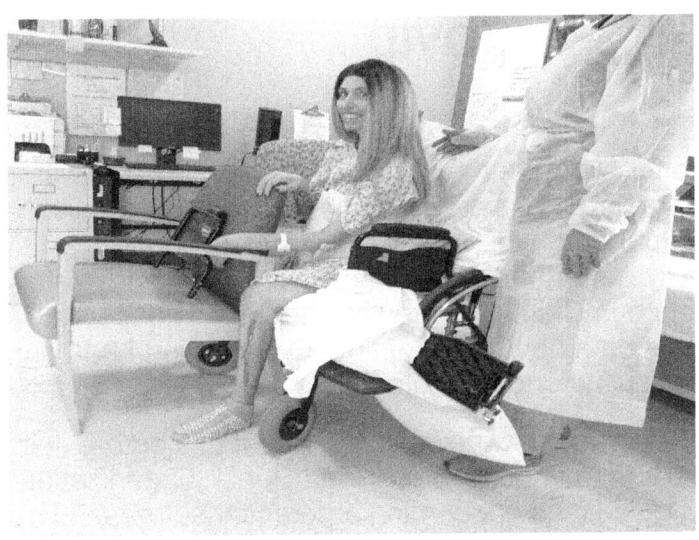

Amanda used her arms to help her sit up. Note a few items... the band around Amanda's waist provided support because her abdomen was still separated which resulted in her having no core strength. Her leg has a wound on it due to the removal of necrotic tissue.

The PT team helped Amanda to stand so she could see what it felt like to stand on her left leg. I believe the staff did this to show Amanda that anything was possible.

COVID

It was just after New Year's Day 2020 when I saw a news article indicating there were cases of individuals in China that had developed pneumonia. There were very few details around this story other than the cases appearing to be isolated to one providence in China. I remember not being concerned. I thought it might be a new strain of flu, but Daryl and I had our flu shots. I figured that should protect us.

A few days later, another news article about this outbreak in China appeared on my phone. The World Health Organization (WHO) issued guidelines concerning a potential outbreak of a new virus worldwide. I remember seeing the words SARS and MERS in the article and recalled how those viruses didn't cause me too much alarm when they were active, so, in my mind, I filed this new virus in the same category.

A few days later, another news article appeared that the virus now had a name. It was called COVID-19. The name was derived from the shape of the virus and the year it was first discovered. The article also said there was a case in Thailand. This was the first time that I was alarmed. The virus was no longer contained in China, and its transmission method was still unknown.

By the end of January 2020, the WHO issued a Public Health Emergency. There were now well over 7,000 reported cases in China and numerous reported cases in 18 other countries. The WHO gave a risk assessment of human-to-human transmission of "High" to the world. This was now becoming more concerning to me. It appeared this virus was contagious and knew no boundaries. It was being transmitted from human to human, but there wasn't an understanding yet of the virus's transmission method.

At this point, I started to voice my concerns to Daryl, Amanda, and Mario. I told them that I hoped this virus would fizzle out because transmission may be complex, but if it wasn't, I was pretty sure that hospitals would begin setting restrictions for patient visitation. We had become relaxed with our visits to Amanda. We would show up when we liked and be able to walk right into her room. We could stay as long as we wanted and interact with the staff without restriction. Having worked in a hospital for a long time, I had seen restrictions put in place during flu outbreaks and an Ebola outbreak. The limitations used weren't too intrusive, but they existed, nonetheless.

In February, air travel restrictions were put in place by many countries, including the US, a public health emergency was announced in the US, the death toll from COVID-19 exceeded the death toll from SARS, and even though a pandemic had yet to be declared, the word "pandemic" was starting to be said out loud.

In early to mid-March, the news about COVID was now at the top of the list. Cases were turning up in the US. A cruise ship was kept at sea off the coast of California because of a COVID outbreak on board, the US government declared the virus outbreak a national emergency, and California became the first state to shut down and issue a "stay at home" order.

At this time, the hospital Amanda was in issued its first restrictions for visitation. Besides visitors having to undergo a health screening, each patient was permitted only one visitor at a time. As a family, via social media, we asked friends and family who wanted to visit Amanda only to visit her before 1 pm and not on weekends unless they scheduled a visit since Mario spent the weekends with Amanda. Daryl and I were granted permission to be in Amanda's room together, and we would stay from 1 pm until Mario arrived after work.

One of the other restrictions was that no one under 18 was permitted to visit. This included Mila. Amanda was not very receptive to this restriction. Her time with Mila was minimal, and this restriction took that away.

When my kids were going through infancy, I got to experience all their "firsts." It was exciting when they did something for the first time, and you took it for granted that you wouldn't miss any of them. Amanda had missed so many "firsts," and now she would miss more. There was no chance she would be a part of those, and I couldn't imagine how much that must have hurt her. There were numerous occasions where she would tell us how unhappy she was at not being a vital part of Mila's life. As hard as Daryl and I tried to minimize the significance of the experience of "firsts," we knew we weren't very convincing. Amanda would be depressed and cry in front of us about missing Mila's first year, breaking my heart. I knew the only thing we could do was hold her hand and let her cry. I don't know how often, when Amanda was alone, she would have nothing else to do but think and question her future. It still breaks my heart just thinking back to this time.

Coping

I don't know that I have documented Amanda's daily life after her AFE and what she would have to cope with. I've been so locked in on detailing her progress and setbacks that I haven't conveyed what waking up in the morning and facing her day was like for her.

Based on my observations and what Amanda would communicate during our hospital visits with her, I will describe this to you the best I can.

Amanda was in constant pain daily. She hurt everywhere on her body. She was on pain medications, but they did little to make her comfortable. The doctors couldn't increase her pain meds because for her to feel no pain, they would have to raise them to a dangerous level, and they needed her to be alert so they could evaluate her daily and so she could participate in her rehab process.

Amanda would sleep in pain, wake up in pain, and be in pain every minute of every day. When Daryl and I would enter her room at the beginning of our visits and ask her how she was feeling, there was never a day where she said "ok." She would usually say she felt the same. As I sat with her and watched her go through her day, I tried to imagine what she was experiencing. I once tore my left biceps tendon from my forearm. The instant it happened, the pain brought me to my knees and put me in a kneeling fetal position. I couldn't move for what seemed like hours. I tried to recall that feeling of pain and then imagined having to endure that for 24 hours a day, seven days a week.

Besides having to live with this type of pain, there was little Amanda could do to help herself. She couldn't reposition her body on her own. She couldn't scratch an itch. She could barely get her hands to her chin; even when she did, her fingers still couldn't move with great range. She needed assistance with everything, and there were numerous times when you were assisting Amanda and didn't understand what she wanted you to do; she would become frustrated and tell you to stop.

Repositioning Amanda was always an effort and would require numerous pillows that would have to be used to prop her into a position that would provide her some comfort. That comfort was usually short-lived, and she would need to be repositioned again.

Her tailbone bed sore had become huge and was one of her most significant pain sources. Amanda could never be placed on her stomach because of the large wound from her initial surgeries when the surgeons saved her liver.

That wound extended from the bottom of her sternum to below her belly button. It was constantly covered with gauze while initially healing, and when I first looked at it, I couldn't believe what I saw. Amanda's internal organs had shifted somewhat from her being open. Even though they had covered the mesh that was holding her intestines within her with skin grafts, you could still see her intestines occasionally move as they digested food.

Amanda's pain medication constipated her, so she was in pain from that, also. The doctors had her taking laxatives, but they did little to resolve this issue.

My daughter was caught in a significant Catch-22 because of her pain. Her wounds needed to heal to help relieve the pain, but they were recovering slowly because of all her trauma.

Amanda's muscles had atrophied while she was in her coma to the point that they were useless. Amanda had Myotonic Muscular Dystrophy. This was going to be a massive factor in Amanda's muscle recovery. It would probably delay her muscles from regaining their full strength and flexibility.

Lastly, Amanda was also in pain because of scoliosis in her back and her lack of mobility. Having her mobility would help her alleviate that pain by being able to stretch her back.

As you can see, when I said Amanda was in pain everywhere, that was not an exaggeration.

Because Amanda's lungs weren't functioning fully and she had a weak diaphragm, Amanda had a hard time coughing up mucus, and when she did, she would have to have someone available to help suction it out of her mouth.

Amanda spent most of her time sleeping when she wasn't being rehabbed or going for some testing or procedure. We never woke her. When she was asleep, we felt like she wasn't in pain even though she was.

I constantly worried about the toll from all of what she was going through was having on her mentally. I desperately wanted to talk to her about it, but I also knew I didn't want her concerned about one more issue. I would ask her on occasion if she wanted to talk with a therapist, but she declined. She was talking to a woman from palliative care, but she was older than Amanda, and I don't think she ever connected with Amanda.

After describing all of this… ask yourself, could you have endured this? I'm not sure I could have.

Therefore, today I look at my daughter as the most courageous woman I have ever known. To this day, she is still in pain and endures. She still gets up every day and tries to be the best mom to Mila that she can be.

My daughter is the epitome of the word 'Coping,' and she does it with grace, style, and willpower only she possesses.

New House Rules

As COVID-19 raced across the country and the reported case and death tolls rose, it became a tough decision to visit Amanda. My biggest concern was for Amanda. With her weakened state and lungs that weren't fully recovered, Daryl and I certainly didn't want to bring anything with us when we visited. If Amanda contracted COVID-19, we knew that it would probably kill her.

I told Amanda about our concerns, but she disagreed. She told us she needed us to be with her during the day. She told us she needed us as her advocates since the hospital staff didn't always respond to her needs.

I knew this was true because when we would walk into her room to begin our visit, Amanda would tell us about something she wanted that the staff wouldn't give her. I would usually find the nurse for her room and ask about it, and they would provide their reason for not responding or following through. Most times, their response was valid, but I would tell them to please reply to Amanda and to do their best to satisfy her when they could.

In my opinion, there would be occasions where the reasoning from the staff was inappropriate, and I would address that with them so that they knew that we were on top of the situation.

It was the middle of March, and word came back to us that Amanda was being transferred to the Rehab Hospital so she could begin what we hoped would be the final leg of her hospital stay.

At this time, hospitals also started to become very strict about visitations. There was massive confusion about how COVID-19 could be transmitted. Most medical experts agreed that the primary method of transmission was via airborne particles. But there was also concern that it could be transmitted via touch, surface transfer, and airborne particles entering the eye.

Hospitals were beginning to see the results of the pandemic with increased emergency room visits for COVID-like ailments. The ICUs were starting to fill up with COVID patients, and protective masks, gowns, gloves, and eye coverings for the clinical staff were in short supply.

Our state was beginning to issue Stay-At-Home orders for counties with the most significant outbreaks.

The rehab hospital put in a strict one-visitor-at-a-time rule. Each visitor had to undergo screening at the hospital entrance to see if a fever was present. If you passed the screening, you were given a mask that had to remain in place.

I told Amanda that we could no longer visit her at this juncture. I was concerned about her health, but I was also worried about Daryl's health.

Daryl was already seeing a Cardiologist because of her muscular dystrophy, and there were reports that COVID-19 may be a vascular disease. With Daryl's heart already compromised by her condition, I was afraid that if she contracted COVID, it would attack her heart and possibly be fatal. It wasn't a chance I was willing to take.

We decided that to protect everyone involved, we would only do video visits with Amanda. We would video visit with her daily, but these visits were very short and left me feeling like I was abandoning my daughter.

I didn't know if I could settle with just video calls. I was torn between what I knew about COVID and my need to continue motivating Amanda and being her advocate at the hospital when I needed to be.

My Heart or My Head

It was becoming painfully clear that scientists and doctors did not understand the COVID-19 virus and the resulting pandemic. New terms were making their way into my everyday language, like "N-95" masks and "Social Distancing." Every day, there seemed to be some new information on the virus that either provided some clarity or muddied the waters.

I was torn between seeing Amanda and possibly bringing a virus home that could put Daryl in danger. Amanda was transferred to the rehab hospital from which I had just retired one year earlier. I knew staff and personnel and thought my being with Amanda could help them see her as more than a patient.

Daryl and I talked about my going to the hospital to visit Amanda and the possible risks. It was a difficult decision.

One of the things that Mario and Amanda had told me was that her day was busy. She had two daily rehab sessions that lasted about one and a half to two hours per session. Before her sessions in the morning, Amanda would have her breakfast brought into her room, and the staff would perform other routine personal care matters with her. After her morning session, she would come back to her room to have lunch and rest until her afternoon session. Due to her condition, these rehab sessions were very strenuous, and she needed to rest after each.

I wanted to see Amanda and hopefully talk to a rehab doctor or one of the rehab therapists to hear what they hoped to accomplish with Amanda. Mario had told us how strict the hospital was about visitors and the procedures and rules they had implemented. Knowing the risks, Daryl and I decided for me to go into the hospital and visit Amanda.

As I drove into the hospital, I couldn't help but hope that I was making the right decision. I always told my children that when making any decisions, they should always "think with their head, not with their heart." I always believed that decision-making based on emotions usually did not provide the results that one would be looking to achieve. I told myself that this visit was more of an evaluation of the safety procedures the hospital had put in place, Amanda's availability outside of her rehab sessions, and what the game plan was for rehabbing Amanda.

I parked in the parking garage across the street from the hospital, put on my facemask, and made my way to the pedestrian walkway that passed over the road below and into the hospital. There were markings on the floor for social distancing purposes and signs stating that you would not be admitted if you had any "flu-like" symptoms.

When I walked through the hospital doors, there was a station that a nurse and a security guard manned. Both had on masks and gloves. The nurse also had a clear plastic visor to protect her eyes.

My temperature was checked, and I was questioned regarding my health and if I had any contact with someone exposed to COVID. After passing the screening, I proceeded to the check-in desk, where I had to sign in and indicate whom I was visiting and what department and room they were in. I knew the greeter behind the desk, and he asked where I had been. I told him about my retirement and that I was in visiting my daughter. I gave him a brief synopsis of my daughter and her current condition. He was shocked beyond belief to hear the story.

It was funny how I had gotten used to this reaction when I told anyone what happened to Amanda. In the beginning, when I would tell someone what had happened to my daughter, I couldn't get through the story without choking up or needing to compose myself. Now I was taking everything one day at a time and was determined to steel myself not to let my emotions show through. He asked me if I knew where I was going but caught himself and told me that I probably knew this hospital better than he did.

I walked down a hallway I knew was not too heavily

traveled by others. With the pandemic firmly in place and all the work-at-home edicts in effect, the hallway was relatively empty. When I did see someone coming, I hugged the opposite wall from them as we passed. I would also hold my breath until I was well past them. I was hoping not to breathe in any COVID particles if the person who walked passed me in the hallway was infected. Yeah… I was that paranoid!

I took the stairs to the rehab floor rather than ride an elevator. I had to walk up a few flights, but at least I wasn't in a box with others who may have COVID.

When I arrived on the floor, I realized that Amanda was on the rehab floor for patients with brain injuries. This was a locked-down unit for patients who suffered a brain injury so they couldn't possibly wander off in a confused state.

I remembered this unit. My mom had been on this floor when she suffered a stroke about ten years before my daughter's event.

I wasn't familiar with any of the staff I was seeing this day, but I made sure to mention to any staff I encountered how I had just retired from this hospital. Amanda's room was spacious and comfortable. It had a motorized Hoyer lift installed above the bed so the staff could remove the patient from the bed without injuring themselves. It was safer for the staff and safer for the patient.

Amanda did not like the lift. They would have to put her in a pouch that would be attached to the lift, and as the lift would rise, the patient would be lifted from the bed within the pouch and then placed in a wheelchair. When the pouch was raised, it would rub on Amanda's bed sore and cause severe pain. After the first try with the lift and Amanda's obvious discomfort, the lift was never used again.

I arrived after Amanda's morning rehab session and stayed until they took her to her afternoon session. It was apparent to me that Amanda needed to rest after her morning session, but between lunch and the need for her to use the bedpan or to have something else done to her or for her, she wasn't going to get the sleep between sessions that she was going to need.

I did note that Amanda did not complain about being tired and went to her afternoon session to put in the work she needed to do to regain her mobility. While I was visiting Amanda, I did get to talk to one of the rehab therapists who was working with Amanda. I don't recall if I asked or if she asked me about goals for Amanda.

I do recall that I made it clear what my goals were. I wanted to see increased strength in Amanda's arms and fingers. I also wanted them to continue to work with her left leg and get it to begin moving better than just the quad muscle twitch that Amanda could do. At this time, I was made aware that these goals would not be accomplished in the time they had with Amanda. I asked what kind of time limit they had. I was informed that most patients usually get six weeks of rehab. Six weeks??!! What could they possibly accomplish in six weeks?

She told me they would work very hard with Amanda to improve her upper body and hand strength, but the leg was different. She did not believe the leg mobility would be addressed. Their goal was to get Amanda in a motorized wheelchair that Amanda could drive using a joystick. This chair would also tilt back so Amanda could make herself comfortable. They were going to train her to maneuver the chair in tight quarters so she could drive in it wherever she desired.

While I was thrilled to hear about the wheelchair, I was expecting much more. I thought Amanda would be in this hospital for months while she rehabbed. I thought they would surely rebuild her hands and arms and begin working on her left leg. I had to readjust my expectations, but I couldn't imagine how much care Amanda would need when she was discharged.

I entered the hospital this day concerned about COVID, but I left worried about what would be required to care for Amanda in a home environment. This day left me with so many more questions than answers.

I remember driving home thinking that this information was not what I desired. I also knew that what I wanted was not significant. I knew that, somehow, we had to make this work for Amanda. Amanda had survived so much to this point, and I was determined to do whatever we could to help her continue her fight to become mobile again. There was Daryl, me, my son Dan, and Mario's parents to make this work. I'd be damned if it wasn't going to work.

Upcoming Move

Amanda had been in the rehab hospital for a couple of weeks, and it was decided that for me to keep coming in to visit her just wasn't an intelligent thing to do. COVID cases were rising along with deaths at an exponential rate.

Daryl and I were both in the age range that made us vulnerable to the more severe symptoms of COVID, and as I wrote earlier, Daryl, due to her Muscular Dystrophy, was at a greater risk.

We would video visit with Amanda but not every day. There were days that she was just too tired. Amanda was measured for a power wheelchair, but in the meantime, she was provided with a loaner while hers was built to her specifications and needs.

Around this time, it was becoming apparent that Amanda would be released sometime in the middle or late April of 2020.

Amanda and Mario were renting a three-story home in the southern suburbs of Pittsburgh, and during this time, Mario would run home daily to feed their dogs and let them outside before returning to the hospital. It wasn't ideal for Mario or the dogs for this to continue, but one of the dogs was a large German Shepard who was challenging to handle due to his size. Finding someone to foster the dogs was difficult.

Because the house was in an older neighborhood in a rather hilly part of Pittsburgh, there were steps from the street to the front door and then to the bedrooms and bathroom. Daryl and I had been having hypothetical discussions about where Amanda and Mario would end up living. Still, we decided to wait to have that discussion until we knew what Amanda's condition would be at discharge. Now knowing that Amanda would be released in late April, we weren't surprised by Mario and Amanda's request to move in with us when Amanda was discharged.

The only reservation I had was the size of our second bedroom. It wasn't a large room, and I knew that Amanda and Mario had a king-sized bed, so I was concerned about how the bed would fit. Other than that, our home was the only logical choice for them.

Our home was in a 55-plus community, and our condo was single-level living. It also had wide enough doorways for a power wheelchair to navigate through.

A couple of days later, Mario measured their bed, and we determined that the bed and a dresser would fit, but there would be little room left. Again, there wasn't much choice, so we would have to make do for as long as it took for Amanda to recuperate and for them to be comfortable with living independently.

We talked about how Mila was living with Mario's parents, which would probably have to continue. With Mario back at work during the day and Amanda's care falling on Daryl and me, having Mila living with us full-time would be too much of a burden. We did work it out where Mila would come over to our place and stay for the weekend when Mario was off from work. It was going to be interesting watching Mario and Amanda begin their parenting in front of us. I hoped that Daryl and I could be good grandparents and take a back seat while they learned how to parent Mila.

The jury is still out on how well Daryl and I did. It all depends on whose perspective you see it from.

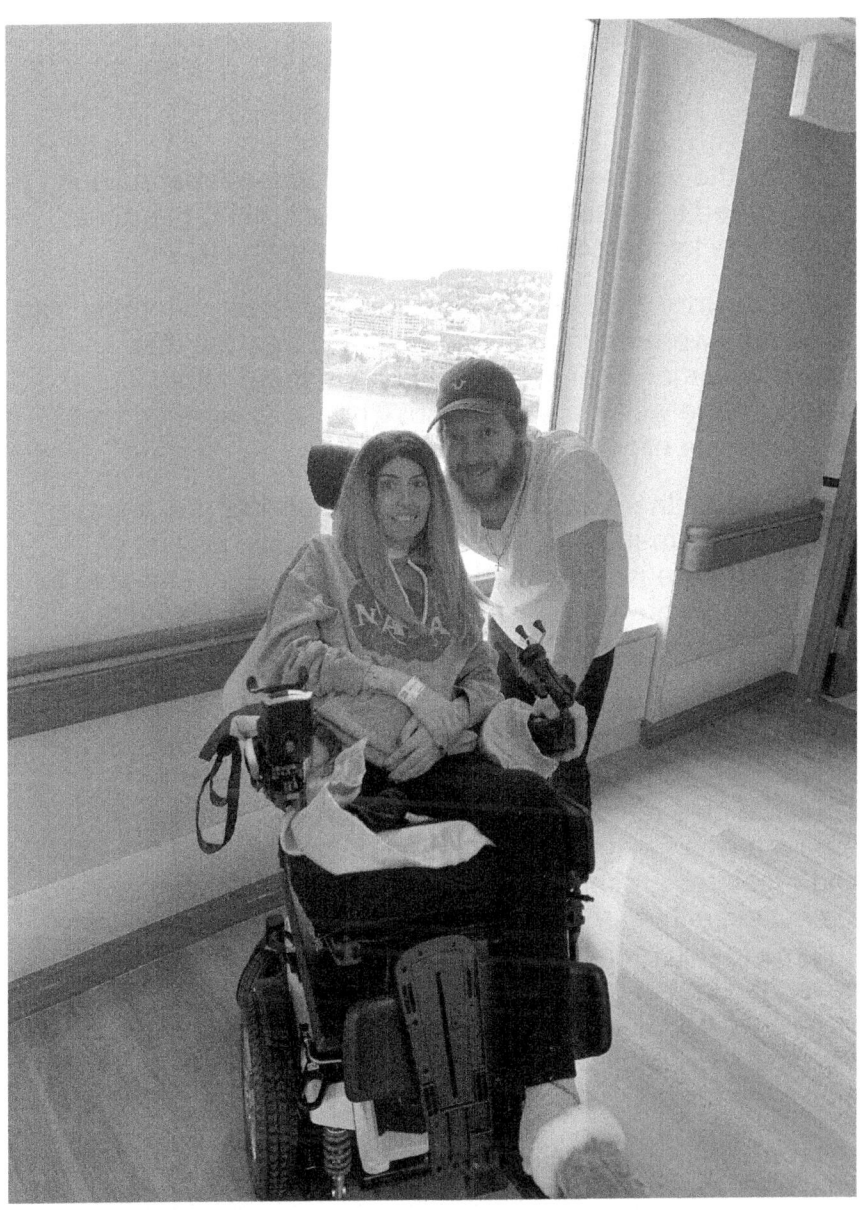

Amanda and Mario when she was an in-patient at the rehab hospital. Amanda is in an electric wheelchair that she could drive using a joystick with her right hand. The chair also could tilt to a reclining position so she could sleep in her chair without having to be transferred to a bed.

The Last Visit

It was the second week of April 2020 when Amanda and Mario called to tell me that Amanda's lead rehab therapist wanted me to come into the hospital to meet with her.

The doctors were getting close to discharging Amanda. Her blood labs were returning to normal, and they felt that tweaking some of her meds would bring them within the normal range within a week or so. Once they were normal, she would be eligible to be discharged.

The rehab therapist was aware of Amanda's upcoming living arrangements and felt that since I would be one of Amanda's caregivers when Mario was away that I needed to be trained on how to transfer Amanda from her bed to her wheelchair and how to transfer her from her wheelchair to the toilet.

This was when Amanda coming to our home became real for me, and I will admit I was very apprehensive about how we would be able to take care of her in the state she was in. Amanda was still in need of a large amount of care. She still had problems grasping items and needed assistance with almost everything. All I knew was that she counted on Daryl and me to help her, and we had to step up and get it done. I'll never say that we were perfect with what we did for Amanda or how we handled her emotions at times, but we always did the best we could, even though I'm sure we came up short on many occasions.

I went to the hospital on the specified day to begin my training. I was nervous about this. I'm not a very big guy, nor did I have the strength of Mario. I hoped they remembered that I was a 63-year-old man with two bum ankles, a surgically repaired left arm, and a right shoulder with a torn labrum from an earlier injury.

When I met with the therapist, I decided to voice my concerns before we started in case she had to adjust any of the methods she was going to train me on. She told me the purpose of the training was to teach me techniques that would keep me from injuring myself or Amanda. That was a relief to hear and put me somewhat at ease.

The therapist talked about how we could use a Hoyer Lift to get Amanda out of bed and into her wheelchair, but I knew that would not happen because of the pain Amanda was still having from the bed sore on her tailbone. She also told me how the therapists worked with Amanda on using a transfer board. They acknowledged that this was also very difficult for Amanda because of the tailbone bed sore.

At this time, I started to get concerned about getting Amanda from one place to the other. The therapist then said there was a way to transfer Amanda by lifting her but that it would require me to use the proper technique not to hurt my back. I can't recall what that technique was, but I remember I was able to get the job done though I had doubts that I would be able to do it on my own without the coaching from the therapist.

I did have a conversation after our training session with the therapist and asked her what she thought about Amanda's progress and if Amanda should be getting discharged so soon. She addressed my concerns with compassion and caring. She said that Amanda was nowhere near the end of her recovery. She would continue therapy after she was discharged, but in our home. She also told me that in a case like Amanda's, a patient would recover muscle mass and mobility better when in their home environment and must begin to learn to do things for themselves. She told me that keeping Amanda in a rehab hospital was not the best thing for her. Amanda had too many people at her disposal at the hospital to do something for her that she needed to learn to do independently. She told me Amanda's young age was a significant positive in her recovery, and she wanted Amanda to flourish.

I was sold. I went home knowing that Amanda would come home to where she needed to be so she could get her life restarted.

D-Day

(Discharge Day)

We knew we were getting close to Amanda's discharge. Her daily blood labs looked good, and the physicians tweaked the medications they felt would give her even better results.

On April 19, 2020, Amanda and Mario called us with the news that Amanda would be discharged the next day. They didn't know what time of day she would be discharged. Daryl and I figured she wouldn't be released until later in the afternoon.

Mario's mom, Debbie, wanted a big welcome home greeting for Amanda. COVID cases were still rising rapidly, so we knew we couldn't do anything indoors but luckily, the weather looked like it might cooperate and provide us with a sunny day. We began calling family members close by to see if they wanted to come to our house and greet Amanda from the street without any contact. We couldn't tell them exactly when she would be home until Mario called us to give us a more accurate time. It wouldn't be a large group of people, but it would be enough.

April 20, 2019, arrived, and it was confirmed that Amanda was being discharged in the morning. She was coming home with a basket of medications, so besides waiting for the discharge papers, Amanda also had to wait for the hospital pharmacy to provide her with all her meds.

The hospital delivered Amanda's power wheelchair to our house so it would be there for her when Mario brought her home. Around noon, Mario called to tell us they were waiting for someone from the Transport Department to get Amanda to Mario's car.

With that news, Debbie and I began contacting members of our family who said they wanted to be at our house to greet

Amanda. About a dozen family members parked outside our house in less than an hour, waiting for Amanda. The weather was a perfect Spring day. It was sunny and beautiful. The sky had very few clouds and was blue, like my granddaughter Mila's eyes.

I remember standing outside and realizing that it was nine months to the day of her AFE that Amanda was coming home. Nine months ago; I thought I would never see my daughter again. She survived the most horrific medical event I had ever heard of by some miracle. The word "miracle" kept swirling around in my brain, and I realized how blessed we all were that this "miracle" had happened.

I was brought out of my thoughts by seeing Mario's car coming around the corner with Amanda in the passenger seat. Handmade signs were being held, taped to our front door, and taped to the garage door, welcoming Amanda home. We clapped and cheered her arrival, and I could see that Amanda was visibly moved.

After they parked in our driveway, Mario picked up Amanda and placed her in her wheelchair. Debbie brought Mila over and gave her to Amanda. It was a moment that, nine months ago, I thought I would never witness. I didn't want to start crying, so I stood to the side and watched as Amanda's family walked over and told her how glad they were that she was home. I couldn't speak; I was so overwhelmed.

My daughter was home. She had made it. She had shown everyone the strength and determination she possessed. She was, and in my eyes, will always be, the most courageous woman I will ever know.

She is... a living miracle.

One of many signs welcoming
Amanda home.

Mila with Mario's father, Joe.

Mila with Mario's mother, Debbie, and members
of the Romanelli family.

Amanda outside our home with myself in the
background.

This is some of our Village… the family that helped us navigate this nightmare, kept us grounded when we went too high, and pulled us up when we went too low.
Thank you all!

Epilogue

Amanda's story didn't end on April 20, 2019. It was the beginning of another chapter.

Six days after Amanda came home, she was rushed back to the Emergency Room by her husband, Mario. She had become a little disoriented the day before, and by the next morning, she was very disoriented. Amanda did not want to return to the hospital, but we all knew there was no other choice.

Before Amanda was discharged, her doctors had made some changes to her meds, and the effects of those changes caused her to be disoriented. It was also discovered that she had an infection in one of her bed sores. She was in the hospital for six weeks because of these issues. This also caused her to miss her first Mother's Day with Mila.

Amanda had many milestones, both physically and mentally. Her hand and arm strength started returning as she progressed in her physical therapy. Her bed sores finally fully healed one year after they first appeared. Those bed sores are what caused her most of her pain. After they had finally healed, you could see the difference in her.

Even with COVID still going strong in 2020, we had an outdoor first birthday party at a local park for Mila. Seeing our family and Amanda's friends scattered around the pavilion, social distancing, and singing Happy Birthday to Mila was heartwarming. Nothing was stopping this birthday party from happening.

Mila's birthday is always a bittersweet day. We are so blessed to have our curly-haired red-headed blue-eyed granddaughter, but it's also the day we lost our grandson Vinny and nearly lost our daughter. I always think about Vinny on this day and wonder what he would be like. I know that someday I'll be reunited with him. That brings me some comfort.

Amanda contracted Shingles in August 2020. I couldn't believe it! I was so confused about how she could have contracted Shingles when no one around us had the virus. The doctors believed this case of Shingles was caused by stress. It took weeks for them to heal, which kept Amanda in extreme pain. It also took Mila away from Amanda so she wouldn't be exposed to the virus. What a bump in the road that was.

Amanda had to return to the hospital for minor surgery, her 40th since her AFE. She was so emotionally scarred from all she had been through that she was stressing over the thought of this surgery. It went well and without a hitch.

Amanda was able to take Mila out for her first Halloween. Little milestones like this were what brought Daryl and me the most joy. It showed the bonding of Mario, Amanda, and Mila as a family and their desire to keep moving forward with their lives.

In December 2020, because of all of Amanda's hard work she put in at rehab, she was able to sit up on a hard surface without losing her balance. Another milestone was accomplished.

Amanda, Mario, and Mila celebrated their first Christmas together. It was a very magical moment during a very magical season.

In early March of 2021, Amanda went back into the hospital to remove the mesh covering her abdominal area and close her abdominal muscles. This was a highly complicated set of surgeries that required multiple surgeons to make sure that all her organs were put back in the correct locations within Amanda's body and then to be able to pull the abdominal muscles back together. This was finally accomplished after four surgeries and another 5-week hospital stay. None of us could visit her due to COVID restrictions. When Amanda was finally discharged, she returned to our house to continue her rehabilitation and reconnect with Mila.

In August 2021, with the assistance of a brace on her left leg, a walker, and encouragement from her PTs, Amanda could stand on her own!

Toward the end of September 2021, Mario and Amanda were able to close on their own home! This was another bittersweet moment for me because even though we had our ups and downs as two families living under one roof, I had grown accustomed to having them with us. Still, I also knew this was the next positive step for them to be the family they wanted, living in their own home. They now live comfortably as a loving family with their two dogs. I am so very proud of them!

Even though this seems like the happy ending to Amanda's, Mario's, and Mila's story, it is just the beginning of their happy ending; every day they spend together adds another page to their story. It is a story that I know will outlive me, and I will always be eternally grateful to God that I was able to witness and chronicle this story to be shared by others who have survived an AFE so that it can provide hope, inspiration, and strength for the journey that they are on.

Mila's First Birthday Party, Covid style!

Mila's first Halloween with Mom & Dad

Mila's first Xmas with Mom & Dad

Mila's second birthday with Mom & Dad.

Mila Cottontail!

Family Vacation

Mila's second Halloween

The beauty of a child at Xmas.

The Romanelli family outside their new home!

With Thankfulness, Gratitude, and Love

We had a motto for Amanda's remarkable recovery that we had printed on T-shirts for a fundraiser. That motto was "The Reason Is Family." I want to acknowledge many people who either were family or became our family because of their actions, support, or the love they shared with us.

My wife Daryl was my rock throughout these very trying years. We have known each other since we were sophomores in high school, which covers a 50-year time span. Even with her Muscular Dystrophy, she insisted on being by Amanda's side every day until we had to begin regulating her visits due to her health concerns. She never gave up on Amanda, even when we did not know what Amanda would be like if she ever came out of her coma. She would stand at her bedside daily and talk to Amanda to let her know she was there fighting with her. Daryl would cuddle and shower Mila with kisses while she was at the children's hospital and anytime she could. I love my wife more than any known words can describe, and I am so grateful she was by my side throughout the horrific beginning days and the miraculous days that followed. You had me before "Hello."

My daughter Amanda was and still is my baby girl. She may not like hearing that, but unfortunately, that is how I believe every father sees their daughter. She has been a challenge for Daryl and me, but her challenges helped make us better parents and human beings. She has taught me many life lessons because of her early challenges, and those lessons helped us through her AFE and the aftereffects. Because of her, I understand that when there is adversity, how you respond to it will define you as a person throughout your life. She was my character builder. She made me examine myself and my beliefs. She made me more empathetic and compassionate about the plight of others. She made me understand the real meaning of unconditional love. I am forever grateful to her for helping me to learn all these lessons. She is a warrior, a fighter, a survivor, and now she is a thriver. She deserves all of life's blessings going forward, and I hope she never loses sight that she is meant to do great things. God would never have spared her so many times if there wasn't something that she still had to accomplish. I hope I'm still on this earth to see what it will be. She is and always will be... this father's daughter.

My son Dan was always Amanda's big brother, and as they grew together, they had typical brother-sister moments. I know Amanda's addiction played havoc with his life. He was angry at the pain it was causing his mom and me. It must have hurt him deeply. I'm so sorry for not addressing his pain during those days. I'm so proud of how he stood by his sister daily while she fought for her life. It reminded me that no pain could break the bond between a brother and a sister. I have become an admirer of my son and how much he values his family. It's difficult for a parent to stop seeing their child as anything but that. Even though you grow and physically change, you are still their baby in a parent's eyes. I stopped seeing Dan that way because of his dedication to Amanda and how he handled and carried himself during her most difficult days. I stopped seeing Dan that way because of his commitment to step up and help Mario and Amanda however he could when asked. He not only showed me that he is a man but that he is a good man, a good brother, and a good son. I love him more than he will ever know.

My son-in-law Mario had his world turned upside down on July 20, 2019. I can never imagine his thoughts when no one knew what would become of his wife. For five months, he never left her side day or night. He lived in the CTICU, studied her daily progress report, asked questions that provided him with the medical knowledge to understand her condition and plan of care, was her 24-hour advocate, and never wavered in his unmeasurable love for Amanda. I could not imagine what it was like to walk a day in his shoes, but I wanted him to know that I was in awe of his resilience, his dedication, and his love for my daughter. I know I will never have to worry about my daughter or granddaughter if he's with them. He is a real-life superhero and inspired many people who were touched by his presence during the most challenging days of his young life.

My granddaughter Mila was just an infant while all the darkest days were closing in on us, but she was the light that kept us going through all of this. I fell in love with her when I first saw her in the hallway outside her mother's room as Amanda was fighting for her life. Her innocence and purity would remind us that we had to provide her with all the opportunities for a semi-normal upbringing. She will always be the new princess in my life and one that I will always protect and help guide with a grandfather's wisdom.

Mario's parents, Joe and Debbie… words cannot describe my feelings for them, but I will try. We shared the same harrowing experience on July 20, 2019. We were shocked by the horror of what was unfolding before us. We cried, consoled each other, and pulled together because we needed to do that. If we weren't family before that day, we indeed became family after that day. Debbie became Mila's surrogate mother and stayed by Mila's side day and night while she was at the children's hospital, fighting her health issues. She did this because of her love for Mila, Mario, and Amanda, and she showed her courage to face this unknown time by doing it with a steely resolve. Debbie and Joe took Mila home and helped raise her through her infant days, knowing and praying that someday they would return Mila to Mario and Amanda to continue the job they had started. I want them to know that they will never be in-laws to me. They are my brother and sister. I always told my children that they wanted to find a soul mate with a great loving family because they knew they had a great character foundation for a lifelong relationship. Debbie and Joe are the definitions of a great loving family. I want to thank them for allowing me, Daryl, and the rest of my family to be a part of their family.

My sister Mary Jo and her husband Alan were instrumental in helping us navigate through some of the many problems we faced as we progressed through Amanda's 9-month hospital stay. My sister was constantly at the hospital in the early days of Amanda's life-threatening event. She provided a shoulder to cry on, a voice of reason on maddening days, and a pillar of support when sanity was weakening. She and Alan would take Mila for a couple of days as often as needed to give Debbie and Joe a break from raising an infant and give them a chance to recharge their batteries. It also permitted Daryl and me to continue visiting Amanda daily, especially when Mario returned to work. I know Mary Jo and Alan loved every minute they spent with Mila.

I hate to group friends and family, but, in this case, friends and family melded together for us. On July 20, 2019, as Amanda's plight spread, family and friends came out of the woodwork. At one point, we had so many people with us at the hospital that they had to give us a private waiting room. With all the confusion, fear, anxiety, and hopelessness we felt, your presence helped us understand that we weren't going through this alone. As days dragged on, many of you shuttled in and out and provided support in many different forms. You helped create the motto "The Reason Is Family."

The CTICU doctors and nurses, NICU nurses, and clinical staff deserve many thanks. These strangers saw a family at its worse and never made us feel unwelcome or intrusive. They answered every question, provided encouragement, and took special care of a young mom clinging to her life minute by minute, 24 hours a day, seven days a week. They helped bring a baby to her momma as often as possible. They consoled us when we were down and shared the joy of seeing a miracle occur right before their eyes. Our time with these dedicated medical angles will never be forgotten. They are a massive part of my daughter's being with us today.

The doctors and clinical staff at the maternity hospital will always be in my thoughts. I cannot express the gratitude I have for them for saving my daughter's life. Without your efforts on that fateful day, a mother may never have had the chance to lay eyes on her baby. Your unwillingness to let her heart stop beating was beyond belief. Whoever heard of 37 minutes of CPR??!! I know that most births are exciting, happy moments for a family, and you are used to seeing and sharing those moments with a family from afar. I know how my daughter's event affected all the staff on that day. I saw your faces. I felt your hurt. I had to come back and tell you how grateful I was for your efforts. You were the beginning of Amanda's miracle recovery, and you should never forget that.

Many more doctors, nurses, therapists, clinicians, and other support staff were a part of Amanda's recovery. Each of you provided care, support, encouragement, and determination to see a young mom survive the most traumatic of injuries to her body. You must also know that you are angels of mercy. You have done more than provide a service… you provided hope.

Amanda required a ton of at-home care once she was discharged. Numerous nurses, therapists, and aides helped us provide care for Amanda that we could never have done on our own. You permitted Mario to go to work and keep his business afloat. Daryl and I could not have done what you did daily, and you did this all during a pandemic. Your being with us helped us hold things together.

Our neighbors in my community also deserve a shout-out. Daryl and I had just moved into our new home when tragedy struck us, and with one little post on our community website, I had more people step up to help us than I could imagine. In fact, I couldn't imagine it. My neighbors took control and provided us with the support we needed. All the cards, the food, and the help were beyond anything I had ever experienced. Daryl and I know we are so fortunate to have such great neighbors in such a great neighborhood.

If you want to help Amanda, Mario, and Mila with their ongoing medical expenses, there is a Go Fund Me setup for them. The URL is posted below.

https://www.gofundme.com/f/vudyr-amanda-romanelli-afe-survivor-fund

If you, or someone you know, have experienced an Amniotic Fluid Embolism, please visit the AFE foundation's website. There you will find educational materials, support, a patient registry, and the ability to donate to the foundation so they can continue their outstanding work.

https://afesupport.org/

About the Author

Born and raised in the Mon Valley of Southwestern Pennsylvania, Domenic Marks never had any aspirations or training in the art of book writing. This venture was embarked upon because of his love for his daughter and the need to share the miracle they experienced.

The author has been an outspoken advocate for families who currently have, or have lost, a loved one who was afflicted with the disease of addiction. While not formally trained or educated on the topic of addiction, the author has spoken at numerous addiction conferences and symposiums. He expounds on his firsthand experiences and insights for the audience in order to enlighten the audience on the family's role in the addiction and recovery process and to deliver a message of hope.

The author, while retired, still speaks when requested. He resides with his wife of 40 years and lives close to his son and daughter. His granddaughter Mila is his "favorite redhead."

Made in the USA
Middletown, DE
13 February 2023

24782988R00215